The Christian Encounter with Muhammad

Also Available from Bloomsbury:

American and Muslim Worlds before 1900, edited by John Ghazvinian and Arthur Mitchell Fraas

A Constructive Critique of Religion, edited by Mia Lövheim and Mikael Stenmark

Qur'anic Hermeneutics, Abdulla Galadari

The Christian Encounter with Muhammad

How Theologians Have Interpreted the Prophet

Charles Tieszen

BLOOMSBURY ACADEMIC
LONDON • NEW YORK • OXFORD • NEW DELHI • SYDNEY

BLOOMSBURY ACADEMIC
Bloomsbury Publishing Plc
50 Bedford Square, London, WC1B 3DP, UK
1385 Broadway, New York, NY 10018, USA
29 Earlsfort Terrace, Dublin 2, Ireland

BLOOMSBURY, BLOOMSBURY ACADEMIC and the Diana logo are trademarks of Bloomsbury Publishing Plc

First published in Great Britain 2021
This paperback edition published in 2022

Cover design by Ben Anslow
Cover images: Gold foil © Leigh Prather / Alamy Stock Photo, Arabic calligraphy © A-Gallery / iStock

A catalogue record for this book is available from the British Library.

A catalog record for this book is available from the Library of Congress.
Library of Congress Control Number: 2020945431

ISBN: HB: 978-1-3501-9121-1
PB: 978-1-3501-9125-9
ePDF: 978-1-3501-9122-8
eBook: 978-1-3501-9123-5

Typeset by Newgen KnowledgeWorks Pvt. Ltd., Chennai, India

To find out more about our authors and books visit www.bloomsbury.com and sign up for our newsletters

For Omar, Ayesha, Zainab and Abdullah
For Brigitte

Contents

Acknowledgements ix

Introduction 1

1 Muḥammad as a Christian catechumen: Sergius-Baḥīrā and a legendary counterhistory 9

2 Muḥammad as a prophet of inferior monotheism: John of Damascus and a new history of the world 21

3 Muḥammad as a retrograde Moses of minimal significance: East Syrian Christians and public discussions with Muslims 33

4 Muḥammad as a carnal warrior and scheming ruler: West Syrian Christians and refutations of the Prophet 45

5 Muḥammad as an anti-saint: Martyr saints and hamartiography of the Prophet 57

6 Muḥammad as a tainted vessel of Christ: An anonymous counter-chronicle of the Prophet 69

7 Muḥammad as a vanquished anti-hero: A convert, a translator and polemic exposing the Prophet 77

8 Muḥammad as a powerless Prophet to the Arabs: Paul of Antioch and letters written to Muslims 95

9 Muḥammad as a Prophet and colonial goad for persecutors: Mary Fisher and a notorious encounter with a Sultan 109

10 Muḥammad as a redundant Gabriel and missionary conscript: Samuel Ajayi Crowther and West African mission to Muslims 121

Acknowledgements

I met Omar and Ayesha just over twenty years ago at the apartment complex we shared in northern California. At the time, their daughter, Zainab, was still quite small and their son, Abdullah, was not yet born. Our friendship developed in the months before my wife, Sarah, and I married. Omar and Ayesha were unable to attend our wedding, but they gifted us a copy of the Qur'ān in order to commemorate the occasion. Inside they placed a small card and wrote on it,

> We have chosen a copy of the Qur'ān translated into English with commentary for your wedding. Since this is the dearest and most valuable thing to both of us and because of a tradition of the Prophet Muḥammad that 'one can never be a Muslim until he/she loves for his/her brother/sister what he/she loves for him/herself'. So please accept our gift and may God guide all of us and bless your marriage with happiness!

We took great delight in accepting their gift. We still have the copy of the Qur'ān along with the card and they have a cherished spot in our library. I am ever so grateful for their gift and friendship and for the example of the Prophet that inspired their love back then. They remain, as ever, loyal to us, a trait that also finds its inspiration in their devotion to God and to Muḥammad.

With this same measure of love and loyalty, I dedicate this book to Omar, Ayesha and their children Zainab and Abdullah. It must be said that many of the intellectuals with whom I interact in this book did not write or talk about Muḥammad with the esteem that Muslims believe he deserves. I hope my friends will not be disgraced by these assessments but instead be able to find honour in my attempt to take the Prophet seriously by considering the ways their forebears transmitted his biography and the ways my Christian forebears tried to understand him. In this, I hope my friends can see me running alongside them towards all that is good (Q 5:48).

I also wrote this book for my daughter, Brigitte. The structure for the manuscript took shape when she was just 1 and I wrote it as she grew up into a 5-year-old. I have never once regretted the open-door policy I established for my study before she was born and she frequently took advantage, rushing in to offer chunks of watermelon, invite me to impromptu dance parties or share the thoughts that most concern her. If there are any sections of the book where my analysis seems especially bright or the prose particularly pleasing, then these were inspired by my daughter and our dear friends.

Finally, I want to thank my colleagues who are a part of the project titled *Christian–Muslim Relations: A Bibliographical History*. They have been delightful conversation partners as we worked to compile the records of past encounters between Christians and Muslims. We discussed the ideas in this book when I was only just beginning to write it and they continued to offer their insights as it came closer to completion. I shall not forget one of our last gatherings when we spent an evening in the Faculty Club at Utrecht University. Their advice and comments on the book were always insightful and their encouragement life-giving. But most of all, it was an honour to be taken seriously by mentors who have become colleagues and realize that, quite serendipitously, we have become friends as well.

Introduction

This is not a book about Muḥammad. Or, at least, this is not a book about Muḥammad per se. Instead, I want to tell the stories of what Christians thought about the Prophet Muḥammad throughout the course of fifteen centuries of Christian–Muslim encounters. From the eighth century all the way through to the twenty-first, what did Christians say about Muḥammad's life and work? Did they think he was a prophet and God's Final Messenger? If so, then what did they think that would mean for Christianity? If not, then what was he, exactly, for Christians? Did they need to account for his presence in history and in the context of religious claims? This book is about the Christian encounter with the idea of Muḥammad and how Christians tried to interpret his prophethood, affirm it to varying degrees or disregard it completely.

The account of a Christian monk named Jirjī helps introduce the stories we encounter repeatedly in the history of Christian–Muslim relations and will consider in the pages that follow. Jirjī was a Melkite, or Chalcedonian,[1] monk from the monastery of Mar Sim'ān al-Barḥī near Antioch. At some point in 1217, Jirjī, well advanced in years by this time, and some of his brother monks travelled east to the city of Aleppo. There they took shelter in the palace of al-Malik al-Ẓāhir Ghāzī ibn Yūsuf ibn Ayyūb (d. 1218), the local governor and a son of the famous Ṣalāḥ al-Dīn (d. 1193). While the governor discussed formal matters with the monks' superior, his younger brother, al-Malik al-Mushammar, chatted with Jirjī about monastic life. The two must have discussed what monks were and were not allowed because Jirjī, an ascetic, began to suggest that Muḥammad was virtually unrestrained in what he permitted for his followers. Just as he did so, three Muslim scholars (*'ulamā'*) entered the room. Their robes, one account informs readers with a wink, 'exhaled the perfume of musk',[2] an observation no doubt meant to validate Jirjī's comment about the lavish nature of Islam. Introductions were made and the Muslims looked at the old monk. 'Everything in him is pleasing and becoming,' one of the *'ulamā'* observed, 'and his countenance is agreeable. What a pity it is that he is a Christian!'[3] Jirjī and al-Malik al-Mushammar were already involved in a religious discussion, but the backhanded compliment and verbal jab from the sweet-smelling *'ālim* were, as they say, fighting words and a full-fledged theological debate ensued. Jirjī and the Muslims argued and deliberated, discussed and questioned one another for two days.

From the moment the *'ulamā'* entered the debate, the Prophet Muḥammad became the centre of concern. In fact, the first theological remark one of them made in their discussion with Jirjī drove straight to the heart of what makes Muḥammad a potentially contentious figure in the context of Christian–Muslim encounter. The *'ālim* declared:

> We reverence your Messiah, and we glorify his power, and we exalt his dignity above that of all prophets, excepting Muḥammad, the prophet and apostle of God. But you Christians lower [Muḥammad's] dignity, and do not attribute to him the honour due to him, although the most high God honoured and dignified him, and sent down to him the Qur'ān, as a light, and guidance, and mercy from the Lord of worlds. And you Christians deny that he is the prophet of God; for which he will certainly bring you to account in the day of the resurrection and judgment.[4]

Muslims honour Jesus, but Christians offer no reciprocal reverence for Muḥammad. Of course, while it is true that Jesus is highly regarded in the Qur'ān, Islamic traditions and Muslim spiritual life, he is only a human prophet and so is not accorded the same status or veneration as he is in Christianity. Likewise, whatever Christians might be willing to grant Muḥammad, most do not, as Muslims do, bear witness that he was God's Final Messenger. But as we shall see, more significant than echoing the Muslim *shahādah*, many Christians throughout history had, at worst, rather dreadful and, at best, terribly nuanced things to say about Muḥammad.

On many occasions, the key to understanding what Christians wrote about Muḥammad is the context that lay behind their writings. For instance, there were times when Christian authors wrote to discuss Muḥammad because conversion to Islam was a pastoral concern for their communities. In such texts, the question of what Christians could or ought to think about Muḥammad while remaining Christians lay in the background of their discussions. In some cases, Christian authors tried to provide their readers with a means for interpreting the events occurring around them. What might explain the rise of a figure like Muḥammad along with the religion and political force that followed him? How should they account for their place as Christians, followers of the true religion as they thought, in a world in which Muslim rule grew in dominance and Christian power receded? And at other times, assessments of Muḥammad's prophethood formed parts of missionary strategy whereby authors sought to redirect Muslim thinking about the Prophet and point it towards the fulfilment they were convinced was found in Christ. What one said about Muḥammad could be a way of answering questions like these and providing Christian communities with a way of seeing the world and their place in it.

In some situations, Christians were responding to direct inquiry from Muslims concerning what they thought about Muḥammad. Or they wrote accounts of their encounters with Muslims, sometimes even structuring their texts so that they looked like actual interactions with Muslims. This added an extra bit of authority to their accounts. Jirjī's debate fits into one of these categories; if it was not an account of an authentic debate, then it at least covered many of the topics about which Christians and Muslims actually spoke. And so throughout the course of Jirjī's two-day debate the *'ulamā'* continually probed the monk for his views about Muḥammad, returning again and again to the question of what Christians thought about him. In fact, at one point an *'ālim* slid in his suspicion about the monk's view in the form of a question: 'And Muḥammad is held by you to be inferior in dignity to Christ and his apostles?' Jirjī's response came with a shrug. 'Is it right to consider the slave equal to the lord, the created to the Creator, a human being to God?'[5] His answer smacked of an uneven comparison between Christ as the divine Son of God and the incomparably human Muḥammad, or at least the comparison ignored Islamic Christology since Muslims do not invest divinity in Christ. In turn the *'alīm* pointedly inquired with frustration, 'Do we not know, oh monk, that Muḥammad is the apostle and prophet of God, that he guided the people of Ishmael, and converted them from idolatry to the knowledge of the living God?'[6]

Did Christians know this? Did they agree? The answers Christians offered could never fully satisfy the Muslims who asked the questions, for the responses would inevitably fall short of a proper Muslim testimony in which he or she would bear witness, not only that God is one – on this Christians agreed (with the necessary Trinitarian qualification) – but that Muḥammad was his messenger, and the final one at that. In this latter claim lay the challenge. But if Muslims honoured figures from Jewish and Christian history, not least of whom was Jesus, then might there be room, or in what ways could there be space, for Muḥammad to appear alongside the already-recognized prophets? Given what Muḥammad had to say about the one God, what did Christians have to say about Muḥammad?

This is a book about Christians like Jirjī and how they tried to make sense of Muslim claims about Muḥammad and of the Prophet's place in sacred history. It is a book about how Christians answered the persistent Muslim question, offered in more or less the same fashion in numerous writings since nearly the dawn of Islam: What do you have to say about our Prophet Muḥammad? What we will find is that Christian texts that addressed this dilemma were less about Muḥammad than they were about the Christians who wrote them. For that reason, this book is not so much about Muḥammad as it is about the ways in which Christians have thought about Muḥammad's person and function, tried to say something about him to those who read their texts and attempted to convince those readers of their interpretation of Muḥammad.

In order to tell these stories, I consult texts in which the question of what Christians thought about Muḥammad was either explicitly asked or lay implicitly behind a discussion. This means that I do not look at texts whose primary concern is a critique of the Qur'ān, even though such a critique would have implications for what an author might in turn think about Muḥammad (e.g. if the Qur'ān was a fabrication, then so might be Muḥammad's prophethood). Similarly, focusing only on texts that directly address the topic of Muḥammad does not mean that I have included *every* non-Muslim author who had something to say about the Prophet. Instead, what I have tried to do is to use each chapter in order to present a Christian view of Muḥammad and include analysis and discussion of an author, or in some cases a group of authors, who characterizes that view. As a result, nearly every major view that Christians have argued is represented.

The chapters progress in more or less chronological fashion. I begin with legends related to Muḥammad and the Christian monk known as Baḥīrā. These likely originate in the early ninth century (though the figure appears in other texts from as early as the eighth century), and so a bit later than John of Damascus who appears in Chapter 2. But the monk Baḥīrā becomes a commonplace in Christian texts devoted to Islam – he is even, as we shall see, an unnamed Arian monk in John of Damascus's work – that he seems a fitting figure with which to begin. I proceed from there through the medieval period and focus on texts produced by Christians living in predominantly Islamic milieus. This means that the Christian authors were living in regions around the Mediterranean basin and even east towards Baghdad. But it also means that some authors originated to the west on the Iberian Peninsula. When I move beyond the Mediterranean, I do not look towards Europe and modernity but instead towards the New World and West Africa. There are two reasons for this pivot. The first is that literature related to Christian views of Muḥammad focus overwhelmingly on Latin Europe and authors writing from this region in the modern period, up to and including the twentieth century. These are important studies and I want to call attention to them,[7] but I do not wish to walk over already well-trod ground where it concerns Christian assessments of Muḥammad. The second reason, related to the first, is that I want to consider texts from modernity that are less well-known in literature related to Christian–Muslim relations, by looking towards different geographical regions and considering how the assessments of Muḥammad that can be found emanating from such locales dovetail with or diverge from much earlier texts.

A few more qualifications. Readers will note that, in my intention to steer away from Latin Europe and modernity, as other books tell those stories, I have nevertheless included sources situated in or related to al-Andalus and England. My justification for this is that al-Andalus (Chapters 5–7), while located on the Iberian Peninsula, can be considered an Islamic milieu and the texts written from there are decidedly medieval. Mary Fisher (Chapter 9) was an Englishwoman, but the story she tells about Muḥammad is largely one based in the Ottoman Empire, not in England, and the transmission of that story also takes us to Colonial New England. And last, it should be clear that I am interested in what Christians had to say about the Prophet, not non-Muslims in general, and, in particular, their theological reflections. I am not, therefore, engaging texts written, for example, by diplomats, emissaries or novelists or pieces produced by artists in which comments are made about Muḥammad.

The focus, then, is upon Christian theologians, understood somewhat loosely to include monastics, priests and laypersons offering theological commentary on Muḥammad. Looking at theological views helps to focus a study that may otherwise become too complex, but it also means that it favours the views of monastic centres, urban centres and the intellectual elite. On the one hand, then, many Christians throughout history might not have formed an opinion about Muḥammad or might not have even known about him. On the other hand, some of the assessments generated by these centres had ways of emanating to peripheries, ensuring their legacies. This book will attempt to set those legacies in perspective, but it will also bring to light assessments that were, or continue to be, less notable beyond the authors who produced them. With this in mind, I have tried to offer fresh insight on how Christians, some well-known to those interested in the history of Christian–Muslim relations and some much less well known, have interpreted the prophethood of Muḥammad.

While this last qualification helps to delineate the religious identification of the authors I will consider, the generic term 'Christian' introduces its own challenges. I will focus in Chapters 1–4 and 8 on the assessments produced by Eastern Christians, that is, Chalcedonians, East Syrians and West Syrians. In some cases, I will note when a figure is situated in a Coptic or Armenian tradition. These Eastern Christian communities will represent the majority of the authors I consider. In Chapters 5–7 I will look at authors from al-Andalus. Most of these were Latin Christians under the canonical authority of Rome. One of them, however, was likely an Arabized Christian, a community quite distinct from Latin Christians even though they shared canonical communion. In Chapters 9 and 10, I consider two figures who were Protestants, though further clarification is even required here. Mary Fisher (Chapter 9) was a Quaker, considered a religious dissident by the Church of England and so marginal to traditional Protestant communities. Samuel Ajayi Crowther (Chapter 10) was a convert to Christianity and became, under the missionary auspices of the Church of England, an Anglican. As such, he was a Protestant, though Anglicans still represent a community distinct from other Protestant groups such as Lutherans or the Reformed traditions. Lamin Sanneh (Chapter 11) was also a convert to Christianity, first to a Methodist community (a Protestant tradition) but eventually to Roman Catholicism. With these qualifications in mind, my goal in what follows is to provide an overview for how these Christian communities encountered Muḥammad and to draw attention to the complexity and variety of the interpretations they offered for his prophethood.

It would be fitting, before we depart, to have a general impression of Muḥammad as a figure in history. In fact, not a great deal of historical information is known about him. Much of what can be said is drawn from traditional sources. Both Muslims and Christians drew from these sources in order to comment on the Prophet, a point to which I will frequently return in the chapters ahead. While many Christians referred to the Qur'ān in order to make certain kinds of arguments about Muḥammad, and while it does indeed make direct and indirect references to him, the Muslim sacred text was not intended as an account of his life. Instead, it is considered by Muslims to be the speech of God. Thus, the sources that have more to do with Muḥammad are largely Muslim traditions related to the Prophet's life and sayings. This is a complex body of literature, developed throughout the early centuries after the Prophet's life, subjected to varying degrees of authoritative scrutiny and frequently used in order to elucidate revelations in the Qur'ān. As such, much of the biographical material related to Muḥammad functions as a way of setting him within an Islamic religious framework. Nevertheless, the essential bits of Muḥammad's life can be distilled.

Muḥammad was likely born in Mecca in 570 into the prominent Banū Hāshim family of the Quraysh tribe. Orphaned at an early age, he was raised by his uncle Abū Ṭālib (d. c. 619). He became a trader and travelling merchant. Being born in Mecca and being familiar with traders and trade routes in Arabia put Muḥammad into contact with a broad spectrum of cultures and religious traditions. He would have been familiar with devotees to a variety of gods, but he certainly would have known Jewish and Christian communities as well. As a spiritual seeker, we are told that he often took leave of his work and companions in order to meditate. And so, in 610, at around the age of 40, Muḥammad had an encounter, according to the Islamic tradition, with the angel Gabriel that resulted in the first revelation of the Qur'ān (Q 96). Divine revelations followed over time and a new religious community eventually emerged, led by Muḥammad the Final Messenger, that told pagans of the one, true God and called fellow monotheists back to pure worship.

Did Christians agree with this previous sentence? How did they respond to such claims?

1

Muḥammad as a Christian catechumen

Sergius-Baḥīrā and a legendary counterhistory

We begin with the narrator of a story concerning the apocalyptic visions of a Christian monk named Baḥīrā (or sometimes Sergius). The monk appears in a great many Christian and Muslim texts, some as early as the eighth century.[1] In the Islamic tradition, he is an important figure in the life (*sīra*) of the Prophet Muḥammad where he purportedly saw a miraculous cloud above the young Muḥammad's head and a tree bow to Muḥammad in order to shade him. In conversation with the boy, the monk recognized a mark – the seal of prophethood – between Muḥammad's shoulders.[2] The story, in Islamic tradition, is meant to demonstrate that Christians acknowledged and foretold the special prophethood of Muḥammad. This rooted the Prophet in a lineage of pre-Islamic monotheism.

The story also had a long life among Christian communities.[3] It circulated in various manuscripts among East Syrian (Nestorian), West Syrian (Jacobite or Miaphysite), Melkite (Chalcedonian or Greek Orthodox), Coptic and Maronite Christian communities.[4] For these readers, it was a part of apocalyptic visions, anti-Muslim polemic and counterhistory. Though the story's earliest forms likely originate in the early ninth century,[5] it was added to here and there over time and used to explain the rise of Muḥammad and the rapid spread of Muslim rule. The ways in which it framed the Prophet and accounted for Islam would nourish beleaguered Christian communities by clarifying a past that now seemed like a deceit and a future that suddenly felt insecure.

The Christian story of Baḥīrā

The events of the story, as they are narrated, are situated in the early seventh century. As the story goes, a traveller wandered into the desert where he saw 'the people of the Sons of Hagar who are barbarian and primitive like wild desert asses'.[6] The reference is, of course, to the Christian Old Testament and God's words to Hagar in which he promised that her son, Ishmael, would be like a wild donkey (Gen. 16.11-12). For Christians, and indeed for the traveller, the Sons of Hagar were Arabs and, eventually, Muslims.

Among the Sons of Hagar the traveller encountered an old Christian monk named Sergius, otherwise known as Baḥīrā. The monk had a story to tell. When he was younger the idea of making a pilgrimage to Jerusalem appealed to him. So he travelled there and stopped at Mount Sinai afterwards to stay in the monastery. When an opportunity presented itself, he ascended the mountain, knowing that whoever spent a night atop it would receive a divine revelation. And that is just what happened. Baḥīrā saw a vision of imminently rising kingdoms. Of particular interest was the coming rule of Arab kings. Some would be peaceful, some would not, but in the end they would pass and be replaced by the Byzantines before the end of time.

Baḥīrā descended Mount Sinai and eventually found himself among the Arabs who, according to his description, were 'primitive and simple-minded and led an awful life'.[7] Even more, they were polytheists – 'everyone worshiping whatever he liked' – and rather foolish. As a result, Baḥīrā 'prophesied concerning them whatever they liked and ... handed down to them this book which they call "Qur'ān"'.[8] The Qur'ān, then, was not a divine revelation sent down from God but Baḥīrā's creation. For his creation and the gift he made of it to the Arabs, the monk was given a place of honour among them, and when he died his bones were allegedly the source of great miracles.

After Baḥīrā's death, another character appeared in the story, a learned Jew named Ka'b. He is described in unseemly terms and accused of corrupting Baḥīrā's teachings by changing what he taught in the Qur'ān. Chief among these alterations was the confused notion that Muḥammad was the Paraclete promised by Jesus in the Gospels. In one version of the story, Ka'b is even said to have prophesied that Muḥammad would rise again three days after his death. When Muḥammad did die, his followers prepared his body, placed him in a room, shut the door and waited to see what would happen. After three days, they opened the room only to find a rotting, stinking corpse.[9] In turn, when Ka'b died he was 'buried like a donkey'[10] because of his false prophecy. Nevertheless, the Arabs continued to follow the corrupted teachings. In other words, Islam – the religion followed and propagated by Arabs – comprised a Christian monk's teachings that were later tainted by a scheming Jew.

At this point in the story, Baḥīrā's tale is retold, this time from the perspective of one of his disciples. Accordingly, Baḥīrā prophesied on more than one occasion that God would raise up from among the Arabs a great man named Muḥammad. Then one day a group of Arabs came to the well that was near where Baḥīrā lived. One young Arab stood out to Baḥīrā and he saw a vision above the boy's head. Baḥīrā knew this was Muḥammad. He told the others about Muḥammad and blessed the boy. He prophesied that Muḥammad would become a great king and lead his people 'from the worship of idols to the worship of the one true God'.[11] This prophecy prompted a discussion between Baḥīrā and Muḥammad about the basics of Christian doctrine and what those who worship the one true God believe.

In the course of Baḥīrā's explanation, Muḥammad interjected and inquired, 'How will my people believe [these things], since I cannot read a book and I do not know anything?'[12] His question led to an exchange in which Baḥīrā arranged for the best way to pass Muḥammad off as a teacher leading his people to monotheism. Baḥīrā would instruct him in everything he needed to know. Muḥammad would claim that his knowledge was revealed to him by the angel Gabriel and would tell his followers that God would send it to them in a book from heaven. Baḥīrā would write this book, but he would place it on the horn of a cow and send the cow to Muḥammad and his followers. Muḥammad could secure his followers' commitment to these instructions by promising them a sumptuous heavenly paradise and by easing the extent to which they must devote themselves to pious religious acts, such as prayer. Another apocalyptic vision follows, but the story of Baḥīrā and Muḥammad ends with a description of the young Muḥammad:

> He was a humble, simple boy, [he] liked the daily teaching of Mar Sergius. And he wrote for them this book which they call 'Qur'ān', at the hands of Muḥammad. They studied it every day of their lives until the death of Baḥīrā, he who prophesied to them.[13]

Muḥammad is also described as 'great and exalted'[14] as well as:

> good-natured, bright and eager to learn. He received knowledge from Baḥīrā, memorized it and devoted himself to it day and night, until the day that the Qur'ān was written. He continued to visit Baḥīrā frequently and to consult him about his affairs and to do what he said. And he visited him every day and he continued that consistently until Baḥīrā died.[15]

Redacting Baḥīrā's story and the making of a legend

Baḥīrā's story comes to us in four main versions: two Syriac recensions – an East Syrian one and a West Syrian one – and two Arabic recensions – a short one and a long one. There are also Latin and Armenian translations.[16] I have summarized above the material that the recensions have in common. One of the intriguing features of the story is the points where the versions deviate.[17] These are likely the result of copyists and redactors who were interested in using the story, but wished to incorporate other elements – many of them topoi of anti-Muslim polemical literature – for the benefit of their communities.[18]

One of the most significant of these points of divergence is the means by which Baḥīrā's message to Muḥammad is contaminated. In the Syriac and short Arabic recensions, a learned Jew named Ka'b took the Qur'ān that Baḥīrā wrote for Muḥammad and corrupted it. In effect, Ka'b reshaped instructions meant to draw the Arabs towards monotheism, resulting in elaborate falsifications such as the notion that Muḥammad was the Paraclete Jesus promised to his followers in the Gospels.[19] In the short Arabic recension, Ka'b remained responsible for the qur'anic corruption, but Baḥīrā also elaborated on the contents of the Qur'ān he wrote. Baḥīrā confessed these elaborations as a sin and he described some of what he wrote.[20] For example, Baḥīrā admitted:

> Then I wrote for him: 'Jesus son of Mary, did you say to the people "take me and my mother as two gods, next to God?" He said: "Praise be to You. I do not say that to which I have no right. If I had said it You would have known it. You know what is in me and I do not know what is in You. Praise be to You. You are the Knower of the mysteries"' (Q 5:116). I wrote this in reply to them as a reproach to them.[21]

For Muslims, this revelation functioned as a reproach of Christians for allegedly and idolatrously worshiping Jesus and Mary. According to the qur'anic text, Jesus made no such claims. For Baḥīrā, the text became a reproach of Muḥammad and his followers for their polytheism.[22]

Baḥīrā also admitted to writing portions of the Qur'ān that justify Islamic marriage practices that Christians found repugnant. Preeminent among these was Q 33:37 where Muḥammad's marriage to Zaynab bint Jaḥsh, the wife of Zayd, is justified. In many Christian polemical texts, this event – Muḥammad's attraction to Zaynab, Zayd's subsequent initiation of divorce and the qur'anic revelation justifying Muḥammad's marriage to her – was used to demonstrate the unseemliness of Islam and draw into question the Qur'ān's status as sacred text.[23] In the short Arabic recension of the story, Baḥīrā confessed to creating the passage as a means for permitting Muḥammad's desire for Zayd's wife. 'And I made many things for [Muḥammad]', Baḥīrā disclosed, 'that do not resemble prophecy nor befit the chosen of God.'[24] In this version of the story, then, a Jew was not to blame for the inception of Islam. Instead, Baḥīrā accepted responsibility.

In the long Arabic recension, Ka'b disappears completely and any Jewish influence on Islam vanishes along with him. Muḥammad is less a promising, malleable youth than he is a leader who requests that Baḥīrā condense the essential points of Islam for the sake of dim-witted Arabs.[25] This not only reflects the supposed mental aptitude of Arabs in general but is also meant to indicate the limited extent to which Muḥammad was able to grasp the details of what Baḥīrā taught him. So, while Muḥammad was capable of greatness, he remained a slightly dim-witted catechumen only able to retain the most basic of doctrinal matters.[26]

Most importantly, Baḥīrā is clearly the inventor of Islam and the long Arabic recension contains many more examples of the texts he wrote for the Qur'ān. This recension even includes his original Christian explanations for the meaning of the Qur'ān. For example, Sergius claims,

> And I also wrote for him: 'When you make a deal let witnesses from amongst you witness' (Q 2:282). I mean the witness of the Father and the Holy Spirit to the Son at the River Jordan, through the voice which John the Baptist heard, with all the people who advocate the testimony of the two hypostases to the one hypostasis through the uniformity of the oneness of the substance, the Eternal, One, Living, Rational God.[27]

Here Baḥīrā not only claimed responsibility for writing the qur'anic passage but also revealed the original Christian meaning he intended for it. In this case, the Qur'ān is made to affirm a theophanic image of the Trinity that was inherent to the event of Christ's baptism. Despite the true meaning of the Qur'ān that Baḥīrā wrote, he knew that there would come those who would alter his message, adding and subtracting to it as they pleased.[28] This prediction carries along with it the ironic insinuation that Muslims tampered with and corrupted their text, a charge usually used by Muslims against Jewish and Christian scriptures.

The long Arabic recension also provides greater details when it comes to the means by which Muḥammad would convince his fellow Arabs to follow him. For example, in the East Syrian, West Syrian and short Arabic recensions,

Muḥammad asked what he was supposed to tell the Arabs when they inquired about the hereafter. Baḥīrā summarized some of the delights, including the heavenly houris, the young virgins purportedly available to those who enter paradise. The Qur'ān refers to these figures without going into much detail, though later Islamic traditions and Muslim exegetes elaborated at much greater length.[29] Many Christian authors also incorporated this theme in their texts but did so in order to impugn Muslims for what they felt constituted the creation of a vulgar paradise that suited Muslims' lusty desires.[30] Similarly, in the long Arabic recension, Baḥīrā provided more detail regarding the afterlife. In one instance, he alluded to a rather graphic feature, noteworthy here for the ways in which it resurfaces in texts I examine in subsequent chapters. 'There are beautiful houris (*ḥūr*) there', Baḥīrā advised Muḥammad to say, 'in whom men take pleasure every day, virgins like moons, who have not been touched by men or jinn, whose length is so-and-so much (*kadhā wa-kadhā*) and whose width is so-and-so much (*kadhā wa-kadhā*) and that which one is ashamed to mention is so-and-so much (*kadhā wa-kadhā*).'[31]

In expanding on the delights of paradise in the long Arabic recension, Baḥīrā generalized his description of the physical dimensions of the houris, though the language employed indicates that the author is drawing upon *ḥadīth* literature that also employs 'so-and-so much' (*kadhā wa-kadhā*) language.[32] But his description is essentially self-censored when it comes to 'that which one is ashamed to mention', which must surely refer to the houris' genitals. Numerous Islamic traditions of varying degrees of credibility offer details describing the houris, and some later Christian texts were not shy when it came to exploiting these descriptions for the ways in which they could make Islam appear to be overly sexual and, in turn, shockingly repulsive.[33] In this light, Baḥīrā's description in the long Arabic recension is rather bashful but achieves the same revolting result.

Each of these redactions served a purpose for specific communities that read Baḥīrā's story. For communities that read about Ka'b, Islam could be blamed on a Jew who corrupted what may have originally helped Arabs draw closer to monotheism. This effectively dulled the power of Islam. For Baḥīrā's original intention was to create Islam as a positive aid. But Muslims fell victim to Ka'b's deceit and, still generations later, were only adhering to a farce. Quite naturally then, at least for readers who followed the implications of Baḥīrā's story, Muslims need not be taken very seriously.

In later redactions, the blame is spread further. In the short Arabic recension, Ka'b makes a brief appearance,[34] but much lengthier passages are devoted to

Baḥīrā confessing his creation of the Qur'ān as a sin.[35] This helped to explain the origins of the Qur'ān to readers, but it is also an interesting shift in a recension likely arising from a Melkite, or Chalcedonian, community.[36] In many Christian texts devoted to Islam, as we shall see in later chapters, Baḥīrā's non-Chalcedonian tradition was highlighted in order to draw connections between Muḥammad and Christian heresy. In the short Arabic recension, then, Baḥīrā's confession could be a way to point the finger of blame not just at Jews but at so-called Christian heretics as well.[37]

The long Arabic recension keeps the blame squarely on Baḥīrā. 'I have committed a sin for which there is no forgiveness', the monk confessed. 'I presented falsity as truth and avouched absurdity.'[38] But why would he do this? Muḥammad, according to the redactor, 'neither went up nor did he come down' – a way of referring to Muḥammad's failure to possess a divine revelation in the way Baḥīrā and others did when they went up to Mount Sinai, received a vision and came back down – 'nor did he prophesy nor was he sent by God'.[39] Nevertheless, he was part of a divine plan. Baḥīrā recognized what was preordained. 'I knew what I knew and comprehended, and I saw that [Muḥammad] would rule and that his rise, his success and the accomplishment of his mission were inevitable.'[40] In this light, Baḥīrā admitted to inventing the Qur'ān as a means for complementing God's divine plan for Muḥammad.

Another area where the versions of Baḥīrā's story diverge is the implications for the lineage of Arab rulers following the 'Sons of Hāshim'.[41] According to the apocalyptic vision, there would be a succession of seven Hāshimite kings. However, the line of Arab rulers did not end at seven but, in fact, lasted longer. This reality severely compromised the utility of the apocalyptic vision and brought its authenticity into doubt. It becomes noticeable in the long Arabic recension that the redactor discerned the need to adapt Baḥīrā's story, reinforcing it so that it can fulfil its apocalyptic purpose. The redactor achieved this by reorienting the doubt and making Muḥammad seem uncertain about the lasting strength of Muslim rule. 'I fear that … me and my companions will withdraw defeated', Muḥammad worried.[42] Then the redactor had Baḥīrā reassure Muḥammad that he will be victorious and his rule will actually remain for a long time.[43]

The redactor could have adjusted his approach entirely. Facing the lasting reality of Islam, he might have simply written a traditional apologetic text asserting Christianity as the true religion over and against Islam. Or he could have focused the text on scathing anti-Muslim polemic. Instead, he attempted to reinvent Baḥīrā's story and the monk's interaction with Muḥammad in a way that placed focus onto Baḥīrā himself. So readers are treated to lengthy, Christian interpretations of the original intent of the Qur'ān. They see Baḥīrā's role in inventing it and instructing Muḥammad, as well as his doubts about whether or not he deviated from God's plan in doing so. Most significantly, we read that Baḥīrā felt compelled to take the course of action he chose. In this way, Baḥīrā's story could be picked up and adapted in order to suit a new community's needs, just as it has been from the early ninth century all the way into the twentieth century.[44] In a process such as this, the story of a Christian monk and Muḥammad becomes a legend.

A promising catechumen in an apocalyptic counterhistory

What did the Baḥīrā legend achieve for its many readers? As an apocalyptic text, Christian authors and redactors were trying to make sense of the rise of Islam and the subsequent rule of Muslims.[45] The legend is thus an attempt to give readers hope by making their past and future conform to a divine plan in which God had their best interests in mind. So, prophecies about the rise and fall of ruling kingdoms reminded readers that God was in control and that Muslim rule would eventually pass, submitting to God's plan. In times when it became clear that Islam would not be a quickly passing threat but a more permanent fixture in the world, the apocalypse could be a reminder of who would win in the end. Readers should, therefore, remain hopeful.

Even the threat posed by Islam in readers' present circumstances could be neutralized by the apocalypse. This was because, as Krisztina Szilágyi surmises, the legend provided 'Arab rule a safe place in the Christian vision of the course of history'.[46] Muslims and Islam had their purpose. They could be used by God to draw Christians' attention, behaviour and worship back towards him. More importantly, however, Islam was powerless on its own because, according to the legend's apocalyptic interpretation, it could only function in the way in which God wanted it. On its own, then, it was powerless in the safe place it was given in the legend.

Most importantly, what of Muḥammad? Many modern readers discovering this legend, or indeed the genre of apocalyptic writing, will want to ask if the events they describe are real. Did Baḥīrā really exist? Did he really see these visions that the texts describe? Did he actually teach or influence Muḥammad? There can be no doubt that many of the original readers of the legend in its various forms believed it. But the question of historicity obscures the legend's essential function. Besides an apocalyptic text, the Baḥīrā legend was not the retelling of a historical event but a carefully constructed frame through which to view the past in a way that helped readers understand the claims of Islam and its leader.[47] The Baḥīrā legend is counterhistory.

In her work on the legend of Baḥīrā and its sources, Barbara Roggema calls the process of writing counterhistory 'parasitical historiography' for the ways in which it draws upon a community's stories 'only to launch a radically different interpretation', sometimes by simply letting these stories 'speak for themselves in a desacralized context'.[48] The example par excellence, in the Baḥīrā legend and in Christian literature devoted to Islam as a whole, was Muḥammad's marriage to Zayd's wife. Despite its treatment in the Qur'ān and Muslim exegetical literature, indeed despite the event being a relatively minor one in the life of Muḥammad, it is offered as *the* sign through which to accurately see and understand the Prophet. Snipped from its sacred context, the affair could now reveal that Muḥammad was actually a scheming womanizer who depended on invented revelations in order to justify his ungodly and sordid affairs.

Counterhistory could also be parasitical in ways that were less fantastic but still equally disorienting. Reflecting on the Jewish historian Amos Funkenstein and his work on Jewish–Christian polemics, Roggema shows how the Baḥīrā legend functioned as counterhistory in its attempt to distort 'the adversary's self-image … through the deconstruction of his memory'.[49] This is certainly the case with Baḥīrā's account for the Qur'ān's origination. In the East Syrian and West Syrian recensions, this counterhistory is offered as a means for explaining the Qur'ān that also strips it of power since it makes it a human invention, not a divine revelation. It also baptizes the process as an effort to draw pagan Arabs away from their idols and towards the worship of the one, true God. Such a noble effort is only thwarted later on by a devious Jew.

In the Arabic recensions, we also find an explanation for the original Christian meanings Baḥīrā intended for his Qur'ān. This is at least ironic since, for Muslims, the Qur'ān is its own counterhistory because it claims to reinterpret – rightly interpret or, better, *counter* interpret – Christ and reclaim God's message to humankind. In turn, Muslim polemicists could use it as a basis to reinterpret Christian history, showing how early followers of Christ departed from his original mission and message.[50] The Baḥīrā legend flips this strategy and the Muslim stories of Islam on their head; now the Christian monk is responsible for this effort in reclamation, showing the Qur'ān's original intent and offering an explanation for how Muslims had gone astray.

Baḥīrā's account of the Qur'ān is the most extensive example of counterhistory in the legend, but the effort to deconstruct and distort the Muslim self-image is also clearly evident when it comes to the legend's account of Muḥammad. Therein Muḥammad is not the Seal of the Prophets (*Khātam al-Nabīyīn*) as he is according to Muslim stories of Islam. He was recognized as one destined for a kind of greatness, but this was not because he was chosen by God to deliver a final revelation. The figure of Muḥammad, looming large in the history and trajectory of Muslim kingdoms, was suddenly made quite small in the legend. He was a simple, humble boy, selected by God in order to draw a pagan and dim-witted people a little ways towards monotheism by the help of an inventive Christian monk.

Furthermore, in the entire creation of the Qur'ān, Muḥammad is essentially ancillary, only serving to make manifest God's divine plan as it was communicated through Baḥīrā. As a result of this counterhistory, Muḥammad was declawed; with his power neutralized, he became the puppet of a God who fashioned time and a Christian monk who told him everything he was to say and do. At best then, Muḥammad was a promising luminary whose message was tragically corrupted by a Jewish scholar. At worst, he was a mere prop in a divine plan whose message was entirely the work of a Christian monk. In either case, the counterhistory of Muḥammad that is offered in the legend of Baḥīrā helped readers see him in the context of divine history, a story that inevitably favoured the followers of Christianity.

It must be said in closing that a key feature of this kind of historiography is not only the way one community can use it to parasitically deconstruct and reinterpret another community's stories. Roggema also points out that counterhistory is frequently 'employed by marginal groups who try to challenge the "superficial" views of history of the majority, by bringing out a "subterranean tradition"'. In this way, counterhistory is 'fundamentally subversive, in that it challenges the intuitive conviction that the truth is in the hands of the majority'.[51] Through this effort, subjected communities employ counterhistory in order to deny the identity their opponents claim for themselves. In other words, a counter, or inauthentic, identity is created for the opponent. Communities that achieve this, however, fuse their identity with an inauthentic one. In doing so, they also deny themselves an authentic identity because their identity is now dependent upon the one they have created for their opponent.[52] When events or opponents fail to conform to a counterhistory, one's own identity is thus called into question; its authenticity crumbles and must be remade. Will it be reconstructed once again on the basis of a new, slightly altered counterhistory?

In the Baḥīrā legend, an identity based on a counterhistory is a fixed part of a divine plan. Muslims would rule for a specified period before passing away. When that plan required readjustment – such as when Islam did not quickly pass away – then depending on that identity became difficult and its artificial nature was suddenly exposed. When it became clear that Islam was more than a passing phenomenon in history, its place in the Baḥīrā legend shifted.[53] As redactors updated the monk's apocalyptic vision, it became possible for Islam to exist *in perputuum* because it was made, in comparison to Christianity, to be the inferior religion of Muḥammad, Baḥīrā's sometimes promising, sometimes dim-witted catechumen. The task of attempting to prove the inauthenticity of that counter-claim would, of course, occupy many Muslim intellectuals and form the basis of much Christian–Muslim theological exchange.[54]

2

Muḥammad as a prophet of inferior monotheism

John of Damascus and a new history of the world

In 754 the Byzantine Emperor Constantine V (d. 775) convened a synod. Its purpose was to condemn the veneration of holy icons and outline the proper means by which to worship God. Those present also anathematized a few particular iconodules whose devotion they felt was rather impious. According to the synod's decree:

> The holy synod cried out: 'Thus we all believe … this is the way [the Apostles] venerated God when they worshiped … . [The synod] has swept away every idolatry … [and] defeated the faith of Germanus, George and Mansour, the misbelievers.'

The decree went on:

> To Mansour the foul-named and Saracen-minded (*tō kakōnumō kai sarrakēnophroni*), anathema. To the iconolater and falsifier Mansour, anathema. To the insulter of Christ and conspirator against the empire, Mansour, anathema. To the teacher of impiety and perverter of the sacred Scripture, Mansour, anathema. The Trinity has deposed these three.[1]

The text names Germanus (d. 740), former patriarch of Constantinople who was deposed in 730 for his refusal to condemn icons, George of Cyprus[2] and, at greater length, Mansour. This latter individual is most likely John of Damascus, the Aramaean presbyter and perhaps monk[3] who was active in the eighth century.[4]

In fact, there is relatively little that is known about John's life. His birthdate is unknown, though it probably lies between 650 and 675.[5] He was born in Damascus to an influential Christian family. According to some accounts, a government official named Manṣūr surrendered the city of Damascus to invading Muslims in 635. This Manṣūr would be John's oldest known relative.[6] Manṣūr's son, Sarjūn ibn Manṣūr al-Rūmī al-Naṣrānī, figures prominently in Muslim sources and was a notable member of the Umayyad court, serving as the caliph's secretary (*kātib*). Though with much less detail, Muslim sources also account for Sarjūn's son, Manṣūr ibn Sarjūn, who seems to have carried on the family's influential role in Umayyad government.[7]

According to this timeline, John would be Manṣūr ibn Sarjūn's son and would have succeeded his father under the Umayyad caliph. In the early years of the eighth century, however, John left the Umayyad court and either became a monk at the monastery of St Sabas near Jerusalem or a patriarchal adviser in the city. Numerous works, written in Greek, are attributed to him, including hymnography, theological and liturgical studies, homilies and poetry.[8] Among his theological works is a defence of Christian icons – a posture for which he was condemned by his pre-monastic family name. John's condemnation was later reversed, and his defence of icon veneration remains one of the standard sources, especially among Eastern Christian communities, for explaining and justifying the use of icons in Christian worship.[9] John died in the middle of the eighth century.

We cannot be sure why John left the Umayyad court in favour of ecclesial life. While his grandfather enjoyed substantial influence in service of at least five caliphs, his father's role was likely more restrained due to reforms set in place, beginning with 'Abd al-Malik ibn Marwān's rule (r. 685–705) and continuing with his successors.[10] Among these reforms was what Sidney Griffith calls the 'twin social processes of Arabicization and Islamicization [that] began in earnest in the territories of the Levant [that] Muslim Arabs had conquered and occupied in the generation prior to John's birth'.[11] These processes were meant to claim the now-conquered public space for Islam.[12] Construction of the Great Umayyad Mosque of Damascus, for example, on the ruins of what was the Church of St John the Baptist would change the way public space appeared in ways that reminded onlookers of Islam's predominance. Other, more mundane efforts would work similarly, such as the minting of new coinage that incorporated the truths of Islam and the authority of Muslim caliphs instead of Greek inscriptions and symbols of the cross. Roadside signs also changed and began to use Arabic and the *shahādah*, the Islamic creedal statement, instead of the cross.[13] Even the standard language of government changed from Greek to Arabic, a transition that would directly affect the work of secretaries like John's father and grandfathers who would have customarily used Greek. There were constant reminders, then, that Muslims now controlled the public spaces of cities like

Damascus. Of course, making Islam public in this way also meant eliminating or suppressing competing symbols. The removal of crosses and similar Christian signs from public view can be understood in this light.

Heresiology as a comprehensive history of the world

The assertion of Arabic and Islam may have worked over time to decrease the kind of influence Christians like John and his ancestors had in the Umayyad court.[14] Significantly, the processes of Arabicization and Islamicization 'set the stage', Griffith writes, 'for the first Christian responses to the social and religious challenges of Islam'.[15] Among these were apologetic treatises and apocalyptic texts. Catechetical texts were produced in order to help Christians understand their faith in light of their changing cultural and linguistic milieus. Polemical treatises attacked Islam and histories were written in order to make sense of a new community's rise.

There were also works like the *Pēgē gnōseōs* (*Source of Knowledge*), written in Greek in the middle of the eighth century by John of Damascus.[16] This lengthy treatise is divided into three parts: *Kephalaia philosophika* ('Philosophical Chapters'), *Peri haireseōn* ('On heresies') and *Ekdosis akribēs tēs orthodoxou pisteōs* ('An Exact Exposition of the Orthodox Faith'). The second section, *Peri haireseōn*, is devoted to a hundred heresies, each one receiving its own chapter.[17] In large part, the section comprises an updated edition of an earlier work by Epiphanius of Salamis (d. 403), the late-fourth-century *Panarion*. Epiphanius' *Panarion* consisted of eighty heresies,[18] so in some ways John brings the list of heretical beliefs up to date in his treatise. In turn, the *Peri haireseōn* can be understood as a heresiology and John announces its function as he transitions into an exposition of orthodox faith in his third section: 'Then, next, after this, I shall set forth in order the absurdities of the heresies hated of God, so that by recognizing the lie, we may more closely follow the truth. Then, with God's help and by His grace I shall expose the truth.'[19]

But the inclusion of Islam as the one-hundredth chapter is awkward in light of traditional understandings of what constituted a heresy. Its inclusion, furthermore, makes John's *Peri haireseōn* unique as a heresiology.[20] To begin with, John does not use the nomenclature of 'Islam' or 'Muslim'. Instead, he refers to the practices of the Ishmaelites and how, at the time of the Byzantine Emperor Heraclius (r. 610–641), Muḥammad appeared among them. In this light, it would seem that John understood the Ishmaelites to be a group independent of Muḥammad but one whose religious practices were later shaped by him. Moreover, John also uses 'Saracens' and 'Hagarenes' to refer to Muslims. Even as late as the seventh and eighth centuries, such terms were the standard ones employed in order to categorize ethnic groups by their alleged founders. 'Saracens' and 'Hagarenes' were common terms employed in antiquity by Roman historians and so John seems to have inherited this vocabulary.[21] It may be, then, that John did not see Muslims as comprising a new religious group or connected in any way to Christian faith.[22] So why include them in a heresiology?

In most cases, heresy (*hairesis*) could be understood as originating within Christian communities. Heretics were usually assumed to begin 'their careers as "insiders" or at the least were perceived as "insiders" or people claiming "insider" status to the Christian community'.[23] Heretics could also be perceived as the victims of demonic possession. As such, they were an illness in need of a cure and a threat to Christian communities that required exclusion.[24] And heresy could also be the result of contamination, itself the result of proximity to dangerous philosophical speculation.[25] John's treatment of Islam does not neatly conform to any of these expected norms of heresy. As I shall discuss more below, Islam does not appear in John's text as a religion claiming to arise from within Christianity or even meant to perfect wayward monotheism. John does not discuss any apparent demonic influence upon Islam or Muḥammad, nor does Islam fit as contagious philosophical speculation. How, then, ought we to understand his decision to round off his list of heresies with the religious practices of the Ishmaelites and Muḥammad's influence upon them, or what we might now term 'Islam'?

Peter Schadler has shown that John's *Peri haireseōn* as heresiology must not be severed from the *Pēgē gnōseōs* as a whole, for the comprehensive nature of the work signals its participation in an 'emerging literary form in the Byzantine world, that of the encyclopedia'.[26] Despite John's tendency to compile the work of previous intellectuals in *florilegia*, he also aims to, as he writes, 'make a beginning of philosophy and to set down concisely … every sort of knowledge'.[27] It was in this sense – the work's comprehensiveness and attempt to address 'every sort of knowledge' (*pantodapēn gnōsin*) – that John's work was a 'fount of knowledge' (*pēgē gnōseōs*). This further indicates that John's work was meant to be read as a single collection, 'not simply referenced when needed', consulted piecemeal as a sourcebook or reproduced as a paradigm for interacting with Muslims.[28] Instead, by reading it in toto, John intended to shape his audience's world view, hoping to frame the way in which they saw their position in history and the place Islam and Muslims held in world events. Including Islam, then, could be interpreted as John's attempt to make his work complete and to ensure that his exposition of Christian orthodoxy was set against the 'full historical market of alternative possibilities'.[29] In this light, the presence of the Ishmaelites in a heresiology was 'required', as Schadler points out, 'in order to fulfil [John's] encyclopedic intentions and offer his reader every sort of knowledge'.[30]

Besides seeing John's *Peri haireseōn* in the context of encyclopaedism, Schadler has also shown that it is equally important to read his heresiology, much like Epiphanius' *Panarion* from which John draws heavily, as a work of universal history. As such, John's treatment of Islam in the context of heresy must be understood as an effort to demonstrate the triumph of Christian orthodoxy over not just doctrinal error but a-historicism as well.[31] So the *Peri haireseōn* helped to explain to John's readers their place in history at a time when their connections to imperial authority had vanished. In John's account, God's sovereignty was made manifest, not in geographical dominance but in superior religious truth. Likewise, John's heresiology is a history of the world that interprets Christianity as triumphant over error. His Christian readers, living as they were under Muslim rule and caught up in the social processes of Arabicization and Islamicization, could see their intellectual and religious predominance over the broadest spectrum of alternative knowledge.[32]

For John, then, heresy could be understood as opinions diverging from the Church's opinions. Like traditional heresiologies, John saw heresy as a collection of lies, but unlike traditional treatments, John did not view heresy as an ecclesiastical sickness in need of a cure. Similarly, traditional views of heretics saw them arising from within the Church and poisoning its sacred sources. For John, heretics, like the Ishmaelites, could also arise alongside Christian communities and develop their own sources. As a result, the Ishmaelites, and the trajectory that linked them with Muḥammad, were worthy of inclusion in a comprehensive heresiology that sought to explain their place in the history of the world.[33]

Situating the Ishmaelites and Muḥammad as the hundredth and final chapter in an encyclopaedic endeavour to account for 'every sort of knowledge' also made the Ishmaelites the 'final bringers of an alternative system of faith and communal order'.[34] In this position, then, readers could also view Islam as the sharpened tip of a heretical spear, a kind of 'summa' of past errors.[35] Understanding Islam in this way could galvanize John's readers for the imminent victory over what had become, in the light of his encyclopaedic account of all knowledge (*pantodapēn gnōsin*), the greatest of foes.[36]

Muḥammad in *Peri haireseōn*

Most of the chapters in *Peri haireseōn* are relatively short, ranging from a few lines to a few paragraphs. Chapter 100, however, is by far the longest chapter in the work, taking up several pages. It is devoted entirely to 'the still prevailing people-deceiving practice (*thrēskeia*) of the Ishmaelites, the forerunner of the Antichrist'.[37] Whereas much of the *Peri haireseōn* is dependent upon earlier heresiology, the *Panarion* in particular, the chapter on Muḥammad and the Ishmaelites appears to comprise John's original work.[38] The chapter marks one of the earliest known attempts by a Christian to respond to Muḥammad in detail.

As I have pointed out, John began his chapter on Islam with a reference to the Ishmaelites, a people who 'worshiped and venerated the morning star and Aphrodite, whom they themselves called Habar in their own language, which means "great" '.[39] The Ishmaelites, then, had always been idolaters, John explained, until 'a false prophet appeared to them named Muḥammad (*Mamed*)'.[40] At that time Muḥammad happened upon the Old and New Testaments and an Arian monk. With the monk's help, Muḥammad 'introduced a sect of his own'.[41] He was able to do so, John informed his readers, because he fashioned himself as a 'God-fearing person' and told them that a Scripture had been 'brought down to him from heaven by God'.[42] John clearly had the Qur'ān in mind when he referred to Muḥammad's Scripture (*graphēn*). But even though he was able to reference the Muslim belief that the Qur'ān was sent down by God,[43] John chose instead to present that alleged revelation as Muḥammad 'having put together some sayings in his book, worthy of laughter'.[44]

In this sense, Muḥammad 'handed down' the Qur'ān to the Ishmaelites; God did not miraculously send it down. In fact, John repeatedly attributed the handing down of the Qur'ān to Muḥammad[45] and he argued that the book's contents comprised Muḥammad's own words. With this assessment in mind, John discussed a handful of passages from the Qur'ān, even identifying the chapter titles where they are found, but was careful to add to his descriptions, clarifying that these were things that Muḥammad himself spoke.[46] Moreover, the things Muḥammad spoke were 'worthy of laughter', 'absurd' and 'foolish'.[47]

John also considered the Qur'ān, by implication, lurid and, in one case, he even seemed bashful about the contents of the Qur'ān. Of particular concern in this regard was the Qur'ān's ostensibly relaxed legislation of marriage and divorce. John cited the pre-eminent example: Muḥammad's marriage to Zayd's wife, Zaynab bint Jaḥsh. But if the prescriptions for marriage and divorce that are related to the story were not enough to devalue the Qur'ān, then John closed off the passage by quoting one of the Qur'ān's pronouncements regarding marriage. According to John's quotation the Qur'ān proclaimed, 'Work the land which God gave you and beautify it.' But then John appended to the quotation his own rather generic phrase, making it a part of the qur'anic text: 'and do this and in this way'. In order to explain the very generalized addition, he then wrote, 'so that I may not say all of his obscenities'.[48]

It seems clear that the quotation is from the second chapter of the Qur'ān: 'Your wives are a place of sowing seed (*ḥarth*) for you, so come to your place of cultivation however you wish' (2:223) – part of the Qur'ān's sexual ethics for marriage. The precise meaning of the verse is not immediately apparent. According to various Islamic traditions, the origin of the revelation was reported as a Jewish concern over a particular position for sexual intercourse.[49] Q 2:223 would seem to solve the dilemma, but since it does so in rather ambiguous terms its exact meaning generated debate among Muslim *mufassirūn*. For instance, al-Bukhārī (d. 870), in his *Kitāb tafsīr al-Qur'ān*, included *ḥadīth* reports from Ibn 'Umar (d. 693) on the verse. According to these reports, Ibn 'Umar would recite the Qur'ān without interruption. Once, when reciting Q 2:223, he paused and inquired about the verse's meaning. 'It was revealed in such and such (*kadhā wa-kadhā*) connection', came the reply, to which Ibn 'Umar added, 'It means one should approach his wife in ....'[50] Al-Bukhārī did not specify what Ibn 'Umar said, instead cutting off Ibn 'Umar's explanation mid-sentence. Later *ḥadīth* and *tafsīr* literature, however, did complete Ibn 'Umar's thought, suggesting that it must have been al-Bukhārī himself who was reticent to repeat the information.[51]

An initial reading of John's reference to Q 2:223 suggests that he was aware of at least some of the Muslim debate over the verse's meaning, even if in the debate's early, informal state, since the traditions related to it would not begin to appear in any formalized fashion until at least the ninth century. His awareness of this Muslim context seems clear from the bashful, generalized manner in which he referred to Q 2:223's suggested meaning; he was reticent to be explicit about it and so he self-censored himself with a delicately obscure 'do this and in this way'. This rhetorical gesture reveals the necessary familiarity with Islamic sources that would be required in order to write what John did: he not only quoted the qur'anic passage but signalled its meaning within Muslim circles as well. Both the text and its interpretation, at least on the surface, would be sufficient to provoke astonishment from John's readers.[52]

Further, the similar unease with which al-Bukhārī discussed the verse makes one wonder if John was not only familiar with the Muslim debate surrounding Q 2:223 but also emulating the kind of generalized language commonly found in *ḥadīth* literature – 'such and such' (*kadhā wa-kadhā*) vis-à-vis John's 'do this and in this way' – and the self-censorship that al-Bukhārī deployed when he compiled his *ḥadīth* collection. In other words, was John's generalized self-censorship a result of his bashfulness or his close familiarity with the exegetical traditions attached to Q 2:223? What seems clear, in either case, is that John was familiar enough with the Qur'ān and Islamic sources to reference them and even reflect some of the Muslim debate over the meaning of their sacred text and traditions. He was not simply inventing an unseemly context from which the Qur'ān emerged. Rather, he was attempting to subject Islamic sources to a kind of critical evaluation that he could put to work in support of his polemic. He did this, significantly, by attending to Muslim literature and internal debates over the meaning of their sacred text. Equally significant, however, was that John's main interest was not the complexities, variegations and processes of authenticating these Islamic traditions. By merely suggesting the presence of unseemly scandal in the Qur'ān he could conjure doubt in his readers' minds as to the authenticity of Muḥammad's claims. Thus, John presented only the surface of Muslim debate in order to draw attention to something that would call the authenticity of Muḥammad into question.

John also cast doubt on Muḥammad's prophetic credentials. 'And who is the witness', John questioned, 'that God gave the Scripture to him, or which of the prophets foretold that such a prophet would arise?'[53] Authentic revelation worked in a certain manner. The people of Israel witnessed Moses on Mount Sinai along with God's theophanic glory – this was a public revelation, a visible handing down of God's word. What is more, Moses and all the prophets succeeding him were thought to have foretold the coming of Christ.[54] How did Muḥammad fit into this kind of revelation? Could he, or any of his followers, produce this kind of evidence for a prophetic nature?

In fact, according to John, authentic revelation required witnesses. Such witnesses were meant to certify a figure's claims to prophethood. Further, Scripture foretold a prophet.[55] Muḥammad lacked such witnesses. Instead, John reported that Muslims maintained he received his revelation while asleep – a claim verified in at least the biographical account (*sīra*) of the first revelation given to Muḥammad[56] but one also twisted by John to mock Muslims and their notion of revelation.[57] For John, the revelations of the Qur'ān were nothing more than Muḥammad's illogical inventions. In all of this, Muḥammad may have been a kind of prophet – he led the Ishmaelites away from paganism and towards monotheistic belief – but he was a false one and was given harsh condemnation by John: Muḥammad's inventions ultimately led his followers, 'like animals', to hell.[58]

History's latest false prophet of an inferior ideology

John's summary of Muḥammad may leave one with the impression that his chapter on Islam was little more than a polemical side to the otherwise encyclopaedic *Pēgē gnōseōs*. In contrast to his hostile tone, however, there also can be heard in *Peri haireseōn*'s one-hundredth chapter whispers of John's familiarity with Muslim belief. He was, of course, raised in a context that more than likely gave him access to some of the best information about Islam and its sources that one could obtain at the time.[59] As a result, he is able to mention qur'anic passages in his text, oftentimes along with the name, or a near rendition, of their corresponding *suwar*. How much of the Qur'ān he had read, or in what form it had come to him, or whether he simply heard portions of it in conversation with Muslims is not altogether certain. It is known that Greek-speaking Christians in the region where John was active were already familiar with portions of the Qur'ān by the year 700.[60] So it is clear that he had heard bits of the Qur'ān, but perhaps he had even seen portions or even read it in Arabic.[61] In addition to the Qur'ān, John also seems to draw from Muslim oral traditions, popular beliefs and stories of the prophets (*qiṣaṣ al-anbiyā'*).[62]

Again, it is not certain whether John accessed these sources independently or if Muslim contacts shared them with him. It would seem, at the very least, that John was representing in some form in his text interactions he had with Muslim conversation partners. This is likely evident from the rhetorical pattern he frequently repeats in the chapter on Islam, a 'we say … they reply … we respond to them'[63] structure. It is not difficult to see in this pattern a possible summary of John's own interactions with Muslims as they discussed Islam, the Qur'ān and Muḥammad.

If not just John's conversations, then the pattern also intriguingly reflects the Qur'ān itself. In numerous passages, a revelation is structured along the lines of a similar 'they say, we say' pattern. For example, Q 2:111 reports, 'And they say, "None will enter Paradise except one who is a Jew or a Christian". That is their wishful thinking, Say, "Produce your proof, if you should be truthful".' In Q 21:24 Muḥammad is commanded, 'Say, "Produce your proof. [The Qur'ān] is the message for those with me and the message of those before me". But most of them do not know the truth, so they are turning away.' Passages like these are structured along very much the same lines as those in John's text, a similarity that suggests that John was familiar enough with the Qur'ān to mimic some of its patterns.[64]

Of course, these kinds of qur'anic passages reveal their own inter-religious milieus – the Qur'ān pushes back against Jews and Christians in the first and against polytheists and Muḥammad's opponents in general in the second. In this, both the Qur'ān and John seemingly formed part of their arguments upon authentic interaction. Along such lines, one must also acknowledge the faint recognition that Muḥammad brought the Ishmaelites away from idolatry and towards monotheism.[65] But nevertheless, John's familiarity with Muslim belief and Islamic sources, along with the way in which he perceived Muḥammad's pursuit of monotheism, did not lend themselves to any observable admiration. The information John shared and the sources he drew upon are instead used to discount Muḥammad's prophetic credentials and invalidate the revelatory value of the Qur'ān. What, then, did John achieve by sharing what he did about Muḥammad in the context of the *Pēgē gnōseōs*?

In simple terms, Muḥammad's monotheism was not purely heaven-sent; it was brokered in John's text by a heretical (Arian) monk. Further, God did not send down Muḥammad's revelations; they were invented and handed down by Muḥammad. It was not so much, then, that Muḥammad's message was false, though John does indeed call him a 'false prophet'; it was simply that Islam was inferior. The nature of Muḥammad's prophethood, then, was linked to the nature of his message. The latter was an inferior ideology, monotheistic though it was, which made Muḥammad an inferior prophet.

With this in mind, John included Islam as a heresy in the *Pēgē gnōseōs* not only as a means for addressing 'every sort of knowledge' but also to show that it fell short of Christian truth and the place Christianity attained in history. In this, Islam was retrograde.[66] Indeed, many Christians in John's environment could begin to accept that Islam was more than just a passing entity. For them, it would be more important to put Islam in context. Thus, while Muslims ruled a growing expanse of territories and comprised ever-more powerful political and military forces, their religion was, simply enough for John, inferior to Christianity.

A final point can be drawn from the physical nature of John's *Pēgē gnōseōs*. Authors who set themselves to the task of writing an encyclopaedic work cannot have grand ambitions for broad distribution or wide popularity. At best, one can hope such a work will become a staple among library acquisitions. Nearly the same might be said for John's work. The expense and effort of writing the *Pēgē gnōseōs*, in terms of parchment and ink alone, would have been immense, not to mention the far exceeding cost of producing copies of a work of such length.[67] It is unlikely that many individuals would have been able to obtain a copy, though monasteries or libraries could possibly afford one.

In this light, John likely had a sense, as any author of an encyclopaedic work might, that the *Pēgē gnōseōs* would be a work of more than passing speculation.

He had to be convinced of this in order to justify producing such a lengthy work, knowing that those who would invest in copying it would see the value in doing so. As it happened, the one-hundredth chapter on Islam, besides being the earliest known Christian text to treat Islam in detail, became one of the most significant sources for Christian knowledge of Islam and Muḥammad among those who read Greek. It further informed texts written in other languages and its themes became staples for Christian treatises devoted to Islam.[68] Not all authors would offer the same assessment of Muḥammad that John did, but his treatment of the Prophet remains a standard source for understanding Muḥammad in the context of the medieval Mediterranean world and in Christian history.

3

Muḥammad as a retrograde Moses of minimal significance

East Syrian Christians and public discussions with Muslims

While John of Damascus is well known to scholars and Christian studies of Islam, the work of Syrian Christians writing in Syriac still remains relatively obscure.[1] This is unfortunate because these Christian communities – both East Syrians ('Nestorians' or the Church of the East) and West Syrian Miaphysites (also known as Monophysites or 'Jacobites') – were among the first communities that Muslims encountered and offered some of the earliest reflections on the rise of Islam and the Prophet Muḥammad. Careful readings of these texts also reveal the use of even older Syriac traditions taken up for use in new, increasingly Islamic contexts.

An East Syrian monk's discussion with an Arab notable

One of the earliest of these Syriac texts comes from the first half of the eighth century, very likely sometime in the 720s. It is an apology for Christian faith written in an Islamic milieu, known to us now as *The Disputation between a Muslim and a Monk from Bēt Ḥālē*. Its author presented it in the form of a report of a 'question and answer'[2] debate in which the Muslim posed various questions for the monk to answer. The discussion purportedly took place between an East Syrian monk and a prominent Muslim in the entourage of Maslama ibn 'Abd al-Malik (d. 738) who visited the monk's monastery of Bēt Ḥālē in Iraq.[3] It is not entirely certain whether or not the text is an account of an event that really took place, or whether or not the neatly packaged exchanges represent the encounter with complete accuracy.[4] What is clear, however, is that the apologetic arguments contained in the text are similar to other kinds of accounts and texts of the same nature. Even if the author concocted the debate, then, he did so on the basis of how authentic Christian communities were actually handling information about Islam and with reference to topics genuinely debated by Christians and Muslims.[5] In other words, the general contours of theological exchange between Muslims and East Syrian Christians are on display in the disputation.

In the case of the monk's debate these topics are employed in an effort to help Christian readers discern the true religion between Islam and Christianity.[6] So the Muslim taunted the monk at the beginning of the debate by asking, 'Is our religion not better than all the [other] religions on earth?'[7] And the Muslim conceded at the end of the debate, 'I acknowledge that your religion is seemly, and … better than ours.'[8] There was certainly good reason to provide this kind of reading material to Syrian Christian communities living under new Muslim rulers. The changes affected by Islam were clearly significant enough that many historians and chroniclers interpreted them as God's judgement for sin.[9] And, alongside political transformations also came the temptation for religious conversion. What, after all, were Syrian Christian communities to make of this new religion and its prophet? Texts like *The Disputation* attempted to answer this question by showing readers how their beliefs and practices were distinct from Islam and how, no matter their social or political circumstances, they could still boast of religious superiority. These arguments, in turn, gave Christians who read the text reason to cling to their faith when the social and economic benefits of converting tempted them to do otherwise.

With respect to Muḥammad, there are a few passages where the author of the account summarized a very general Islamic assessment of the Prophet. According to the Muslim, Muḥammad was worthy of his followers' attentive obedience (by this he meant to indicate that Muslims did not 'create a son for God'),[10] that he was a prophet (*nbiyā*)[11] and that he said Christian monks would 'enjoy the kingdom [of God]'.[12] These details are mentioned somewhat casually, but at one point the Muslim flatly asked, 'Tell me the truth, Muḥammad our prophet, how is he reckoned in your eyes?'[13] The monk responded with a strikingly appreciative answer: Muḥammad was 'a wise and God-fearing man, who freed you from the worship of demons, and caused you to know the one true God'.[14]

This seemingly favourable response prompted an almost incredulous rejoinder. If Muḥammad was so wise, the Muslim inquired, why did he not then 'teach us from the beginning about the mystery of the Trinity?'[15] The debate, up until this point, focused on explications of basic Christian doctrine and the Muslim's question immediately preceding his query about Muḥammad was,

'Given that [God] is one, [why] do you say "Father, and Son and Holy Spirit"?' The monk's response to this question included both philosophical and biblical reflection, but qur'anic nomenclature for Christ was also discussed. In particular, the Muslim and the monk pondered Muḥammad's 'saying' that Christ was a word and spirit of God (Q 4:171).[16] According to the monk, the qur'anic phrase was similar to the angel Gabriel's announcement to Mary in the Gospel of St Luke (Lk. 1.35). There, the angel declared, as the monk put it, 'the Holy Spirit shall come, and the power of the Most High shall rest upon you'.[17]

The connection between the announcement in St Luke's Gospel and the qur'anic phrase is not clear. It would seem, therefore, that the author assumed his readers would be aware of a Syriac exegetical tradition that made the connection plain. According to St Ephrem the Syrian (d. 373), the 'power of the Most High' was identified with the 'Word'.[18] In such a case, the angel could be understood to say that the Spirit and the Word, that is, the Most High, would rest upon Mary. As a result, the Qur'ān could be said to echo this phrase, in the monk's view anyway, and in so doing made the divinity of Christ implicit in the Qur'ān for those who were able to see it there. In turn, this demonstrated that God was a Trinity in Unity. So the Muslim inquired why, if Muḥammad was everything the monk said that he was, would he be so cryptic about the triune nature of God in the Qur'ān. Why would he not make that clear to Muslims from the very beginning?

Muḥammad did not make explicit his knowledge of the Trinity, the monk responded, because the Arabs who were known to him were 'childlike in knowledge'. Knowing that they were incapable of fully understanding Trinitarian doctrine, Muḥammad offered them a simplified form of monotheism. Drawing them a certain distance towards the truth in this way prevented the otherwise foolish Arabs from warping Muḥammad's message back into polytheism. And, just as Muḥammad took his knowledge of Christ from the Gospel of St Luke, so his message about monotheism was taught to him, according to the monk, by none other than 'Sergius Baḥīrā'.[19] At this point, the discussion shifted to matters of Christian piety and religious practice.[20]

In the entire debate, then, Muḥammad is given relatively little space, almost as if Muḥammad was a bit incidental to the economy of revelation presented to the Arabs. Notably, he is called 'wise and God-fearing'. He is credited with turning the Arabs away from polytheism and drawing them towards monotheism. That is really all that the monk has to say about Muḥammad and even this magnanimous offering requires clarification. Muḥammad drew much of what he knew – essentially a kind of primordial Christianity – from the Bible and was mentored in doing so by Sergius Baḥīrā; his guided efforts only informed the infantile Arabs of partial truth. This is all that readers are told. The result, when it comes to Muḥammad, is barely a thumbnail sketch; he seems admirable but rather peripheral – very nearly inconsequential – to the religious concerns presented by Islam. Why?

It might be said that because the text is a kind of summary of the topoi in Christian–Muslim apologetic literature, the author chose to briefly discuss the status of Muḥammad so he could also address other matters, giving more space to some and less to others. So he flagged a topic that Muslims were known to question (what do we do with Muḥammad?) and provided a basic Christian response. This explanation is certainly plausible, and I will return to it further on, but it is not entirely satisfactory since the monk's comments about Muḥammad seem to settle into a larger context. In this light, a clue to the relative paucity of Muḥammad in the text is offered in the Muslim's final question. 'Tell me the truth in as much as you know it', he pleaded with the monk. 'Will the sons of Hagar [i.e., Muslims] enter the kingdom, or not?'[21] Readers of *The Disputation* can recall in this question the Muslim's earlier claim in which Muḥammad granted that Christian monks would enter God's kingdom. Does Christianity allow a reciprocal place for Muslims? In reply, the monk said that only those who were baptized would enter the kingdom of God. 'But', he intriguingly clarified, 'if there should be someone who has fine deeds, he may live through grace in (those) mansions which are far removed from the torment, but he shall be considered as a hired hand, and not as a son (and heir).'[22]

The monk appealed here to Christ's words in the Gospel of St John about the Father's many mansions (Jn. 14.2) and, for their interpretation, he looked once again to St Ephrem the Syrian. According to St Ephrem, 'in the delightful mansions on the borders of Paradise do the souls of the just and righteous reside'.[23] Baptized souls *enter* Paradise. The unbaptized righteous souls reside just beyond the gates, away from eternal torment, but nevertheless, outside the kingdom. The monk drew on this exegetical tradition, appearing to take for granted his readers' knowledge of it. More importantly, the tradition was used in order to suggest that Muslims, by virtue of their good deeds, might spend eternity *near* the kingdom but simply not enter fully into it. Insofar as Muslims were brought near to monotheism and close to the fullness of truth found in Christianity, so they were brought near to the kingdom of God.

With this reply, the monk seems to have flattened the distinctions between Islam and Christianity. Accordingly, Islam was hardly a religion in its own right; Muslim beliefs were really only derivatives of Christianity. Muḥammad's message could be made to echo Christian belief if only it was understood correctly. A Christian, after all, taught Muḥammad. And Islam's confession of monotheism, which was a helpful, even if rickety plank leading towards the fullness of Christian faith, was quite enough for virtuous Muslims to make their way to a place nearby the kingdom of God.[24] The deep divide worn between *tawḥīd* and Trinitarian thought was very nearly filled in with the monk's estimation, all in order to downgrade Muḥammad's message to a simplistic derivation of Christian truth.

There is also a less scheming explanation for the ways in which the monk handled the differences between Islam and Christianity. In the early Islamic period, even in the eighth century when *The Disputation* was written, the ways in which one defined what it meant to be Muslim were not always applied equally and were still very much fluid in certain contexts. Conversions to Islam, however frequently they may or may not have occurred, were not always a highly organized affair and usually occurred in groups. These communal conversions regularly happened, moreover, for political reasons. Oftentimes these conversions occurred with very little catechism so that many new adherents of Islam did not know their faith well. Some still requested baptism for their children; others recited pagan poetry in mosques simply because it had the sound of the Qur'an when it was chanted in Arabic.[25] In this light, the renowned Muslim annalist al-Ṭabarī's (d. 923) remark – a Muslim was anyone who 'prays as we do, who prays [whilst] facing the [proper] direction as we do, and eats meat ritually butchered as we do' – reflects a similar flattening of the religious identifiers that might mark one out as distinctly Muslim.[26]

All of this is not to say that there were no individuals who converted to Islam in these early periods, that no one ever did so for purely spiritual or dogmatic reasons or that there were no converts who could boast a firm grasp of their new faith.[27] To assume, however, that all conversions took place because individuals decided on their own on the veracity of one set of beliefs over and against another set is to impose a decidedly modern view of religious conversion on an early medieval context. In the early Islamic period, with Muslim-controlled regions still expanding and Muslims themselves remaining numerical minorities in the lands in which they resided, the ways in which Muslim identity was defined simply fell short of what could be considered orthodox, or at least what would be considered orthodox by later periods. There were often matters of political and tribal expediency as well as social belonging to consider in addition to religious faith.[28] With this in mind, the monk's comments about where Muslims might reside in the kingdom of God may have less to do with an intentional flattening of the differences between Christianity and Islam and more to do with an awareness of the narrow extent of differences that existed in his time and context.[29] In either case, the result was that Islam became much more of a derivative of Christianity than an independent belief system in its own right.

To put the matter bluntly, then, Muḥammad appears peripheral in *The Disputation* because its author minimizes his religious impact. His religious impact is minimized, moreover, because he is Christianized.[30] In the account of the debate Muḥammad became a quasi-Christian – a wise monotheist drawing here and there from Christian sources – who preached a religion that was merely derivative, parasitic even, of Christianity. Muḥammad is sidelined, then, because he simply served a narrow and, ultimately, incomplete role. This he did well. Islam, at least from what can be gathered from *The Disputation*, really only functioned to draw Arabs a little closer to the fullness of faith. As a result, Muḥammad need not be demonized or dehumanized by the author. In turn, a more nuanced way of describing the text's function may not be to only think of it in terms of discerning right religion from wrong religion. Rather, if Islam only aped Christianity by drawing on and learning from its sources, then the debate was really a matter of superior versus inferior religion.[31] In the presentation of an inferior, parasitic faith can be found a prophet of only marginal importance.

An East Syrian patriarch's discussion with a caliph

Another early Syriac text was written in the late eighth century. It, too, is an apologetic text and is presented as an account of a theological discussion between East Syrian Patriarch Timothy I (d. 823) and Caliph al-Mahdī (d. 785) in Baghdad.[32] The debate purportedly took place in Arabic (the account is written in Syriac) over the course of two days in 782 or 783. After the debate, Timothy wrote down a record of the exchange in a letter to a friend.[33] Such discussions were not uncommon and a genre of religious treatises arose based on them, what Sidney Griffith calls 'the monk in the emir's *majlis*'.[34] Not unlike question-and-answer texts, in these accounts a monk or ecclesiastic is summoned by or found in the presence of Muslim authorities whereupon he is asked to defend Christian faith and practice with a caliph, emir and/or Muslim scholars. Frequently, authors of such texts had a narrator tell the story of the exchanges. As a result, the accounts are highly readable and engaging, intended to circulate among communities of Christian readers.[35] In turn, they could encourage and inform them, helping to shape and affirm their identities as Christians living in Islamic milieus. Stories of theological triumph in which one of their own bested Muslim elites could be nourishing. And, since such accounts often reflected authentic contexts in which such exchanges took place, they could also equip readers with strategies to overcome their Muslim interlocutors in debate.

In Timothy's discussion, the patriarch offered detailed explanations on topics ranging from Christology and the Trinity to the nature of scripture and miscellaneous ethical concerns.[36] In the course of their conversation, the Caliph made several inquiries about how Timothy understood the identity of Muḥammad. In the first inquiry, the Caliph asked, 'How is it that you accept Christ and the Gospel from the testimony of the Torah and of the prophets, and you do not accept Muḥammad from the testimony of Christ and the Gospel?'[37] For the Caliph, the implication was that, according to the Qur'ān (61:6), Muḥammad was foretold in the Gospels and that Christ testified to his coming. Timothy replied, noting the places where Christ was foretold in the Hebrew Bible. 'These and scores of other passages of the prophets', he concluded, 'show us Jesus Christ in a clear mirror and point to Him. So far as Muḥammad is concerned I have not received a single testimony either from Jesus Christ or from the Gospel which would refer to his name or to his works.'[38]

Unconvinced, the Caliph waved off this response. 'Who is then the Paraclete?' he pressed further.[39] In the Caliph's mind, the one promised by Christ in the Gospels – the one referred to as the Paraclete – was none other than Muḥammad.[40] Timothy responded with yet more biblical evidence that clarified the identity of the Paraclete as the Spirit of God. He even drew from theology and the Qur'ān in order to discount the possibility that Muḥammad might be this promised helper.[41] 'Muḥammad is not the Paraclete', Timothy concluded, 'and … I have not received a single testimony from the Gospel about him.'[42] So Muḥammad lacked scriptural witness and did not exhibit the characteristics attributed to the Paraclete, rightly identified as the Spirit of the Triune God. But who, exactly, was Muḥammad and how did God use (or reject) him?

From here the debate shifted to matters of scripture and doctrine, but the Caliph eventually returned to the topic of Muḥammad in what has become a well-known passage in the account of the exchange. He asked pointedly, 'What do you say about Muḥammad?' Earlier in the debate, in their discussion about Muḥammad in the Bible, Timothy asserted that 'after the coming of Christ there will be neither prophet nor prophecy'.[43] But in response to this question, Timothy proclaimed:

> Muḥammad is worthy of all praise, by all reasonable people … . He walked in the path of the prophets, and trod in the track of the lovers of God. All prophets taught the doctrine of the one God, and since Muḥammad taught the doctrine of the unity of God, he walked, therefore, in the path of the prophets. Further, all the prophets drove men away from bad works, and brought them nearer to good works, and since Muḥammad drove his people away from bad works and brought them nearer to the good ones, he walked, therefore, in the path of the prophets. Again, all the prophets separated men from idolatry and polytheism, and attached them to God and to His cult, and since Muḥammad separated his people from idolatry and polytheism, and attached them to the cult and the knowledge of one God, beside whom there is no other God, it is obvious that he walked in the path of the prophets. Finally, Muḥammad taught about God, His Word and His Spirit. Muḥammad walked, therefore, in the path of all the prophets … . Who will not praise … the one whom God has praised, and will not weave a crown of glory and majesty to the one whom God has glorified and exalted? These and similar things I and all God-lovers utter about Muḥammad.[44]

Timothy's answer is not at all unlike the much more compact response given by the monk of Bēt Ḥālē in reply to the same question about Muḥammad. It would seem, in this light, that both the monk and the Patriarch drew from a common Syriac tradition for understanding Muḥammad. The author of the Bēt Ḥālē debate recorded a response in abbreviated form, either transmitting the gist of the tradition or simply condensing what he knew his readers would understand. Patriarch Timothy recorded this same tradition, expanding upon the abbreviated details of the earlier debate. Taken together, Muḥammad appears as a wise figure worthy of praise because he functioned *like* a prophet (a clarification to which I shall return below). He did so by condemning polytheism and bad works, by preaching about the one God, his Word and his Spirit, and by drawing his followers towards good works.

Beyond an apparent expansion of what the monk from Bēt Ḥālē said, Timothy's answer surely reflects the care he took to be diplomatic when answering a question about the Prophet in front of the Caliph. Even more, though, Timothy's answer is also quite eloquent. Muḥammad 'walked in the path of the prophets, and trod in the track of the lovers of God'. He 'taught about God' and was 'worthy of all praise' from anyone who might give him a fair assessment. He functioned in his context in the same way those sent by God had functioned in theirs. Even considering all that Timothy had to say to the Caliph, his evaluation, in the end, placed Muḥammad alongside the prophets who came before him and acknowledged his love for the one true God.

Such high appreciation, however, only went so far and one must discern the limitations that lay beneath the Patriarch's high praise. Without discounting his generosity and eloquence, Timothy never actually called Muḥammad a prophet; he was merely prophet-like insofar as he walked in the path of prophets. He did similar things, in other words, and attempted to follow their example. That is no small compliment, and yet it stops short of what the Caliph and other Muslims would want to hear.[45] This clarification becomes clearer in the light of the way Timothy elaborated upon Muḥammad's zeal for God.[46] All the good work Muḥammad did, Timothy clarified, was restricted to Arabia and to a formerly pagan people. He was not, then, a universal prophet with a message applicable to all humankind. Further, much of what he proclaimed could be found better explicated, according to Timothy, in Christian doctrines and sources.[47] In these ways, Muḥammad really only mimicked in his Arabian context what the previous Hebrew prophets, such as Moses and Abraham,[48] did in theirs: in Timothy's estimation, Muḥammad prepared the way for Christ. Due to his efforts, former pagans were made better able to comprehend the precise nature of Christ and his work.[49] And so, much like the assessment from the monk of Bēt Ḥālē, Muḥammad was for Timothy a kind of quasi-Christian pointing Arabs to Christ.[50] He loved God but was only prophetesque in character.

An East Syrian master's discussion with a student

In perhaps 791 or 792, not long after Patriarch Timothy I wrote the letter describing his discussion with Caliph al-Mahdī, another East Syrian Christian recorded an exchange. This one is Theodore bar Kōnī's *Book of Scholia*, a wide-ranging theological treatise meant for students. Theodore structured the text as a question-and-answer interaction between a master and his student. The interaction was a rhetorical device, not an account of an actual exchange, but the structure helps to make the *Book of Scholia* a ready-made sourcebook that Christians could use in their discussions with Muslims.[51]

Theodore devoted the tenth chapter of his *Book of Scholia* specifically to issues of controversy between Muslims and Christians, matters of dispute concerning religious beliefs and practices. In these passages, the rhetorical student played the part of the Muslim opponent with the rhetorical master, Theodore, continuing on as the wise instructor.[52] Muḥammad is not mentioned by name in the text. Instead, the student referred to him as 'the one who had handed over this teaching to us'.[53] Despite the student's generic references, Theodore made his estimation of Muḥammad and his teaching rather more explicit. In one instance, when the student and master were discussing baptism, the student remarked that the Christian practice was not given much value by his teacher, that is, Muḥammad. Theodore demurred,

> Did the one who has handed this teaching over to you get it from God or from his own conscience that he should speak in this way? If it is from his own mind, we shall not leave the teaching of the scriptures, following after human thoughts. And if you say 'from God', then where has this God been who has taught this, who was misunderstood for more than six hundred years after Christ appeared?[54]

In essence, Theodore's argument assumed that Christ's teachings were from God. If Muḥammad's teachings were also from God, then a gulf of disorientation appears between Christ and Muḥammad. How could confusion over God's message exist for so long? Such a proposition was preposterous. Therefore, Muḥammad's teachings must be his own creation and, as such, mark a deviation from scriptures.

Later on, in the same discussion, the student asked the master, 'If all that you have said is true, why at a certain time did a teacher arise from among yourselves and denounce all of it?'[55] The 'teacher' he mentioned was a reference to Sergius Baḥīrā who, in the Christian tradition, was thought by many to have deliberately misled Muḥammad. Though in the Islamic tradition the monk purportedly recognized the prophethood of Muḥammad, he was used in Christian texts to call into question the authenticity of Islam and his suitability to be an authentic messenger from God. At the very least, Muḥammad's teachings came, for Theodore, from a deceptive Christian. The implication was that Muḥammad and his message could not be trusted.

An inconsequential, retrograde Moses

In other places in the *Book of Scholia*'s tenth chapter, Theodore was more explicit when it came to his view of Muḥammad and Islam. This is particularly poignant in a remark the master offered to the student, 'As I see it, you are believing as a Jew.'[56] In other words, Muslims accepted parts of Christian scripture and affirmed that

Christ was the Messiah. But, like the Jews, they rejected other parts of scripture.[57] In turn, they rejected beliefs in the Trinity and in the divinity of Christ.

Intriguingly, this assessment is not altogether distant from what we find in the debates with the monk of Bēt Ḥālē and Patriarch Timothy I and their Muslim interlocutors. In these discussions, Muḥammad is depicted as bringing a message that was an inferior derivative of Christianity. At best, it was a virtuous, monotheistic step away from paganism that put Arabs in a better position to receive the fullness of (Christian) truth. In this sense, Muḥammad could be seen to represent a step forward. But Theodore places that step into a specific context: Muḥammad had really only brought the Arabs as far as the Jews; they stepped towards monotheism but stopped well short of (Christian) truth. As a result, it was not so much that they had been made more receptive to the fullness of truth, according to Theodore, but that they had simply not come far enough. Theodore's likening of Muslim belief to the Jews, in this way, clearly echoes Patriarch Timothy I who, in another letter in which he recounted a debate with a philosopher, referred to Muslims as 'the new Jews'.[58]

In the end, if Muslims were for these East Syrians the new Jews, then Muḥammad could be nothing more than a new Moses.[59] He brought a law about the one God. But, after Christ, that was not necessary, much less of any benefit. Christ was the one who truly achieved what Moses could not by standing on a mountain and proclaiming a new law, the Gospel, which surpassed what had come before it. Muḥammad, proclaiming his law, simply repeated what Moses had done but in doing so failed to surpass Christ.[60] Muḥammad, for all of his advancement beyond paganism, was, in this light, rather repetitive and certainly unnecessary. As a prophet he was, ultimately, retrograde. And this only confirmed Muḥammad's message as inferior to Christianity and his significance as really only minimal.

It must be said that, despite the rather stark implications for Muḥammad's prophethood that attach somewhat subtly to these figure's arguments, the remarks the monk from Bēt Ḥālē and Patriarch Timothy I offer are remarkably free from vitriol. This is somewhat less the case for Theodore bar Kōnī. But even in his *Book of Scholia* Muḥammad is excused from *severe* treatment. In fact, some of what is said about Muḥammad in the early East Syrian tradition is certainly eloquent and very nearly appreciative, an observation that will become all the more apparent in many of the chapters that follow. For this was certainly not always the case in the bulk of Greek and Latin texts,[61] in many Arabic treatises and not even the case for all Syriac texts, especially for two West Syrian authors to whom I now turn.

4

Muḥammad as a carnal warrior and scheming ruler

West Syrian Christians and refutations of the Prophet

The texts in the previous chapter demonstrate that not all assessments of Muḥammad are entirely antagonistic. Instead, some of the earliest texts to consider his prophethood, and some of the Christian authors in nearest proximity to Muslims early on, had much to say about Muḥammad that was surprisingly appreciative even as they found ways to assert the superiority of Christian claims. The significance of these views notwithstanding, this chapter adds further nuance by problematizing the notion that the earliest Christian encounters with Muḥammad, his message or his followers were always irenic or even primarily amicable. They also challenge the idea that Syriac texts or ones written by Christians situated in the Syrian liturgical traditions were generally affirming when it came to Islam and its Prophet.

A West Syrian's letter in response to a Muslim

It was likely during the first half of the ninth century when a Muslim named ʿAbdallāh ibn Ismāʿīl al-Hāshimī wrote a letter describing his faith. He sent the letter to a West Syrian Christian named ʿAbd al-Masīḥ ibn Isḥāq al-Kindī and called upon the Christian to consider Islam and convert. Al-Kindī, in turn, responded with a lengthy *Risāla*, contesting each of al-Hāshimī's claims and exposing what he argued was the incoherence and unseemliness of Islam, the Prophet Muḥammad and the Qurʾān. The exchange is a veritable summary of the major topoi of Christian–Muslim disputational literature and it became an important source of information about Islam. Other authors, some of whom I discuss later on, depend quite heavily on al-Kindī and the text was even translated into Latin in the twelfth century as a part of the *Collectio Toletana* produced under the auspices of Peter the Venerable (d. 1156).[1] As a result, the text took on new life and became an important source for still later texts on Islam and Muḥammad. In fact, 'the arguments [al-Kindī] puts forward may now seem to be cliché', Sandra Keating surmises, 'because they became so integral to Christian apologetical literature, especially in Europe, over the centuries'.[2]

It must be said that the epistolary exchange between al-Hāshimī and al-Kindī may not be authentic. And it may be the case that the Muslim al-Hāshimī never existed. Instead, it is possible that a Christian author invented a Muslim's presentation of Islam and call to convert for rhetorical purposes, using it to create a foil upon which to build a defence of Christianity and an attack upon Islam.[3] The identity of the Christian is also uncertain, with many scholars placing him within a variety of Christian communities, including the East Syrian tradition.[4] Samir Khalil Samir and Sandra Keating, however, have argued that the author is a West Syrian Christian, at home in the context of Christian–Muslim debates of the ninth century.[5] Keating further speculates that this author wrote in the 'second half of the 820's' and was 'associated with the court of al-Ma'mūn, and in conversation with a Muslim who has invited him to Islam'.[6] Their conclusions rest on the similarities the *Risāla* shares with other, comparable texts confidently attributed to the West Syrian Abū Rā'iṭa al-Takrītī in the early ninth century.[7] Abū Rā'iṭa wrote one of his *rasā'il* in response to a request from another Christian engaged in religious discussion with Muslims and, indeed, al-Kindī's text follows Abū Rā'iṭa's suggested line of argumentation. Evidence like this suggests that a fellow West Syrian known to Abū Rā'iṭa engaged in religious dialogue with Muslims and produced a text very much like what we have from al-Kindī.[8]

When it comes to al-Kindī's *Risāla*, the text is essentially divided into three parts: the first is an explanation of Christian doctrine; the second, an examination of Muḥammad and the Qur'ān; and the third, a defence of Christian truth vis-à-vis Islam.[9] Material in the second section is, of course, especially important here. This material, however, is premised, as is al-Kindī's entire response, upon al-Hāshimī's summons to convert to Islam. In particular, he entreated al-Kindī 'to bear witness, and confess the prophetic rank of my master, the lord of humankind, friend of the Lord of the universe, seal of the prophetic order, Muḥammad'.[10] Al-Hāshimī went on to describe Muḥammad's prophetic ministry: his rejection of idolatry, his penchant for mercy and good works, his success in terms of followers and the miracle of the Qur'ān that was revealed to him.[11]

Al-Kindī began in his response, with respect to Muḥammad, by acknowledging al-Hāshimī's claims about the Prophet's greatness. He took no issue with a Muslim extolling the greatness of another Muslim figure. He did, however, bristle 'when you summon us to admit his prophetic office as genuine and binding'.[12] Al-Kindī's solution was to examine 'the history of your master'.[13] What follows in the text, then, is a reasonably detailed examination of Muḥammad's life with an intention to discern the qualities that might validate or invalidate his prophethood.

Al-Kindī's central argument was that Muḥammad lacked the necessary characteristics of a prophet. Some of these shortcomings pertained to Muḥammad's personal character. For instance, al-Kindī argued that Muḥammad was a scheming trickster. Having come from relatively little means, he was made rich by virtue of his marriage to Khadījah, a wealthy merchant. With his newfound power and wealth, he made a grab for authority but was unsuccessful. So he claimed to be a prophet and an apostle as a means to garner authority over his fellow Arabs. In large part, this worked since the Arabs were unable to discern the truth of his claims or the purity of his motives.[14]

Al-Kindī also portrayed Muḥammad as excessively violent. Al-Kindī went to reasonably great length to detail various Arab raids led by Muḥammad and the barbarity that accompanied them. 'Is it on such grounds', al-Kindī questioned Muslims, 'that you hold your master to have been a prophet? What has a prophet to do with plunder and raids, infesting of roads, intercepting and taking the property of men? What has your master left for thieves and highwaymen to do?'[15] Of course, some Muslims may have wanted to use the wide success of Muḥammad's military exploits as proof of his prophethood or at least as a sign of God's endorsement. Al-Kindī questioned this line of reasoning and noted that an oppressor's success was often less about him and any alleged divine approval he might have and more about the transgressions of nations who fell to oppressors.[16] Nations fell because of their sin. Muḥammad, then, was just one more violent and barbaric oppressor.

The most striking examples of excessiveness that al-Kindī used to discredit Muḥammad concerned the Prophet's sexual ethics and descriptions of related sexual prowess. According to al-Kindī, Muḥammad 'was a man who had no thought or caring save for beautiful women whom he might marry, or men whom he might plunder, shedding their blood, taking their property and marrying their wives'.[17] As proof of his allegation, al-Kindī cited an Islamic tradition in which Muḥammad reportedly admitted that God had given him two passions: perfume and women.[18] Then al-Kindī inquired, 'Are we to hold him a prophet because God gave him strength of loin to deal with as many women as forty ordinary men?' The description of Muḥammad's alleged sexual prowess could have been drawn from a number of Islamic traditions. One describes how Muḥammad balanced marital relations with each of his wives. It was reported that he 'was given the strength of thirty [men]' as a way of hyperbolically responding to the question of whether or not he had the stamina to visit each of his wives.[19] Others simply report that he had the stamina of 40 men, a strength that would double in heaven.[20] Christian authors such as al-Kindī looked at traditions like these, especially in the context of polygynous marital relations, and saw them, regardless of their varying degrees of reliability, as made-to-order for polemic against Muḥammad. Whether or not he knew the function of such traditions, al-Kindī used this one about Muḥammad's sexual prowess in order to cast shocking doubt upon his claim to prophethood. Related in the way al-Kindī used it, the tradition also became dehumanizing for the ways in which excessive sexuality is used to degrade Muḥammad.[21]

A final proof that pertained to Muḥammad's excessive sexuality was drawn from his household. Here, al-Kindī referred to the pre-eminent example of Muḥammad's disqualifying infidelity: his marriage to Zaynab bint Jaḥsh. Al-Kindī recounted the details of the marriage – how Zaynab's husband divorced her so that Muḥammad could marry her and how the Qur'ān justified the entire arrangement (al-Kindī used Q 33:37 in order to summarize the event).[22] Al-Kindī also highlighted Muḥammad's other marriages and the seeming chaos naturally resulting from a household in which a man kept multiple wives. He concluded:

> Now if a man cannot serve one wife and please her without forgetting his Maker, how much less can he bend all his energies to please 15 wives and two concubines? Besides, he was, as you know, absorbed in other pursuits … how could he find time to fast and pray, to collect his thoughts and to turn himself to other matters which were involved in his sacred duties? Certainly we have here a novel and original conception of the prophetic office.[23]

In al-Kindī's *Risāla*, Muḥammad's other shortcomings pertained to qualities that would typically accompany a genuine prophet but were not apparent in his life. For instance, the stories of Muḥammad's military exploits were often accompanied by examples of him being wounded in battle, facing significant adversity without any divine assistance and protection or lacking prophetic foresight. So al-Kindī wondered why, if God sent Muḥammad, was he absent when Muḥammad's teeth were broken, his lip split and his cheek gashed in battle? Surely a prophet would have been spared from such war wounds.[24] Why did no angels come to help Muḥammad or his armies when they faced adversity and insurmountable odds in battle?[25] Finally, the word 'prophet', al-Kindī contended in a grammatical argument, meant one who foretold information no one else knew or explained previously known information that was otherwise mysterious.[26] Why, then, was Muḥammad unable to foresee military setbacks so that he could avoid them or approach them differently? Such foresight 'was truly the sign of a prophet, with insight to see things both past and future, one who can publish them, predicting them before they can come to pass and heralding them before their advent'.[27] In fact, according to al-Kindī, Muḥammad never claimed to possess the gift of foreknowledge and all of his religious proclamations were things Christians 'already know'.[28] They were, in other words, hardly mysteries anymore and so the claim of Muḥammad's prophethood failed.

For al-Kindī, another significant feature missing from Muḥammad's life was the presence of miracles. Of course, Muslims had a number of responses to this argument and offered various examples that they argued should be understood as miraculous. For example, al-Kindī referred to the story of the Jewish woman, Zaynab bint al-Ḥarith, who attempted to poison Muḥammad's food. According to the tradition, a piece of the food, a lamb shoulder, that Muḥammad had eaten warned him that it was seasoned with poison. The poisoned meat did not kill Muḥammad, but it did cause the death of one of his companions, Bishr ibn al-Barā', who was eating alongside him.[29] The story is thought to constitute a miracle that validated the special status granted to Muḥammad by God, a characteristic unique to prophets. Examples like these, however, were unconvincing to al-Kindī. Perhaps the poisoned meat was the cause of Muḥammad's *eventual* death. If Muḥammad was made aware of the poison, then why did he not prevent his companions from swallowing it? Why did he not implore God to heal Bishr? 'That would have been a sign worthy of a prophet', al-Kindī remarked.[30] In any case, al-Kindī added that Muḥammad himself never claimed to have been able to perform divine signs. Those who made claims on his behalf 'have no ground to stand on'. On the contrary, al-Kindī concluded, Muḥammad 'was sent with the sword, enforcing his pretensions and those who did not confess that he was a prophet were slain or paid a heavy fine'.[31]

Typifying his assessment of Muḥammad's prophethood was al-Kindī's account of Muḥammad's death. According to al-Kindī, Muḥammad claimed that, like Christ, God would raise him to heaven before three days had passed beyond his death. Muḥammad's companions laid him out after his death, feeling confident that God would take him. Three days came and went, with Muḥammad's body beginning to decompose and rot. On the fourth day, his companions simply buried him. Upon his burial, the Muslim community descended into chaotic division. Through force and fear and bribery, some sense of unity was restored, but many who said they remained faithful to Islam after Muḥammad's death did not do so truthfully.[32] So Muḥammad died the ignominious death he deserved, at least according to al-Kindī, and the fruit of his life was the same violence, discord and untruthfulness that he sowed now made manifest in the Muslim community.

In fact, much of al-Kindī's recounting of the events following Muḥammad's death conforms to various Muslim traditions. As Krisztina Szilágyi has shown, traditions surrounding Muḥammad's death and delayed burial circulated among early Muslim communities where there was debate about a possible resurrection of Muḥammad, an ascension to heaven and the time that elapsed between his death and burial. In this light, it cannot be said that al-Kindī invented the details in order to malign Muḥammad. Instead, he culled details from Islamic traditions that fit the agenda of his polemic.[33] In that agenda, Muḥammad could not have been further from the example of Christ and the previous prophets. Al-Kindī repeatedly compared them to Muḥammad, showing how the former brought peace and virtue, acted under God's direction, were validated by miracles and could discern the future.[34] Muḥammad, by contrast and in the light of al-Kindī's relentless attack, fell rather short. Thus, al-Kindī offered a very curious summary assessment of Muḥammad's prophethood. First he concluded that 'God never sent' Muḥammad and then he reminded al-Hāshimī of what he claimed were Christ's words:

> All the prophets prophesied [until] the time of My coming, and at My coming prophecy ceased, and no prophet shall arise after Me. Those who come after Me and claim to be prophets are thieves and robbers; ye shall not hear them.[35]

Al-Kindī asserted, in summary, that there was no place for a prophet, even if he was not like Muḥammad, after Christ. But what is curious about his claim is that al-Kindī placed many of the words in Christ's mouth. The first portion of the quotation is reminiscent of Mt. 11.13, but the rest of the phrase – that no prophets would arise after Christ's coming – does not appear in the Gospels at all. The second portion of the quote – that those coming after Christ who claim to be prophets are thieves and robbers – appears to be drawn from Jn 10.8, but al-Kindī severely altered it. In the Gospel text, Christ says that he is the gate for the sheep. Anyone who enters the fold by any other means is not a sheep but a thief. Those coming before Christ were indeed thieves and robbers, but the sheep did not listen to them. It would seem that al-Kindī wanted to see Muḥammad in this text, and so he rearranged Christ's words and made Muḥammad the thief who wished to sneak in the fold and steal Christ's sheep.[36] And, since Muḥammad followed after Christ, his claim to a prophetic voice should be ignored.

For al-Kindī, then, Muḥammad was not a prophet. Unlike al-Kindī's East Syrian contemporaries whom we met in the last chapter, Muḥammad was not a virtuous Arab sent to his people with a message of monotheism. He was not a kind of primordial Christian who, even if inadvertently, brought Arabs closer to the fullness of Christian faith and pointed them to Christ. Instead, Muḥammad was excessive in every personal shortcoming that disqualified his prophethood. His claims to prophethood really only masked his political ambitions. In this way, he was a warrior. But even in this category he was a conniving, unduly violent and ruthless murderer.[37] He was, furthermore, excessively lascivious, boasting sexual prowess that made him more animal than man. His polygynous household was a chaotic mess of disunity and sordid affairs. Besides these personal flaws, Muḥammad also simply failed to possess the necessary qualities of a prophet. He boasted of no miracles. The evidence, at least as it was presented by al-Kindī, made it clear that he could not foresee the future and lacked divine assistance. The best of his religious proclamations represented details with which Christians were already well acquainted. In this, Muḥammad was simply rather dull. The story Muḥammad's followers told in order to address such claims were, according to al-Kindī, nothing more than 'poor stuff, the idle tales of bearded dotards'.[38] In short, God did not send Muḥammad.

The stark contrast with which al-Kindī assessed Muḥammad, compared to someone like Patriarch Timothy I, led P. S. van Koningsveld to write that the *Risāla* 'can be read … as one long refutation of Timothy's reconciliatory debate with Caliph Al-Mahdī'.[39] As I detailed in the last chapter, Timothy's remarks are not altogether 'reconciliatory', but van Koningsveld's comment remains an intriguing argument because al-Hāshimī, in the letter he addressed to al-Kindī, described East Syrians at length and praised their generally favourable posture towards Muslims, a feature clearly evident, even if only on the surface, in the account of Timothy's debate. Al-Hāshimī also spoke of his interactions with East Syrian monks, bishops and metropolitans. In one way, it is an impressive résumé, but it really only served as a target that al-Hāshimī could destroy in the rest of his letter. Likewise, al-Kindī was able to demolish the seeming rapprochement towards Muḥammad of someone like Timothy in an assessment that was highly and comparatively antagonistic.

A West Syrian metropolitan's response to Muslims

A second text comes from the twelfth century and was written by Dionysius bar Ṣalībī (d. 1171). Where al-Kindī's biography and Christian tradition are relatively obscure and open to speculation, Bar Ṣalībī was most assuredly a West Syrian metropolitan situated in the eastern region of what is now Turkey. Not only did he function as an ecclesiastic but his writing also reflects the work of a philosopher, theologian and historian. His refutation, *A Response to the Arabs*, is the most comprehensive assessment of Islam written in Syriac, and he pulled into this work many of the expected topoi of refutational literature devoted to Islam, including the interpretational traditions of Syrian authors who wrote before him.[40] His work also drew upon previous texts from the East and West Syrian traditions devoted to Islam. So, Bar Ṣalībī's discussion of scripture sounds very much like Timothy I and his overall approach to Muḥammad is reminiscent of al-Kindī. But, as I highlight below, Bar Ṣalībī also struck new ground in his work, particularly when it came to considering Islam.[41]

A Response to the Arabs functioned as a kind of disputational sourcebook. By covering a wide range of topics – historical sketches of Islam, Muslim objections to Christian doctrine and practice and common points of disagreement between Christians and Muslims over matters related to prophethood and scripture – Bar Ṣalībī provided readers with strategies for responding to Muslims in debate.[42] Towards the beginning of the work, he even offered his view on who might best be engaged with such apologetics: certainly not 'ignorant' or 'deceitful' Muslims but instead the 'dialecticians and the learned'.[43]

Bar Ṣalībī's initial thoughts about Muḥammad are offered at the very beginning of the text when he commented on the rise of Islam. According to Bar Ṣalībī, Muḥammad chatted with Jews along his journeys as a trader. From these Jews he learned about the belief in one God 'and one hypostasis'.[44] In turn, when he saw his people worshiping idols, Muḥammad taught them monotheism. He quickly gained a following and asserted himself as the new community's leader.[45] The new Muslim community grew, both in numbers and in geographical area, by force of power. Its growth was encouraged by Muḥammad who promised his followers an abundance of riches in return for their devotion.[46] Besides converting polytheists to the worship of one God and raiding surrounding areas, Muḥammad also created a system of laws for his new community and claimed that the angel Gabriel gave the laws to him. The list of laws Bar Ṣalībī enumerated is really an account of basic Muslim religious beliefs and practices.[47] Based on Bar Ṣalībī's brief biography, Muḥammad appears as a cunning political leader and a greedy general who just happened to have monotheistic allegiances.

Bar Ṣalībī's next remarks on Muḥammad focused on ways in which he fell short of the requirements meant to validate a figure's prophetic status. Bar Ṣalībī led up to this argument by applying a typological hermeneutic to Old Testament passages, demonstrating how biblical prophets bore testimony to Christ.[48] Following on this, Bar Ṣalībī offered a similar argument, this time drawn from the witness of non-Christian philosophers.[49] This approach allowed Bar Ṣalībī to suggest a taunt of Muslims: 'What do you say, O sons of Hagar? Who of them prophesied concerning your Muḥammad? Not a one!' As a result, Muḥammad lacked the necessary scriptural precedence required of prophets.[50]

Other arguments concerning Muḥammad's inability to perform miracles or predict future events followed, but the question of how Christians ought to assess Muḥammad is focused in three sections in particular. In the first, Bar Ṣalībī recognized, 'But they say: Why do you not acknowledge Muḥammad?' The answer, for Bar Ṣalībī, came back to the absence of any witness that would point towards Muḥammad. More importantly, Bar Ṣalībī argued that Muḥammad could not be acknowledged as a prophet by Christians because his law either contradicted Christian truth or repeated it. With this in mind, he taunted Muslims again: 'Now show us what is in your scripture that was not said by Moses or the Gospel. And if there is nothing additional, then neither is there any need of it'.[51] Where in earlier Syrian texts Muḥammad was said to accomplish what previous prophets did – he prepared his people for a proper understanding of Christ – in Bar Ṣalībī's text Muḥammad was, at the very best, obsolete. In this way, his services were not required.

In the second section, Bar Ṣalībī observed that Muslims 'ask whether Muḥammad is a prophet, or not'. He advised that,

> If he who asks is a reasonable inquirer, we should answer him: If you seek to learn from us, he is not a prophet as far as we are concerned because it is written in your scripture that God said to Muḥammad: 'If you are uncertain about anything we have revealed to you, ask those who read the scriptures before you' (Q 10:94). It is clear from these words that [God] sent [Muḥammad] to us who possess the books of the prophets and the New Testament so that he might learn. If he were a prophet in our estimation, we would accept his scripture, believe as he does, and follow his practice.[52]

Muḥammad was meant to learn from Christian scripture. In this light, he did not offer anything that was new. So not only did he fail to function as a prophet – he lacked prophetic witness, performed no miracles and was unable to discern the future – but he was also redundant. What he did preach that was new contradicted Christian truth; it could not be accepted and, by implication, represented cases in which Muḥammad failed to learn from the (Christian) texts to which he had been pointed.

Finally, Bar Ṣalībī reframed the Muslim question. 'Why do you ask us', he wrote, 'to testify whether or not your *rasūl* (the Arabic term for 'apostle', which Bar Ṣalībī transliterated into Syriac) is a prophet?'[53] In response, Bar Ṣalībī explained that being sent by God did not necessarily equate to being a prophet. Even 'locusts and hail and plagues' were sent by God, 'but no one says that these are prophets'.[54] Bar Ṣalībī thus repeated the qualifications of a prophet sent by God, in particular the grammatical argument that a prophet is one who makes things known. At best, Muḥammad only 'repeated and set down various earlier accounts'.[55]

Bar Ṣalībī concluded his commentary on the prophethood of Muḥammad with a question for Muslims. 'Who is more honourable in the sight of God: people who fast and pray and avoid fornication, or those who pursue lustful desires?'[56] Everyone could agree upon the virtues of previous prophets. 'So tell us', he entreated in yet another taunt, 'what is written concerning your prophet in his scripture?'[57] Bar Ṣalībī answered his question with a death knell of salacious details. He quoted Q 33:50 – a revelation that sanctioned Muḥammad's marriages – in order to point out the seemingly excessive marital allowances given to Muḥammad. 'Now who extols someone as a prophet who marries all these women?' he wondered.[58]

Then Bar Ṣalībī turned to the delights Muḥammad promised in Paradise, which seemed to him to be terribly scandalous. 'Who will verify', Bar Ṣalībī demanded, 'intercourse with seventy women, who you claim are given to all of you, and the pudendum of each one of them of seventy miles long?'[59] The graphic description is similar to, though more explicit than, a comparable depiction provided in the long Arabic recension of the legend of Sergius Baḥīrā.[60] It is possible that Bar Ṣalībī's knowledge of these descriptions came from Christian texts that referred to them. It could also be that Bar Ṣalībī encountered them in conversation with Muslims or by reading Islamic traditions. In fact, descriptions of the houris are abundant in *ḥadīth* literature. Many such traditions have very questionable chains of transmission (*isnād*),[61] but they do, in any case, appear frequently. Importantly, the details used to describe them and Paradise in general often include the numbers seven, seventy or seventy thousand, suggesting a kind of symbolic, cosmological perfection.[62] So, not only is it possible that Bar Ṣalībī preserved a tradition he heard, but it could also be that he misheard information and applied to anatomical dimensions something that originally referred to other kinds of metaphorical measurements.[63]

From whichever source Bar Ṣalībī drew his information – and however accurately or inaccurately he preserved the details – the apparent sensual descriptions clearly struck him. Even with their graphic detail, how could he not pass them on to his readers? Any temptation they might have to give some space to Muḥammad would surely be swept away by such a lurid portrayal. And it was not only lurid. It was also unsuitable for heaven – the Christian conception, as Bar Ṣalībī recounts, was thoroughly ascetic[64] – and unbefitting a prophet. The truth, according to Bar Ṣalībī, was that Muslims and their Prophet would 'be tormented eternally'.[65] By implication, it would seem, Muḥammad would not even find a place near the kingdom of heaven. In general, he was simply not accepted as a prophet and what good he did was either theologically redundant or ultimately rooted in his political aspirations.

A warrior and scheming ruler

Dionysius bar Ṣalībī's account of Muḥammad is not altogether the same as al-Kindī's *Risāla*. There is space in *A Response to the Arabs* for Muḥammad's monotheism and a turn away from polytheism. But much of the rest of Bar Ṣalībī's assessment follows the lines of al-Kindī's account. Muḥammad fell short of the necessary requirements a prophet should meet. His message was either redundant when compared to Christianity or simply contradictory. Most troubling, he was a power-hungry warrior and lascivious ruler. For Bar Ṣalībī, as for al-Kindī, Muḥammad was not a prophet and there was nothing virtuous that could be said about him, at least nothing that might have a bearing upon how these West Syrians assessed him.

Considering these authors alongside the East Syrian figures introduced in the last chapter, one must wonder how, with a group of texts that share so much in common, the drastic differences that lay between their assessments of Muḥammad can be explained. What might account for the stark shift between the assessments offered by East Syrians like the monk from Bēt Ḥālē or Patriarch Timothy I and the ones asserted by al-Kindī and Bar Ṣalībī?[66] Is there anything that can mark the apparent shift to the blatant polemic of the latter two authors? One must first note the shift in literary genre. The East Syrian texts purport to be accounts of specific interactions, the circumstances of which may have called for more measured responses to Muslim questions. It is difficult to imagine Timothy, in the presence of Caliph al-Mahdī, responding to questions about Muḥammad with details furnished by al-Kindī. Quite the opposite, the West Syrian texts are purposely written as defences of Christianity vis-à-vis Islam or outright attacks aimed at Muslim beliefs and practices. As such, the texts by al-Kindī and Bar Ṣalībī are much longer, comprehensive and, perhaps in turn, able to give space and voice to details the others were not.

Mere constraints of space, however, would not likely give full account for such a marked difference in information shared about Muḥammad. It may also be a matter, then, of historical context. Perhaps by the ninth century, the earliest possible dating for al-Kindī's *Risāla*, conversions to Islam had begun to increase, even if only slightly by this time, and the doctrinal lines distinguishing Christians and Muslims had begun to solidify and thicken. Texts intent on highlighting the differences between the two faiths and making more plain the reasons Christians should distance themselves from Islam would become more important. Whereas demographic changes of a drastic nature are unlikely by the ninth century, this would surely be the case by the time Bar Ṣalībī wrote his refutation in the twelfth century.[67] The contexts of conversion that may have existed in the ninth, and especially the twelfth, century compared to the eighth century of the East Syrian texts may have influenced al-Kindī and Bar Ṣalībī to write more biting assessments of Muḥammad. One might even blend the influence of genre and context by indicating that certain kinds of texts were thought by authors to be best suited to certain kinds of contexts.[68] Hence, sharper refutations may have been more suited to al-Kindī's and Bar Ṣalībī's contexts.

While each of these explanations may have something to do with differences between the East Syrian and West Syrian texts, another, more significant observation begins to emerge: particular views of Muḥammad do not seem to have been fixed to a single region, time period, language, Christian tradition or literary genre. Instead, an assessment of Muḥammad that might be relatively appreciative is just as likely to appear in one genre from one period, region or Christian tradition as a much more negative assessment is likely to appear in another.

5

Muḥammad as an anti-saint

Martyr saints and hamartiography of the Prophet

Perfectus was a monk of the St Aciscus Basilica just beyond the city walls of Córdoba, Spain. On a spring day in 850, while on a walk and tending to personal business, he was confronted by a group of Muslims who asked what he thought about Christ and Muḥammad. The monk was quick to acknowledge the divinity of Christ, but when it came to Muḥammad he was less than forthright, knowing the possibly hazardous repercussions of a response. He agreed to a pact of friendship with the Muslim inquirers that left him free to speak his mind. And so he held little back in his opinion that Muḥammad was:

> seduced by demonic illusions, devoted to sacrilegious sorcery, he corrupted with his deadly poison the hearts of many idiots and condemned them to eternal perdition. Lacking any spiritual wisdom, he made them subjects of Prince Satan, with whom he will suffer the most abominable punishments in hell.[1]

For Perfectus, Muḥammad was a heretical false prophet. He was in league with Satan and, as Perfectus went on to say, he was a lecherous fool. For evidence, Perfectus cited Muḥammad's marriage to Zaynab bint Jaḥsh, which we have seen was a Christian staple of the Prophet's allegedly adulterous tendencies.[2]

The Muslims surrounding him were obviously incensed with this assault upon their Prophet, but they allowed Perfectus to continue on with his business in accordance with their friendship pact. Several days later, the monk's fortunes changed. The Muslim inquirers found him and accused Perfectus of blaspheming the Prophet. They took him to the *qāḍī*. Realizing his fate, Perfectus denounced Muḥammad again and, after a month in prison, was brought before the *qāḍī* on 18 April 850. He refused to renounce his abuse of the Prophet and was summarily executed. Within 15 months, similar examples began to occur with curious regularity. From 851 to 859, nearly 50 Christians – most of them born in Spain but a few from outside the Iberian Peninsula – were executed by

Muslim authorities for the crimes of apostasy and/or blasphemy of the Prophet Muḥammad.

The question of what motivated the martyrs to take the actions they did has understandably puzzled scholars. Was it a matter of communal, penitential angst? Was the movement a response to social unrest in ninth-century Córdoba? Further complexity comes from the relatively few sources that describe the events. Only two figures, as far as is known, wrote contemporary accounts about the martyrs: Eulogius, a priest from Córdoba who eventually joined the martyrs' ranks in 859, and his friend, the layman Paulus Alvarus (d. c. 862). Eulogius' relevant texts are almost entirely hagiographical and seek to honour the martyrs' actions and deaths, connecting them to the early Christian martyrs of antiquity. He also devoted some texts to defending the martyrs since their actions drew the ire of some Christian communities in Córdoba.[3] Eulogius also threaded through his treatises a highly polemical view of Islam and Muḥammad. Alvarus wrote to defend the martyrs, too, in addition to producing a hagiographical account of Eulogius' life and martyrdom. Like his friend's work, Alvarus' treatment of Islam and Muḥammad is highly antagonistic. There is very little manuscript witness that accompanies their texts, which suggests that their work was not widely read. This casts some doubt as to how well the martyrs' actions were known outside of ninth-century Córdoba, but even regardless of their notoriety, the texts Eulogius and Alvarus produced come to us in such arduous Latin that it is difficult to imagine many readers making much sense of their writings.[4] So a fair bit of obscurity attends the authors, their texts and the martyrs.[5]

In what follows I will not offer any further speculation on what motivated the Cordoban martyrs to seek their deaths in the ways they did, how we might best understand the texts devoted to them or how we might further categorize Christian communities in ninth-century Córdoba.[6] Instead, I would like to focus on how Muḥammad was depicted in texts related to the martyrs' movement and its surrounding milieu, particularly how his life was set into the context of Christian hagiography as a means for understanding his person and prophethood.

Eulogius and Alvarus on Muḥammad

Taken together, much of the literature produced in connection to the Cordoban martyrs was written as martyrology and hagiography. Some texts were much more polemical in nature, but even these were written in order to defend the executed Christians as saints worthy of martyrs' crowns. So like other accounts of saints' and martyrs' lives, Eulogius followed a general pattern when he described the martyrs' actions, their virtuous lives, the circumstances of their arrests by or betrayals to Muslim authorities, their valiant defences before their accusers and judges, their imprisonments and, finally, their executions.[7] Unique to his Islamic milieu, however, were the words Eulogius recorded the martyrs using in order to insult Muḥammad and earn their deaths. We catch a glimpse of this in the account of Perfectus and his description of Muḥammad. Alongside the martyrs' words, Eulogius added his own descriptions of Muḥammad in order to bolster the martyrs' actions and galvanize support for them. In these descriptions, Muḥammad was consistently portrayed as a false prophet who was possessed by a demon and led his followers to hell. He was licentious, a forerunner of the Antichrist and an enemy of the Church.[8] The martyrs' actions were, in this view offered by Eulogius, valiant. In turn, they were worthy of support and even emulation.

Eulogius also coupled his accounts of the saints with details about Muḥammad that framed his alleged wickedness as a foil to the martyrs' sanctity. A preeminent example is a comment Eulogius made about Muḥammad and Mary, the Holy Mother. His hesitancy is palpable when he wrote:

> I will not repeat the outrageous sacrilege … that the impure dog [Muḥammad] dared to say about Mary, Blessed Virgin, Queen of the World, holy mother of our venerable Lord and Saviour. In effect he declared – I speak with respect for so great a Virgin – that in the world to come he would violate her virginity.[9]

In other words, Muḥammad would either consummate a marriage to Mary or simply deflower her in Paradise. This is a shocking claim. That Eulogius purported to delicately *repeat* something Muḥammad said, however, is a clue that he was not inventing an outlandish accusation but somehow drawing upon a source for an Islamic tradition. In fact, there was some disagreement with *ḥadīth* collections about the rank of the Prophet's wives in the afterlife. According to one, the Prophet was reported to tell Fāṭima, 'You are the chief lady of Paradise, with the exception of Mary the daughter of ʻImrān.'[10] Another reports that 'The Messenger of God said, "God married me in Paradise to Mary the daughter of ʻImrān and to the wife of the Pharaoh and the sister of Moses".'[11] Later traditions mention these *aḥādīth* in order to draw into doubt their authenticity, but the tradition nevertheless circulated and was certainly known in Muslim circles in the ninth century.[12] It is not clear how Eulogius learned of the tradition and he referred to it without remarking on the seeming conflation of the Holy Mother with Moses' sister, both called Mary. It is almost as if Eulogius chose to repeat a claim he came by way of hearsay. From wherever Eulogius gathered the tradition, he detached it from its context within an Islamic debate and used it in order to impugn Muḥammad in a manner that could hardly appear more iniquitous to Christian readers. And it made Muḥammad the very antithesis of holy martyrs whose aggressions Eulogius wanted to set out as noble.

It would hardly seem possible, but in comparison to his friend Alvarus, Eulogius' remarks are almost restrained. Though Alvarus echoed Eulogius' general denunciations of Muḥammad (although he mentioned nothing of the Holy Mother in Paradise), the layman also devoted roughly half of a thirty-five-paragraph polemical treatise to what he saw as the wretchedness of Muḥammad and Islam.[13] Therein, Muḥammad was depicted as a forerunner of the Antichrist, a claim to which Alvarus gave exegetical support by tying Muḥammad to biblical passages and apocalyptic hermeneutics about those who opposed Christ.[14] Alvarus also went further in his characterization of Muḥammad as a lascivious man. Though Alvarus claimed to restrain himself due to the sheer embarrassment of the descriptions he intended to employ, he is in fact rather relentless in his portrayal of Muḥammad's sexual prowess, some of which was the result of Alvarus' own work and some of which is reminiscent of descriptions in Eastern sources like 'Abd al-Masīḥ ibn Isḥāq al-Kindī's *Risāla*.[15] In short, Muḥammad was, in Alvarus' estimation, utterly repulsive and nearly inhuman in his animalist lust. As a result, the martyrs were correct to insult him as they did and rightly earned their martyr's reward for doing so.[16]

Hagiography and anti-hagiography

Within the corpus of literature connected to Eulogius and Alvarus there also appear *vitae*, biographical accounts of Muḥammad. Set alongside the Cordoban martyrs, these accounts do not function as mere biography. Their contents, some of it rather inventive and salacious, make this clear. But as we shall see, the manner in which they recount Muḥammad's life suggests that they are not concerned with historical biography or, more importantly, the kind of traditional hagiography that was being written for the martyrs. Quite the opposite, the *vitae* of Muḥammad come to us and to those who first read them as anti-hagiography,[17] or what I will call hamartiography. Here *hamartia* can be likened to a character's tragic flaw, or even sin. In such treatments we see Muḥammad, real or imagined, at his absolute worst so that we might see others as their very best. And the same can be said in reverse: the Cordoban martyrs were portrayed in the most sacred hagiographical light so that Muḥammad could be utterly desacralized.

As Eulogius himself tells us in his final work honouring and defending the martyrs, the *Liber apologeticus martyrum* (written c. 857), he found in the Monastery of Leyre in Navarre an anonymous *vita* of the Prophet Muḥammad.[18] We know this short biographical account of Muḥammad's life now as 'Istoria de Mahomet'. Though a version of it appears in another manuscript, Eulogius also preserved it in his *Liber apologeticus martyrum*.[19] Little is known about the text's original provenance except what can be inferred from its own introductory remarks. There, comments about ecclesiastical architecture in Spain suggest that the author was a cleric from southern Spain.[20] He was familiar with Islamic sources and, as I discuss below, he appears to have adapted the biography for his polemical purposes along the lines of Eastern Christian biographical accounts of Muḥammad. So it seems he was familiar with this source material as well, perhaps even dependent upon it. The 'Istoria de Mahomet' was found in northern Spain, so the author may have migrated there from the south of the peninsula, or the manuscript itself had made its way there.

Examining the 'Istoria de Mahomet' as Eulogius copied it we read that Muḥammad was a 'heresiarch' (*haeresiarches*) born in 618 and a contemporary of Isidore of Seville (560–636). His rule lasted ten years, after which he was buried in hell. Going into more specific detail, the account related that Muḥammad was an orphan. He grew up and became a greedy businessman. In the course of his business travels, he found himself in the company of Christians and, shrewd as he was, began to commit some of the things they said to memory. In turn, he became wiser than all the other Arabs who were otherwise a rather uncivilized lot. Though he grew in (Christian) wisdom, he did not alter his natural lasciviousness and eventually developed a relationship with the widow who employed him. Soon after, an evil spirit appeared to him in the form of a vulture. It said that it was the angel Gabriel and convinced Muḥammad to present himself to his fellow Arabs as a prophet.

Pressed on by the vulture and by his own pride, Muḥammad preached unheard of things, moving his foolish listeners to abandon their cult of idols in favour of 'a corporeal God in heaven' (*Deum corporeum in caelis*).[21] He also ordered his followers to take up arms; those who opposed them were to be killed. With divine support, Muḥammad and his violent followers spread their kingdom widely.

There are also some details in the 'Istoria de Mahomet' about Muḥammad's revelations. According to the *vita*, these were psalms composed by a false prophet for animals, the author of the *vita* thinking here of the names of various *suwar* in the Qur'ān.[22] Muḥammad wrote these so that, as the author charmingly puts it, the one animal could burp out disgust and the other could babble nonsense incessantly, a concoction 'seasoned' (*condimentum*) with stories of biblical figures like Joseph and Mary, the Mother of God.[23]

While carrying on with his prophetic charade, Muḥammad continued to indulge his desire for women. Here, the author of the *vita* inserted the story of Muḥammad's marriage to Zaynab and the claim that it was divinely sanctioned. In the *vita* the event is rooted completely in the Prophet's lust and power: Muḥammad wanted the woman and her husband could not refuse him. And the author even included a translated passage he claimed was from Muḥammad's 'law' (*lege*). The revelation was, according to the author, 'Since that woman was displeasing in the eyes of Zayd and he repudiated her, we joined her to our prophet in marriage, as an example to the others and to future followers wishing to do the same that it not be reckoned a sin.'[24]

This story would become a topos of anti-Muslim polemic where it was used to highlight the unbecoming character of Muḥammad that seemed apparent to many non-Muslim interpreters of his life. But the use of the Zaynab story in the 'Istoria de Mahomet' marks a very early appearance in a Christian text. One of the only earlier examples is in John of Damascus's account of Islam in his *Pēgē gnōseōs*. In fact, the account of the story in the 'Istoria de Mahomet' is strikingly similar to John's account of and commentary on the marriage. Both even included alleged quotations from the Qur'ān regarding the marriage, though their quotations do not actually appear in the Qur'ān where there is only an allusion to Zaynab's marriage and the accompanying revelation (Q 33:37). As I noted in Chapter 2, John seems to have been working from Muslim traditions alongside the Qur'ān. It seems likely, then, that the author of the 'Istoria de Mahomet', rather than simply inventing a qur'anic passage, incorporated elements from Muslim traditions of which he was aware, either directly or through Eastern Christian sources such as John of Damascus. His inventive interpretation is seen, then, not in the quotation but in his *use* of the quotation.[25]

In fact, on more than just this occasion we see the author flipping traditional material on its head so that instead of praising the Prophet, he was slandered. In no place is this more apparent in the 'Istoria de Mahomet' than in its account of Muḥammad's death, which follows the author's reference to Zaynab. According to the account, Muḥammad, nearing death, predicted that three days after he passed, the angel Gabriel – or really the spirit who appeared to him as a vulture – would resuscitate him. Upon his death, guards were posted nearby. When no resurrection took place and Muḥammad's body began to rot, his followers suggested that perhaps Gabriel was afraid of the guards. So they left Muḥammad's body unguarded. But instead of the angel coming to him, dogs followed the scent of his rotting body, found him and devoured his side. The rest of his body was buried and left to decay. In retribution, Muḥammad's followers ordered dogs to be killed annually so that they might join him in death. The author determined that Muḥammad's unsavoury end was appropriate for someone who had led so many to hell. He concluded, writing that many more of Muḥammad's sinful deeds could be recounted, but that the details he shared were sufficient in order to help readers deduce Muḥammad's character.[26]

While it may seem that the author has invented this story of Muḥammad's death in order to slander him – a deceptive prediction, the failure to resurrect after three days like Christ, a rotting body, a partially eaten corpse and a departure to hell – many of the details actually conform to Muslim traditions of the Prophet's death. As I discussed in Chapter 4, traditions surrounding Muḥammad's death and delayed burial circulated among early Muslim communities where there was debate about his possible resurrection, ascension to heaven and the time that elapsed between his death and burial. Christian authors, some of whom we have met with the Baḥīrā legend and others like al-Kindī, picked up the legends for use in their texts, too. In fact, the author of the 'Istoria de Mahomet' did not invent much of the death account, but instead merely preserved what was known from a variety of Muslim traditions. He did so, either by virtue of his direct acquaintance with these Muslim traditions or, as is more likely, indirectly by virtue of his familiarity with Eastern Christian sources.[27] The only details that appear to have been created by Christians, and again this likely originated among Eastern Christian authors, were those about the dogs devouring Muḥammad's side. This seems to have been a deliberately slanderous invention.[28]

In this light, although the author of the 'Istoria de Mahomet' may not have invented all of the details in his biography, he used and fashioned them in order to support his polemical agenda. This was a process begun by Eastern Christians from whom he at least indirectly had assistance. The same explanation can shed light on the author's intriguing claim that Muḥammad's followers, though they turned away from their idols – an admission many Eastern Christians conceded – nevertheless 'worshiped a corporeal God in heaven' (*Deum corporeum in caelis*).[29] In both Christian and Islamic theology, God is said to be incorporeal, or having no physical substance. So the claim in the 'Istoria de Mahomet' that Muslims worshiped a corporeal God is an extremely odd one until we turn, once again, to

Eastern Christian sources. In approximately 870, Nicetas of Byzantium wrote a refutation of the Qur'ān in which he offered commentary on much of its contents. Therein, he refers to Q 112:2 where God is described as 'the Eternal' (*ṣamad*), but he translated the Arabic *ṣamad* into Greek as *holosphairos* (something like 'all-spherical') in one case[30] and in another instance as *holosphuros* ('made of solid beaten metal').[31] The Greek translation at first seems odd and, without careful consideration of the Arabic term and Muslim readings, could give the impression that Muslims worshiped a God that had physical form. In fact, this is very much the argument that Nicetas and other Byzantine theologians used in their polemical refutations of Islam.[32] At around the same time that Nicetas was writing his refutation, a Greek translation of the Qur'ān, now known to us only in fragments, was produced. It is not certain whether or not Nicetas was working with this translation, but he does incorporate the same Greek vocabulary for Islamic terms that it does and so it appears that he has failed to appreciate how the Greek may accurately represent what Muslims intended by *ṣamad*.[33]

How the Greek may actually be a fair representation of *ṣamad* becomes clearer by considering another text. In the same century, but likely earlier than Nicetas, a deacon named John compiled into a text refutations of Islam from the Melkite bishop Theodore Abū Qurrah.[34] In one section on Muḥammad, Abū Qurrah argued that Muḥammad was a false prophet. Quoting from Q 112, Abū Qurrah asserted that Muḥammad was under the power of a demon when it was revealed to him that 'God is one, barren-built (*steiropēktos* or *sphuropēktos*), who did not beget and was not begotten, who has no partner.'[35] Here again, the Greek is thought to be a confusing mistranslation of *ṣamad*, one with polemical potential. However, early Muslim readings of Q 112 include reflection on the notion of God as *ṣamad*, as self-sufficient, an idea with connections to the idea of God as 'barren-built' or 'solid'. In this light, it could be that Greek translators and those like Abū Qurrah were attempting to accurately represent *ṣamad* and the Qur'ān's notion of God's eternal permanence, a concept with connections to notions of self-sufficiency and, in this sense, solidness, a concept shared by both the Arabic and Greek vocabulary.[36]

Just as Nicetas and other Byzantine theologians misunderstood these nuances, so the author of the 'Istoria de Mahomet' misunderstood his Eastern Christian sources. Like Abū Qurrah, he wrote an account of Muḥammad in which the Prophet was under the influence of an evil spirit, but unlike Abū Qurrah he translated the Muslim conception of God as *ṣamad* with the Latin *corporeum*, representing the Byzantine misunderstanding in which God had bodily form. In turn, he had Arabs turning from their idols to an idolatrous form of God. Here again, then, the polemic is not necessarily based upon an intentional, slanderous invention, but instead upon a mistaken and/or agenda-driven reading of the sources.

It must be said that other elements of the 'Istoria de Mahomet' seem to have their origin entirely in polemical twists. Such is the case with descriptions of Muḥammad as full of lust or as a power-hungry ruler. More significantly, the notion of an evil spirit disguised as a vulture is difficult not to understand as a foil of the Holy Spirit represented by a dove. In this way, it was a polemical invention intended to discredit any notion that Muḥammad had received a revelation from God. Taken together, both the twists of Muslim traditions and the outright inventions work to highlight the *hamartia* of Muḥammad and set these unholy characteristics against the lives of the martyr saints.

Desacralizing Muḥammad and creating an anti-saint

Intriguingly, further reflection on the *vita* of Muḥammad in Spain can be added by referring to a note appended to a letter John of Seville sent to Eulogius' friend Alvarus.[37] John does not tell us anything about how he acquired the information, only that 'we direct to you this note of Muḥammad (*Mammetis*) the heretic'.[38] And it is not at all clear what John intended for the note. In his letter, it awkwardly follows a grammatical discussion and it has no relationship to the rest of the letter's contents.[39]

It could be that he wanted to compare the information he had with what Eulogius had acquired, and so he included an abbreviated form of it, or it may be that he was in possession of another version.[40] But the note's contents are almost identical to the 'Istoria de Mahomet' and I include it in its entirety here:

> A note on Muḥammad, chief of the Arabs: in the time of Heraclius, in his seventh year and in the current era 656 (618), there arose the heretic Muḥammad, seal (*sigillus*) of the false prophets of the Arabs, forerunner of the Antichrist. At that time Isidore of Seville excelled in our doctrine and Sisebut held the throne in Toledo. His followers say that this aforementioned wicked prophet shone out by his many miracles, such as that he took the wife of another by reason of the ardour of his lust and joined her to himself in marriage; and that, as we have read no prophet to have done, he held mastery over a camel, controlling its will. When death was approaching, he promised to rise up on the third day, but by negligence of the guards he was discovered devoured by dogs. He held the leadership for ten years, at the end of which he was buried in hell.[41]

Muḥammad appears in the same guise in John of Seville's note as he does in the *vita* Eulogius preserved: he was a heresiarch and false prophet who suffered a ghastly, unbecoming demise.

Conspicuously different, however, is the manner in which some of the descriptions were ascribed to Muḥammad. For example, the marriage between Muḥammad and Zaynab, noted for its scurrilous nature in the 'Istoria de Mahomet', is cited in John's note as an example Muslims use for one of Muḥammad's miracles. In their native Islamic context, the story of the Prophet's marriage and the subsequent revelations intended to justify it have a special function. According to one historical tradition,[42] Muḥammad unintentionally encountered Zaynab in a state of undress. He saw her and found her attractive, but he nevertheless humbly and respectfully turned away in order to preserve her honour. When Zaynab's husband, Zayd, heard about the encounter, he visited the Prophet and wondered if he should, as a result of their meeting, take Zaynab as his wife.[43] Even after repeated interactions, Muḥammad refused and urged Zayd to continue his marriage to Zaynab. Despite these exchanges, a revelation came to Muḥammad (Q 33:37) allowing the Prophet to marry her. According to this account, the marriage was not so much a scandal as it was a blessing to those involved, an indication of the Prophet's honour and a sign of his divine approval. In this way, Muslims could understand it as one of the ways in which Muḥammad 'shone out by his many miracles', to use John of Seville's phrase.

In Christian contexts, however, the story is received quite differently as an outlandish affair, unbecoming of anyone claiming to be sent from God. As we have seen, John of Damascus refers to the marriage in his *Pēgē gnōseōs*, one of the earliest Christian discussions of the event. According to summary there, Muḥammad was attracted to his friend's wife. 'Sitting together, Muḥammad said to him: "God commanded me to take your wife" ', and so the story goes.[44] John of Damascus included all of the necessary elements, but his summary reflected a Christian perspective in which the marriage is simply untenable. He made his perspective all the more plain by linking Muḥammad's marriage in the *Pēgē gnōseōs* directly to other matters of Islamic marital and sexual ethics, which, as I pointed out in Chapter 2, appeared even more outlandish to John of Damascus than the relationship between Muḥammad and Zaynab.

Al-Kindī created the same link in his refutation of Islam and Muḥammad. In his *Risāla*, the story of the marriage to Zaynab is summarized, not before unseemly sexual details like John of Damascus offered, but afterwards. Al-Kindī referred to traditions that report Muḥammad's love of women and his alleged sexual prowess and immediately linked them to the marriage to Zaynab, even quoting Q 33:37.[45]

John of Seville, Alvarus and Eulogius surely read the details of Muḥammad's relationship with Zaynab in much the same manner as John of Damascus and al-Kindī did. Intriguingly, though, the way the marriage is mentioned in John of Seville's note carried echoes of the tension between the story's original Islamic context and its reception in Christian contexts. This is likely because, in the note, the story came without a frame in which to mark out its function as biographical or polemical or part of any other genre of literature. John of Damascus, al-Kindī and the author of the 'Istoria de Mahomet' added their polemical frames to the story and used it accordingly. And so the marriage transitioned from a miraculous demonstration of Muḥammad's prophethood for Muslims to an example of his pseudo-divinely sanctioned lust for Christians.[46]

It could also be the case that reaction to the story in ninth-century Córdoba, and indeed by those like John of Damascus and al-Kindī, picked up on an internal Muslim debate. According to Muqātil ibn Sulaymān's (d. 767) interpretation (*tafsīr*) of the relevant material in Q 33, not everyone in the Muslim community approved of Muḥammad's marriage to Zaynab. In fact, some thought it might constitute incest since Muḥammad had adopted Zayd as his son. According to Muqātil, the first portion of Q 33:38 – 'There is not to be upon the Prophet any discomfort concerning that which Allah has imposed upon him' – represented the disapproval of unidentified critics who were shocked by what amounted to Muḥammad's marriage to his daughter-in-law. To them, the qur'anic revelation seemed to function merely to gratify the Prophet's sexual desire. The larger context of Q 33, then, represents the legal ramifications of the marriage and an effort to placate discord within the Muslim community. In such a case, Christian use of the marriage story as ammunition in polemical attacks upon Muḥammad and the Qur'ān might actually reflect and, much like our other examples of Christian polemic, conveniently draw upon Islamic tradition or, as in this case, an internal Muslim debate.[47]

The note from John of Seville also mentioned a story of Muḥammad's control of a camel. Again, John of Seville surely found the story ridiculous – no other prophet was said to have claimed such a feat. Nevertheless, the story of Muḥammad subduing a wild camel is attested in Islamic traditions.[48] Yet again we see Christians drawing on some authentic Islamic sources, but pulling them into entirely different contexts where they are used not to support Muḥammad but to malign him. And adding to this denigration was the story of Muḥammad's death with the addition of the dogs devouring his rotting body. Again, the story had a native Islamic context that was grounded in Muslim traditions and debates, but the flourish of hungry dogs helped to add an interpretive frame ensuring that the biographical detail, now an element of hamartiography, could be used for the desecration of Muḥammad's memory.

That so much of what contemporary authors wrote about the Cordoban martyrs appeared in or is connected to hagiography is significant for how it framed their presentation of Muḥammad. For in this hagiographical context, the lives of the martyrs were glorified and their deaths were sacralized. Quite the opposite for Muḥammad for whom Eulogius and his companions located *vitae* that nestled comfortably into their anti-Muslim agendas. The information at their disposal already cast Muḥammad in a dark shadow, but in their hands, they used the information as a jaggedly inverse mirror of the martyrs. And so the life of the anti-saint[49] Muḥammad was vilified, not glorified; his death was sullied, not honoured; and his soul made its way to hell.

6

Muḥammad as a tainted vessel of Christ

An anonymous counter-chronicle of the Prophet

Eulogius, Paulus Alvarus and the Cordoban martyrs did not represent all Christian communities in ninth-century Córdoba. In particular, we know from various comments Eulogius made that there were those in Córdoba who were very much opposed to the martyrs and who represented views of Islam, Muslims and Cordoban society that were quite different from the ones portrayed by Eulogius and Alvarus. It is difficult to reconstruct the views of this segment of the Cordoban Christian community because, without any evidence coming from them directly, we are forced to discern their views upon the basis of what Eulogius and Alvarus wrote about them. According to Eulogius' remarks, critics of the martyrs condemned their actions because they failed to live up to the ideals of the early Church's martyrs. What they meant was that, not only were they not slowly and painfully killed, but more importantly, they were also not executed by polytheists, which is what the pagan Romans were. Instead, the Cordoban martyrs, as Eulogius put his critics' words, were 'quickly put to death ... by men who venerate God and confess to heavenly laws'.[1]

This one remark is not a lot on which to go, but it is a very revealing one. It tells us that, alongside their unwillingness to support the martyrs' movement and honour those who sought their deaths as martyrs, some in the Cordoban Christian community were convinced that Muslims worshipped God. Moreover, they performed this worship of God on the basis of divine revelation. Such a position tore at the very centre of Eulogius' position in which the martyrs were worthy opponents of those who followed a 'disciple of Satan'.[2]

So it would seem that there was a fracture in the Cordoban Christian community. There were surely a handful of positions that this fracture created, some of which represented those who fretted very little about Islam and Muslims. But two positions appear rather stark and an allusion to these came in a letter written by Saul, a bishop from Córdoba, that he sent to Alvarus. Therein, he claimed that some Christians in the city rightly drew a hard line between them and other Christians who seemingly colluded with Muslims. That line created a break in Christian communion between those like Eulogius and Alvarus – they represented a view that saw Muslims as a creeping deterioration of Christian thought, society and culture – and those like secular priests in an urban centre for whom daily interaction with Muslims and Islamic government required, at least in their minds, a different posture towards Muslim rule and belief.[3] For those from this latter position, Muslims were those 'who venerate[d] God and confess[ed] to heavenly laws'.

As I pointed out in the last chapter, Eulogius preserved a *vita* of Muḥammad, the 'Istoria de Mahomet', which helped to ground his disdainful views of the Prophet and his defiant approach to Muslim life and culture. John of Seville and Alvarus had discussed a similar *vita*, if not the same one. Unfortunately, there are no extant sources – no comparable *vita* – written or preserved by Christians who fell on the other side of the fracture in ninth-century Córdoba. What does exist, however, is a *vita* of Muḥammad that represents a very different view of him than the 'Istoria de Mahomet'. While there is no way to connect this *vita* to Cordoban Christians who thought Muslims worshipped God on the basis of a revealed law, the biography could nevertheless support such a position.

The 'Tultusceptru de libro domni Metobii' and a different view of Muḥammad

Known as the 'Tultusceptru de libro domni Metobii', this *vita* of Muḥammad, like the 'Istoria de Mahomet', originated in Spain and was written by the tenth century, very possibly in the ninth century.[4] Despite these shared characteristics, the author of the 'Tultusceptru' offered a very different view of Muḥammad's origins and prophetic function than what we find in the 'Istoria de Mahomet'. According to the 'Tultusceptru', an angel of the Lord appeared to a bishop named Osius, a possible conflation of the fourth-century Bishop Osius of Córdoba (d. 359).[5] The angel instructed Osius to go to the people of a region known as Erribon who had fallen away from the true faith and into error. 'But go and tell them,' the angel said, '"Be not unbelievers but believers".'[6] Regrettably, Osius fell ill before he could leave on his journey in order to deliver the angel's message. So he ordered a young monk named Ozim to go in his place.[7] Ozim listened to the message he was asked to proclaim in Osius's place and set off to deliver it.

Nearing the region of Erribon, Ozim encountered an 'angel of temptation who resembled an angel'.[8] Standing by an oak tree, the evil angel asked Ozim, 'What is your name?' Ozim replied:

> I am called Ozim. I have been sent by my teacher Father Osius to speak the words that he spoke to me, for the angel of the Lord had ordered him to speak these words, but the day of his summons came and his spirit was called to the celestial kingdom.[9]

So Ozim carried with him a divine message revealed by God. But the evil angel spotted his chance and cunningly flipped the narrative on its head. 'I am the angel who was sent to Father Bishop Osius,' he lied. 'I will tell you the words that you are to preach to the satraps to whom you are sent.' And then the evil angel gave the young monk a new name, almost as if he was commissioning him to offer his new message. 'You are not called Ozim but Muḥammad (*Mahommad*)' he proclaimed.[10]

After changing Ozim's name, the evil angel 'ordered him to say, so that the satraps might believe: "*Alla occuber alla occuber situ leila citus est mohamet razulille*" '. This resembles the *shahādah*, the Muslim profession of faith, which proclaims: *lā 'ilāha 'illā llāh muḥammadun rasūlu llāh* ('There is no god but God and Muhammad is the messenger of God'). So, while the author is clearly familiar with the Islamic creed, he represented it in a rather distorted form and inserted into it the frequently heard Muslim *takbīr*, '*Allāhu akbar*' ('God is greatest'). The author of the 'Tultusceptru' also gave a new meaning to the creedal statement. He noted that 'The monk did not know that by [saying the phrase] he was invoking demons, for every *alla occuber* is a summoning of demons.'[11] In effect, by uttering this phrase and by teaching others to say it Ozim was spreading an evil incantation. By implication, the more people who repeated the incantation and the more frequently they did so, the further the evil angel's message spread and the more tightly it gripped its followers.

In case readers might wonder why Ozim, now Muḥammad, did not question the evil angel and his instructions, the author added that 'already [the young monk's] heart had been turned away by the unclean spirit and the words that the Lord had narrated to him through his teacher had been lost to oblivion'.[12] In this, Muḥammad is not portrayed as a fool or a naïve catechumen. He had, more or less, arrived at the wrong place at the wrong time and fell victim to evil. Without any means for discerning truth from falsehood – and again, there is no indication in the 'Tultusceptru' that an older or wiser monk might have fared better – Muḥammad had simply fallen under evil's spell and the rest was history.

The closing lines of the 'Tulusceptru' are eloquent and telling, especially with respect to how readers ought best understand Muḥammad and Islam. The author concludes:

> And so, although he was a vessel of Christ, [Muḥammad] became a vessel of Mammon to the ruin of his soul, and all who converted to this error and those whom they induced to do so by persuasion, are said to be sheaves for burning.[13]

It is clear from this final remark that Islam, according to the author of the *vita*, was the creation of an evil angel and led those who followed it to hell. But more significantly, Muḥammad appears in the account as an innocent soul. Even more, he was a 'vessel of Christ'. It was the angel that was to blame; he changed Ozim's name, corrupted his message and sent Muḥammad's followers to hell. The author of the 'Tultusceptru' placed the accent, so to speak, on Muḥammad's starting point as a God-follower with a divine message. When it came to the origins of Islam he was quite marginal.

Setting aside this fascinating assessment of Muḥammad for a moment, among the most immediately noticeable features of the 'Tulusceptru' are its author's familiarity with bits of Islam and with sources devoted to Islam. As I have already pointed out, the author knew the *shahādah*, or at least *of* it since he recalled it in a rather jumbled form. One wonders how familiar he may have been with the Qur'ān, not just because of his attempt to reproduce the *shahādah* but also in light of what the original angel instructed Osius to preach to the inhabitants of Erribon. 'Be not unbelievers but believers', he said, a phrase with a rather qur'anic ring to it. The Qur'ān is, of course, replete with references to the unbelievers (*al-kāfirūn*) and the believers (*al-mūminūn*), even devoting whole chapters to them.[14]

The author of the 'Tultusceptru' was also familiar with Muḥammad's connection to the city of Medina. This becomes clear when we reference the *Apocalypse of Pseudo-Methodius*, originally written in Syriac in the late seventh century but translated into Greek and Latin by the following century. In this text, the author posited an explanation for the collapse of Christian hegemony and the rise of the Arabs (described as Ishmaelites). In the *Apocalypse*, Arabs are linked to Ishmael who was described as fleeing from the dessert of Yathrib or Ethribum, referring in all likelihood to what became known as Medina.[15] Erribon, so it would seem in the 'Tultusceptru', was likely a form of Ethribum.

In this way, the author of the 'Tultusceptru' suggested that God intended for Osius to proclaim his message to the Arabs in Medina (i.e. Erribon), but that an evil angel sabotaged this mission. Similarly, Ozim (or Ocim as it is variously used in the 'Tultusceptru') was likely an attempt to represent Hāshim since the clan from the Quraysh tribe from which Muḥammad descended was the Banū Hāshim. Indeed, a Latin genealogy of 'Saracens' (*sarrazenorum*) in the late-ninth-century *Prophetic Chronicle* rendered Hāshim into Latin as 'Escim'. It would not be difficult to arrive at Ozim from there, and it is telling that the only known version of the 'Tultusceptru' appears in the Codex of Roda where, among other texts, the *Prophetic Chronicle* can also be found.[16]

Perhaps more significantly, there are also the readily apparent thematic similarities in the 'Tultusceptru' to features of the Baḥīrā legend.[17] In Chapter 1, I noted that Baḥīrā was purportedly a Christian monk who recognized Muḥammad. In the 'Tultusceptru', Muḥammad was the monk. In Christian versions of the Baḥīrā legend, Muḥammad is guided in his proclamation of Islam. In the 'Tultusceptru' the evil angel deviously guided him and in both texts there is a sense in which Muḥammad is towed into his role as prophet and leader, either by way of duping him or evil incantation. In the Syrian recensions of the Baḥīrā legend, pre-Islamic Arabs were said to worship a false demon named 'Awkbar'.[18] In the 'Tultusceptru', demons were invoked when one uttered, wittingly or unwittingly, 'alla occuber'. In fact, a common accusation in Eastern Christian texts was that Muslims invoked both Allāh and a god named Akbar when they proclaimed '*Allāhu akbar*'.[19] Finally, in the Muslim versions of the Baḥīrā legend, Muḥammad is recognized as a prophet while sitting beneath a tree.[20] Trees were even reported to bow towards him. Curiously, in the 'Tultusceptru', the evil angel is found 'standing by an oak tree'.[21]

Far from inventing material by which to lampoon Muḥammad, then, it would seem that the author of the 'Tultusceptru' drew from a number of different sources in order to weave together an explanation for Muḥammad's emergence. This emergence was, according to the author, grounded in a divine concern for the spiritual well-being of Arabs, a spiritual state that hinged upon a divinely revealed message. It was only when an evil angel intercepted the young Muḥammad who carried that message that a lie was formed, perpetuated and, as a result, drew its followers to the condemning fires of hell. But in all of this Muḥammad remained a relatively innocent youth. It could be that he was naïve and susceptible to manipulation, but that is not exactly straightforward in the 'Tultusceptru'. What is certainly clear is that, before his corruption by the evil angel, he possessed a divine revelation given by a messenger of God that was meant to draw the Arabs towards pure worship of the one, true God. This was a completely different view of Muḥammad than the one offered in the 'Istoria de Mahomet', the one to which Eulogius, Alvarus and John of Seville looked for support of their view of Islam.

The 'Tultusceptru' and ninth-century Córdoba

As I have already pointed out, there is very little information that can be used to reconstruct the views of Christians who opposed the martyrs of ninth-century Córdoba. There are certainly no textual resources like those produced or transmitted by Eulogius and Alvarus and those like them. All we really know is that their Christian opponents refused to honour the martyrs and had concluded that Muslims 'venerat[ed] God and confess[ed] to heavenly laws'. In light of this paucity of evidence, however, Kenneth Baxter Wolf has argued that the 'Tultusceptru', even if not a biographical source ninth-century Cordoban Christians produced or drew upon, nevertheless could *functionally* represent their views about Muḥammad in a manner directly inverse to the way in which Eulogius used the 'Istoria de Mahomet' to undergird his views of Muḥammad. In this way, Wolf suggests the author of the 'Tultusceptru' was attempting to address questions for a Christian community that may have looked upon Islam, Muslims and their Prophet with a degree of assent, or at least much less hostility than those like Eulogius and Alvarus.[22] His proposal becomes clear when we consider why the author of the 'Tultusceptru' wrote the *vita*. Or, as Wolf asks, 'What were the conceptual needs of his audience that he aimed to address?'[23]

Finding an answer to that question begins with a turn back to Eulogius and the 'Istoria de Mahomet'. For Eulogius, the 'Istoria de Mahomet' helped to affirm his position that Muḥammad, despite his claims to monotheism, was a destructive force whose sheer ungodliness threatened Christian communities in ninth-century Córdoba. As a result, Christians should either follow along the pathway of the martyrs or, at the very least, support their efforts.[24] Of course, Eulogius' opponents saw matters differently. Their condemnation of the martyrs, as far as we can tell, was rooted, in part, in their view of Islam and its Prophet. For them, Islam was monotheistic and, though it may have been in some ways a corrupt monotheism, it had connections to pure, divine revelation. Such a view effectively mirrored the Islamic position that Christianity (like Judaism) was a corruption of pure monotheism. Christians espousing such a view were only claiming for Islam what Muslims claimed for Christianity. In this way, Islam's monotheism could become the basis for viewing Muslim rulers and a society that grew increasingly Islamic in a much more convivial way. It provided, as Wolf argues, 'an ideologically grounded modus vivendi that served both [Christians and Muslims] in their day-to-day interactions'.[25]

A text like the 'Tultusceptru' could provide the affirmation that Islam was not something to resist, as Eulogius and Alvarus saw the martyrs doing; since it was a derivative of Christianity, Christians could more comfortably participate in a society where they had become politically disenfranchised. The author of the 'Tultusceptru' may well have been attempting to speak to an issue just like this by providing Christian readers in Spain with an understanding of Islam that not only affirmed their religious superiority to Islam but also provided a framework for accepting life under Muslims. Such a view pivoted on the way one understood Muḥammad and his origins. Hence, Eulogius' opponents may not have known the 'Tultusceptru', but the *vita* does, functionally, support their concerns and lend credence to their view that Muslims could in some ways worship God and confess to what was originally a heavenly law. This interpretation would be much more likely if Muḥammad was not demonized, such as he was in the 'Istoria de Mahomet', and instead given some connection to pure monotheism, such as the 'Tultusceptru' does.[26]

Again, none of this is to say that the 'Tultusceptru' *was* taken up by those who opposed the martyrs or that it was even necessarily known in ninth-century Córdoba. But analysis of the 'Tultusceptru' does help us to add further detail to Eulogius' statement that his opponents saw Muslims as 'venerat[ing] God and confess[ing] to heavenly laws'. What is more, it suggests that there were those in medieval Spain who were drawing upon older and geographically widespread evidence in order to assess Muḥammad.

Counter-chronicling the life of a prophetic vessel

Reflecting on the reasons why the author may have written the 'Tultusceptru' helps us to see its probable, original function and can even lend some aid to understanding the position of Christians in ninth-century Córdoba who opposed Eulogius, Alvarus and the martyrs. It is still further interesting to consider the only surviving copy of the 'Tultusceptru' and its inclusion in the Codex of Roda, most of which dates from the tenth century. This codex consists largely of Latin chronicles. Two-thirds of the manuscript reproduces Paulus Orosius's *Historiarum adversum paganos libri VII*. There is also Isidore of Seville's *Historia de regibus Gothorum, Vandalorum et Suevorum*, genealogies of Jesus and Iberian rulers and chronicles of Arab and Christian kings from medieval Spain.[27] So the Codex served in large part to legitimize Christian rule in Spain, link it to the Visigoths who ruled before Muslims entered the peninsula and place into a historical context the shifting zones of Muslim rule in Spain.

Curiously, the 'Tultusceptru' appears as folio 185v, sandwiched directly in between the *Chronicle of Alfonso III* and the *Prophetic Chronicle*. In fact, it was added after the completion of the Codex and written on the empty page that separates the two chronicles. As a result, its insertion appears slightly awkward at first glance and rather out of place. The *Chronicle of Alfonso III* attempted to demonstrate the continuity between the earlier Visigoths who ruled Spain and the later rule of Christian kingdoms. In this way, the Christian kings who vanquished Muslim rulers marked a return of pre-Andalusī rule. The *Prophetic Chronicle* alleged to predict the downfall of Muslim rule on the peninsula.[28] Towards the beginning of the *Prophetic Chronicle*, on folio 187r, there appears a genealogy of Arabs and, just below a miniature illustration of a serpent coloured in deep green, blue and yellow with a flickering red tongue, we find a version of the 'Istoria de Mahomet' (ff. 187r–188r). How does the 'Tultusceptru' fit in between these two ideological proclamations and the more vitriolic biography of Muḥammad?

If one of the functions of a historical chronicle was to document the events of significant figures, political rulers in particular, so as to lend them legitimacy and solidify their place in a society's record, then the inclusion of a brief *vita* of Muḥammad would seem to function as a counter-chronicle by delegitimizing his place vis-à-vis his counterparts. In this way, the author's account of Muḥammad and the explanation for Islam that appears in the 'Tultusceptru', for all the credence it lends to Islam as a corrupted divine revelation, delegitimized the Prophet and added biographical credence to the prophecy of Muslim demise. Significantly, Muḥammad may have been an innocent young man and a 'vessel of Christ', but he was exploited and his message corrupted. In turn, the Muslim claims that he functioned as the final prophet of a revealed message needed to be contextualized and walked back. Muḥammad may not have been an anti-saint, as he was in Eulogius' 'Istoria de Mahomet', but as a *tainted* vessel of Christ, he was, in the end, an illegitimate prophet.

7

Muḥammad as a vanquished anti-hero

A convert, a translator and polemic exposing the Prophet

'Now when I was a pilgrim [in Mecca] in the time of my infidelity'.[1] So remarked the author of a medieval anti-Muslim treatise before his descriptions of the *Ḥajj*. Nearer to the beginning of his text he condemned 'the infidelity which the devil had stamped upon our hearts', implying that he wrote as a convert to Christianity from Islam.[2] His claim is entirely plausible, especially since the text exhibits a clear familiarity with the Qur'ān and other Islamic sources, a feature to which I shall return below. It was not at all unknown, after all, for figures to convert from one religion to another and then to write scathing critiques of their former religion. For example, 'Alī Rabban al-Ṭabarī (d. c. 860), a ninth-century East Syrian Christian, converted to Islam, likely in his seventies, and then wrote his *Al-radd 'alā l-Naṣārā* (*Refutation of the Christians*).[3] And there was also Būluṣ ibn Rajā' (d. c. 1020), a Muslim who became a Coptic priest and wrote *Kitāb al-Wāḍiḥ bi-l-Ḥaqq* (*Clarity in Truth*) as an evaluation of Islamic origins and the Qur'ān.[4]

But this particular author who claimed to be a convert is unnamed in the text and his identity has puzzled scholars, in large part because, until very recently, information about him was restricted to the only known manuscript of the work: a sixteenth-century Latin manuscript originating in Italy with the title *Liber denudationis siue ostensionis, aut patefacientem*, or *The Book of Denuding or Exposing, or The Discloser* (henceforth, *Liber denudationis*).

It is clear from this manuscript that its Latin represents both a translation and an abridgement of what was originally a longer Arabic treatise.[5] This can be deduced from a number of the text's details, but its transmission history is particularly helpful here. We know that the Dominican monks Ramon Martí (d. c. 1284)[6] and Riccoldo da Monte di Croce (d. 1320),[7] as well as the Majorcan intellectual Ramon Llull (d. 1316),[8] used the text as a source in their productions of polemical treatises. But in Martí's work, his *Explanatio simboli apostolorum* in particular, passages drawn from the text, though they contain the same content, references to the Qur'ān and arguments, are reproduced by Martí in rather different language. The conclusion is that not only did Martí have a copy of *Liber denudationis* next to him as he wrote but that he was also reading the text in Arabic and translating it into Latin as he went along. Not only did he select different Latin vocabulary for his translation but he was also referring to an Arabic text that, unlike the manuscript we have, was not yet abridged.[9]

Given the reasonable certainty of an Arabic original and the *Liber denudationis*' translation and circulation in the western Mediterranean, scholars assumed that the author also originated in the same region. Knowledge of Arabic and, as is evident from the text, familiarity with Islamic sources would seem to support the author's claim to have converted from Islam. But there was something different about the author who claimed to have been a pilgrim in Mecca and was now writing to condemn his former faith. To begin with, although he drew heavily from Islamic sources, the style of his argumentation and the topics he discussed make it clear that he was also very familiar with Eastern Christian sources. Some of the details he shared about Muslim pilgrimage practices are generic enough that they could be drawn from such sources instead of direct experience.[10] What is more, the text not only circulated in the western Mediterranean, as I have shown, but also conforms to the manner in which a western Arabized individual might refer to Muslim intellectuals. Dāwūd al-Iṣfahānī, for example, the Iraqī founder of the Ẓāhirite school of jurisprudence, is referred to by the author as 'David the Oriental' (*Dauid Orientalis*), the kind of reference that only a Western intellectual would make.[11] And so scholars have speculated, with reasonable certainty, that the author of the *Liber denudationis* must surely have been an Arabized Christian.[12] As such he would have been fluent in Arabic and thus conversant with Muslims and Islamic sources as well as Eastern Christian literature. His claim to be a convert from Islam more than likely functioned as a rhetorical device used to lend authority and credibility to his text.

The most fitting milieu for the author's text is Toledo, a city that was a centre for Arabized Christian communities in the medieval period. From the text we know it was written between 1010 and 1132.[13] Within this period, it would then most likely have been written after Toledo's recapture by Christian armies in 1085.[14] It was at this point that the author would have been less restricted in writing such a scathing work against Islam. Readers of the treatise would most likely have been fellow Arabized Christians. In post-conquest Toledo, such communities would have found themselves in a reasonably precarious position. Muslims, with whom they shared matters of language and culture, would be leaving the city or finding ways to maintain their residence under new conditions. Latin Christians, with whom Arabized communities shared a religion, were moving to the city in increasing numbers. But Arabized Christians in Toledo were not Muslims and they were not like their Latin co-religionists. For this reason, their former Muslim rulers viewed them as outsiders because they were non-Muslims, but Latin Christians viewed them in the same suspicious manner because they looked and sounded like Muslims. As a result, Arabized Christians became a fifth column in post-conquest Toledo and tension emerged: they shared cultural and linguistic affinities with defeated Muslims and religious connections with victorious Latin Christians. With whom did their allegiance lie?

The *Liber denudationis* did not answer this question for its Arabized readers directly. Instead the text would have softened the tension by offering to Arabized Christians a means by which to navigate their multireligious and multicultural milieu. They read a text in a language they understood using thought forms with which they were familiar. But the text also articulated the differences between Christianity and Islam. In these ways, their cultural and linguistic distinctions were affirmed as much as their religious superiority.[15] And so the *Liber denudationis* exposed Islam and its Prophet for who they really were and, in so doing, disclosed the superiority of Christ and his followers, a function as potentially useful to Arabized Christian audiences as it may have been for Latin Christians encountering Islam in the western Mediterranean and perhaps reading the text in its Latin translation.

All of this speculation about the *Liber denudationis* and its author has been considered rather sound and very plausible. However, David Bertaina has recently shown that the author is in fact none other than Būluṣ ibn Rajā' and that the original Arabic treatise, of which the *Liber denudationis* is an abridged translation, is actually Ibn Rajā''s *Kitāb al-Wāḍiḥ bi-l-Ḥaqq*.[16] As I point out above, Ibn Rajā' was an Arab convert to Christianity from Islam, making him an ideal candidate to write a text refuting his former faith built upon a familiarity with Islamic sources and Muslim intellectuals. And Ibn Rajā' was alive and flourishing between 1010 and 1132, the range suggested by the text, though we can now assert that it was written towards the beginning of this range.[17]

A comparison of the *Liber denudationis* and the *Kitāb al-Wāḍiḥ bi-l-Ḥaqq* reveals that they share the same structure, information and details. The text by Ibn Rajā' is simply much longer and various details in the *Liber denudationis* have felt the slight alterations of a scribe's hand as he translated and abridged the text for a new audience. For example, the translator was happy to refer to Dāwūd al-Iṣfahānī as an 'Oriental', given his Western origins and perspective, but Ibn Rajā' simply referred to him as one of the imams from Iraq.[18] Likewise, the translator's abridgement and translation of descriptions pertaining to the *Ḥajj* accurately reflect what Ibn Rajā' related, but he has sharpened their polemical edge for a new context. In doing so, the details become less believable as the personal observations one would make in situ and cast doubt upon their authenticity. The details in the *Kitāb al-Wāḍiḥ bi-l-Ḥaqq* are not all accurate – Muslim pilgrims throw seven, not seventy, stones (the translator has them throwing the stones at themselves, but Ibn Rajā' did not write this) – but this does not necessarily mean Ibn Rajā' never visited Mecca. He has simply come to view such piety with the scrutiny of an unbeliever.[19] More importantly, the differences between the *Kitāb al-Wāḍiḥ bi-l-Ḥaqq* and the *Liber denudationis* reveal some of the translator's goals in producing an abridged translation. For while the *Liber denudationis* is a reasonably faithful thumbnail sketch of what Ibn Rajā' wrote, the translator was clearly intent on maintaining the text's polemical punch. He recognized in the *Kitāb al-Wāḍiḥ bi-l-Ḥaqq* a useful and seemingly authoritative resource, culled from it what was most important with respect to a Christian understanding of Islam and highlighted, at times even embellished, details that he saw as particularly damaging to Muslim belief and practice.

With all of this in mind, the speculation about what was thought to be an anonymous Arabized Christian author from Spain can now be redirected and applied, not to the author of the text but to the likely identity of the scribe who translated and abridged Ibn Rajā''s *Kitāb al-Wāḍiḥ bi-l-Ḥaqq*. We must continue to speculate, however, about how an early-eleventh-century Arabic text written in Fatimid Egypt by a Coptic priest made its way to the western Mediterranean and circulated among Christians reading texts in Arabic and producing translations in Latin. Ibn Rajā' seems very far removed from an Arabized Christian in Toledo or Dominican monks in Spain and Italy. But, in fact, the channels for transmitting religious texts and knowledge back and forth from one end of the Mediterranean to the other were well worn. Monks from Palestine travelled to Córdoba in the ninth century, bringing with them religious treatises and knowledge about Islam. And Latin texts made their way to St Catherine's Monastery in Sinai as early as the seventh century.[20]

So it is not at all unlikely for a text from someone like Ibn Rajā' to make its way west and his *Kitāb al-Wāḍiḥ bi-l-Ḥaqq* would have as much utility in his own community as it would among other Christian communities for whom interaction with Islam and Muslims was not uncommon. Ibn Rajā' sought to provide clarity about the true religion between Christianity and Islam. He likely felt well positioned to offer such insight as a convert and many readers of his text surely found his analysis authoritative on the basis of his conversion. For this reason, the text transitioned from its origins as point of clarity for Ibn Rajā' to a tool for exposing truth for the text's translator and for those who read and used the text as it circulated in the western Mediterranean.

Exposing Muḥammad as an imposter

One of the main ways the allegedly true nature of Muḥammad was exposed in these texts was through an attack upon Islam's authoritative sources: the Qur'ān, Ḥadīth and interpreters of Islam (*al-fuqahā'*).[21] So besides referring to Islamic traditions, the Qur'ān in particular was quoted repeatedly in the texts in an attempt to expose the seeming inconsistencies and lurid details that were unbecoming of a so-called sacred and revealed text. These were two-pronged attacks meant to discredit the Qur'ān directly and to indirectly cast doubt upon the legitimacy of Muḥammad's claim to be the bearer of divine revelation. How could a messenger sent by God proclaim what, in the *Liber denudationis* and the *Kitāb al-Wāḍiḥ bi-l-Ḥaqq*, was utter nonsense? Was Muḥammad a legitimate prophet or an imposter?

There is also space in the texts alongside their two-pronged attack upon the Qur'ān to focus directly on Muḥammad. This focused barrage first appeared in sections where Ibn Rajā' and the translator assailed Muslim claims that the Bible foretold the Prophet's arrival.[22] According to the argument, the coming of a universal prophet was an event foretold either by a person or by a book. The Bible certainly foretold true prophets – such was the case for Christ – but it did not mention Muḥammad. Here, the texts reflected upon the popular Muslim beliefs that saw portions of the Bible as having been corrupted in order to erase any mention of Muḥammad. The claim was countered by drawing from the Qur'ān, observing that God instructed Muḥammad – he 'pretends that God said to him', the translator wrote in the *Liber denudationis*[23] – to consult the scriptures that were sent down previously (i.e. the Torah and the Gospels) when in doubt about any revelation (Q 10:94). In other words, this verse, properly elucidated in the *Kitāb al-Wāḍiḥ bi-l-Ḥaqq* and the *Liber denudationis*, indicated that Christian scripture was meant to interpret the Qur'ān. If this was true, then the Bible could not be a corrupted text, which in turn signified that Muḥammad was left without prophetic witness. Cut off from this necessary lineage, Muḥammad could hardly claim to be doing anything more than impersonating God.[24]

Having made this argument, the texts returned to the Qur'ān in order to demonstrate that the Bible was untainted. In fact, the Qur'ān's only references to Muḥammad appeared when it referred to false prophets and, as the *Liber denudationis* added, 'workers of iniquity'.[25] By comparison – and here we begin to see one of the texts' dominant comparative strategies, a point to which I will return below – Christ stood uniquely apart from Muḥammad. He sent prophets before him so that they could herald his coming incarnation, virgin birth, death and resurrection and ascension to heaven. These same prophets foretold Christ's divine nature that worked the miracles only prophets could perform in order to validate their office.[26] The implication of the comparison is that biblical prophecy pointed solely towards Christ. Its silence regarding Muḥammad was matched only by the silence of evidence demonstrating any miracles Muḥammad performed.[27] These were significant shortcomings and readers are led to conclude that Muḥammad was not a real prophet but an imposter.

Besides lacking necessary scriptural support and the corroborating witness of prophets and miracles, the *Kitāb al-Wāḍiḥ bi-l-Ḥaqq* and the *Liber denudationis* also attempted to expose Muḥammad's other personal deficiencies. Accordingly, without the necessary qualifications of a true prophet, Muḥammad resorted to violence and deception in order to create followers.[28] To deal with Muḥammad's violent tendencies, the texts drew from both Islamic traditions and the Qur'ān. Several Islamic traditions are cited in which Muḥammad justified the murder of anyone who did not confess the *shahādah*. Muḥammad purportedly claimed that anyone who performed such violence would enter paradise.[29] When some of Muḥammad's followers asked for proof of his prophethood, citing the usual signs that would accompany such a calling, he replied that prophets were frequently taken for liars. For this reason, God sent Muḥammad, not with signs but with the sword. In turn, his followers became known for their fearlessness in battle.[30] As the text went on to argue, many Muslims did not genuinely follow Muḥammad since their conversions really came only out of fear for their lives.[31]

Another strategy emerged here: the frequent and consistent use of *ḥadīth* literature. Though these can usually be traced to authoritative collections, they frequently appear, in both the *Liber denudationis* and the *Kitāb al-Wāḍiḥ bi-l-Ḥaqq*, in ways in which they were disconnected from their historical and interpretive contexts. In the case of Ibn Rajā', his reference to Islamic traditions in the *Kitāb al-Wāḍiḥ bi-l-Ḥaqq* reflects the intra-Islamic debates with which he was familiar in twelfth-century Fatimid Egypt. The arguments applied to other

Muslim communities, oftentimes based on interactions with Islamic traditions, are re-applied by Ibn Rajā' to Islam as a whole. In this way, the Islamic traditions suffer only a narrow detachment from the original interpretive framework. By the time we arrive at the *Liber denudationis*, however, the translator strained the detachment even further by forcing the traditions to support arguments meant to convince a new audience of Christian readers.[32] In this way, Ibn Rajā' and the translator used *ḥadīth* literature to undergird the arguments *they* wanted them to make.

'Now', the translator interpolated in the text, 'to the violence of his message was added the seduction of supposedly divine advice'.[33] So Muḥammad deceived his followers, leading them to believe that he received revelations from God. A few examples were given in order to substantiate this claim and portray Muḥammad as a charlatan. In the first, the texts recounted how a Muslim once asked Muḥammad for advice. Muḥammad did not have an immediate answer but suggested that the angel Gabriel would come to him with God's response. 'He sat thus for an hour thinking', the texts related. 'And when an answer came to him, he fell on his face and twisted his hands and feet, and thus they saw him until he raised his head and said, "Where is the questioner? An answer," he said, "to your question came to me through Gabriel, and it is such and such"'.[34] Intriguingly, the Islamic tradition from which Ibn Rajā' drew the story portrayed the Prophet receiving a revelation from God via Gabriel, but without the description of physical contortions.[35] As a result, in both the *Kitāb al-Wāḍiḥ bi-l-Ḥaqq* and the *Liber denudationis*, Muḥammad looked like a trickster and his followers appeared gullible and foolish. It would seem doubtful in the text, as a result, that Muḥammad's revelations were actually from God.

In a second example, both texts recount that 'Ā'ishah, Muḥammad's wife (she is mistaken as the Prophet's daughter in the *Liber denudationis*), asked how he received his revelations. Muḥammad responded, 'O daughter, just like the sound of a bell, and when it comes I cannot keep from falling on my face, and then it will withdraw from me; even on a cold day I remain in a profuse sweat'.[36] In general, this is an accurate account of the Islamic traditions,[37] but Ibn Rajā' and the translator have added the description of Muḥammad falling on the ground. This addition, along with the description of Muḥammad's spasms in the previous example, helped to suggest that Muḥammad may have had epilepsy – this is an explicit accusation in the *Liber denudationis* but only intimated by Ibn Rajā' – and that this might explain the convulsive nature of the so-called revelations by which he deceived his followers.[38] Accordingly, Muslims not only followed a swindler, they also foolishly believed a man whose claims were quite possibly rooted in a neurological disorder.

As a final example of Muḥammad's deceit, the story of the *mi'rāj*, the Prophet's night journey in which he ascended to the heavens, is recounted and particular attention is given to the event in which Muḥammad interceded for angels.[39] Ibn Rajā' considered the story a lie. In the *Liber denudationis*, the assessment is embellished: 'O unspeakable presumption and unrestrained lies!'[40] To both Ibn Rajā' and the translator, the Muslim tradition was beyond reason and logic and even accounted for tens of thousands of Muslims leaving Islam.[41] Readers of the *Kitāb al-Wāḍiḥ bi-l-Ḥaqq* are left to draw the obvious conclusion as to what this would mean for Muḥammad's claims to prophethood. The scribe translating and abridging the *Liber denudationis*, however, did not leave anything to chance and made plain for his readers that Muḥammad's deceit made him an 'imposter and pseudo-prophet' (*impostorem atque pseudoprophetam*).[42]

One of the basic claims of Islam is that Muḥammad turned his followers away from polytheism and pointed them towards the worship of the one God. Even some of the Christian authors I have examined thus far were willing to grant this to Muḥammad. Both Ibn Rajā' and, following along, the translator disagreed with such a claim and attempted to expose the idolatry that lay beneath Muḥammad's apparent monotheism. To do so, the traditions and practices surrounding the *Ḥajj* were subjected to criticism. Of particular interest was the Black Stone of the Ka'bah (*al-Ḥajar al-Aswad*). This stone was built into a corner of the Ka'bah, the large cube-shaped structure near the centre of the Sacred Mosque (*al-Masjid al-Ḥarām*) in Mecca. During the *Ḥajj*, Muslims circumambulate the Ka'bah seven times and touch the Black Stone or gesture towards it. A number of Christian authors, including John of Damascus, seized upon this act of piety in order to accuse Muslims of worshipping a created object.[43] So, too, in the *Kitāb al-Wāḍiḥ bi-l-Ḥaqq* and the *Liber denudationis* where idolatry was assumed to lay cloaked beneath the Black Stone. 'What is the difference', Muslims were asked directly, 'between this stone and the statues or idols which [Muḥammad] prohibited you from adoring?'[44] In response, several explanations were offered for the Black Stone's origins, a few of which were drawn from Islamic traditions. For example, both texts observed that some Muslims considered the Black Stone to be 'the right hand of God and an oath by which there will be atonement for sinners'.[45] Indeed, Ibn 'Abbās (d. c. 687) reported that the Black Stone was God's right hand on earth and that touching it indicated a renewal of God's covenant with humanity. Ibn Qutaybah (d. 889) later attempted to clarify and emphasize the figurative nature of Ibn 'Abbās' report.[46] In his text, Ibn Rajā' engaged some of these traditions, subjecting them to scrutiny and, ultimately, disagreeing with them. His response to the notion that the Black Stone was God's right hand did not interact with any of the Islamic traditions but was simply swept aside as illogical and idolatrous.[47] The translator of the *Liber denudationis* significantly abbreviated this section, lopping off any mention at all of Islamic traditions and the Muslim intellectuals who interacted with them, and proclaimed that Muslims simply made God a stone god.[48]

There was also the parochial nature of Muḥammad's prophethood. In other texts we have seen, authors found ways to at least partially affirm some prophetic aspect of Muḥammad's life and work by allowing that he was sent as an emissary of monotheism to the Arabs. The translator of the *Liber denudationis*, abbreviating several sections from Ibn Rajā',[49] picked up on this theme, too, but in a decidedly different way. 'If you say that he taught the Arabs with great eloquence in the Arabic language, which was his own, we will answer that in many places he used a foul manner of speaking.' Three examples follow in the *Liber denudationis* in which the Qur'ān's Arabic was deemed clumsily repetitive. The implication was that Muḥammad's Arabic was far from eloquent.[50]

Beyond mere linguistic inferiority, a far grander point is made with respect to Arabs and Arabic. 'Previously you were saying that you were a prophet sent to the Arabs, since they had not had a messenger of God.'[51] But had not the Arabs already heard from the Holy Spirit at Pentecost (Acts 2:11)? Here, Ibn Rajā' and the translator of the *Liber denudationis* found what they thought was a damning argument. The translator of the *Liber denudationis* went further and interpolated another argument, observing that prophets like Moses were sent to their own people; 'The Hebrew Moses was sent to the Hebrews alone', he wrote.[52] But the Apostles, 'to whom the Spirit gave all knowledge of languages necessarily were sent to the totality of nations'.[53] Where other authors might have grounded Muḥammad in a monotheistic prophetic tradition by linking him to those like Moses, the translator of the *Liber denudationis* exposed the parochial limitations of such a move. For him, and for Ibn Rajā', too, Muḥammad was only as valid as the extent of his linguistic abilities and geographic presence. The benchmark was the Holy Spirit's work through the Apostles who were sent to 'all nations' (*omnes gentes*), not simply to the one that could understand them.[54]

Taken together, the examples of Muḥammad's shortcomings – the contradictions in his Qur'ān, the lack of prophecies foretelling him, his inability to perform miracles – along with his reliance upon violence, the idolatrous underpinnings of Muslim worship, his parochial limitations and the way he deceived his followers, even by possibly covering over epileptic seizures with a mask of divine revelation, exposed Muḥammad's true identity. For Ibn Rajā' and the translator of the *Liber denudationis*, Muḥammad was nothing more than a liar and an imposter who masqueraded as a prophet from God.

Exposing Muḥammad's perversion

In both the *Kitāb al-Wāḍiḥ bi-l-Ḥaqq* and the *Liber denudationis*, it was Muḥammad's alleged predilection for sex that was perhaps his greatest personal deficiency. The texts turned for evidence to Muḥammad's marriages and supporting material from both the Qur'ān and Islamic tradition. Of course, the marriage to Zaynab made an appearance for all the same reasons it appeared in other works I have looked at thus far.[55] But the texts also noted the marriage to Māriyah the Copt (*al-qubṭiyah*),[56] referred to as a Jacobite (*Iacobitam*) in the *Liber denudationis*,[57] and introduced the story by quoting Q 66:1–2:

> O prophet, why do you anathematize or prohibit those things which God has conceded regarding that which you seek, [that is], to do the will of your wives? God is well-disposed and merciful. God has already laid down a law for you so that you may break your oaths.[58]

The texts explained the origins of these revelations by referring to common explanations drawn from *tafsīr* literature.[59] Accordingly, Māriyah's father presented her to Muḥammad. The Prophet's other wives became jealous, especially when he was caught by some of them having sex with Māriyah. Embarrassed, Muḥammad vowed to keep himself from Māriyah, but he was unable to keep his vow, and in turn, the revelations were sent that allowed Muḥammad to sidestep what he had promised. The texts' engagement with Muslim explanations of the verses is limited, though even a more vigorous interaction with *tafsīr* may not have diminished the resulting shock for Christian readers, many of whom may well have concluded, as the translator of the *Liber denudationis* put it, that Muḥammad 'perjured himself and had sex with [Māriyah] again. See how much impiety he officially established on account of this in order that he might commit adultery freely.'[60] These unseemly relationships and the link they had to related revelations in the Qur'ān only seemed to expose an inborn shortcoming in Muḥammad's character: he was licentious, a perversion he gave merit by ascribing to it divine approval.

In both the *Kitāb al-Wāḍiḥ bi-l-Ḥaqq* and the *Liber denudationis*, there was more to Muḥammad's perversion than his marriages and the way he made God approve them. In a chapter devoted to ways in which Muḥammad contradicted himself (primarily in the Qur'ān),[61] the texts raised the subject of Paradise. They balked at the notion that Paradise was 'the width of … the heavens and the earth' (Q 3:133) and that those who resided there would eat and drink in the hereafter just as they did on earth.[62] Of course, the physical dimensions of Paradise were a preoccupation not only of *ḥadīth* literature but also of Christian anti-Muslim literature. Likewise, the activities in Paradise were also a concern. Christians, for whom the afterlife would largely be an ascetic experience, were troubled by Islamic notions of Paradise where earthly joys would be experienced in the afterlife as well.[63] In his text, Ibn Rajā' discussed some of the allowances that Islamic traditions ascribed to the hereafter and even wondered where there might be time for fasting if one does so much eating in Paradise.[64]

The translator of the *Liber denudationis* abbreviated this discussion, but both texts use the absence of heavenly fasting as a springboard to launch into an attack on Muslim sex in Paradise. For Ibn Rajā', this followed the illogical notion that one might engage in sexual activity while in a period of fasting; for the translator of the *Liber denudationis*, sex was just one more example of Muslim gluttony carried forward from earth into Paradise. 'And they will devote themselves to this work in Paradise', the translator wrote with an almost palpable shake of the head, 'and they will have beautiful and chosen women.'[65] For support of his claim, both texts turned to the Qur'ān (36:55), the *Liber denudationis* with a rather curious Latin rendering, 'Today … the lords of paradise are fruitful' (*Hodie … domini paradise sunt fructificantes*).[66] Ibn Rajā' quoted what one might expect: 'The companions of Paradise, that Day, will be busy in their rejoicing' (*inna aṣḥaba al-jannati al-yawma fī shughulin fakihūn*).[67]

To what 'work', exactly, would Muslims devote themselves in Paradise with such fruitfulness or, following Ibn Rajā', for what reason would Muḥammad's companions be so happily busy upon their entry into Paradise? For an answer the texts turned to an intriguing bit of exegesis attributed to the Muslim intellectual al-Ḥasan al-Baṣrī (d. 728). The author of the *Liber denudationis* wrote:

> And [al-Ḥasan al-Baṣrī (*Elhassen Elbassari*)] responded [that the 'work' was], 'the joining of male and female'. It is also related [by al-Ḥasan al-Baṣrī] that he said that the length of the instrument [for impregnating] a woman from among those who are in Paradise will be *berid imberid*, which is said about a horse recently exhausted in [another] horse, and the manly rod will be elongated to that measure. And because a Muslim will not be able to carry the burden, he will compel seventy from the Jews and seventy from the Christians to carry those

> rods. Even if it were a question of a paradise of horses and mules and asses or any other of the brutes, it would be vile even to think of such things.[68]

Ibn Rajā''s reference is a bit different:

> Al-Ḥasan al-Baṣrī was asked and it was said to him: 'What makes them busy that day?' He said: 'Sex'. It was reported from him further that he said: 'The length of the clitoris of the virgins is a sizable distance (*ibarīd fī ibarīd*). God lengthened the penis of every one of them on the Day of Resurrection so that its length would be so sizable (*barīdā*) that he is not able to hold it. Then God would employ seventy Christians and Jews to carry his penis'. If its length is sizable (*barīd*), then God should employ the people of his own religion to carry it, since they have more right to be employed than Christians and Jews. Such minds that would accept this are inferior minds. How amazing![69]

There are some intriguing discrepancies between what Ibn Rajā' wrote and attributed to al-Ḥasan al-Baṣrī and what the translator placed in the *Liber denudationis*. The translator left aside Ibn Rajā''s reference to the female anatomy, a comment reminiscent of the generic remarks in the long Arabic recension of the Baḥīrā legend and of the more graphic descriptions in Bar Ṣalībī's twelfth-century *A Response to the Arabs*.[70] However, he followed along with the reference to male anatomy, adding to this the comparison to horses, an addition reminiscent of a comment Paulus Alvarus made in his ninth-century *Indiculus luminosus*.[71] Both Ibn Rajā' and the translator noted the number of Christians and Muslims responsible for carrying the oversized male member in Paradise – seventy – and both concluded that the attribution of such a tradition to Muḥammad made him infamously unlike any other prophet and, in turn, unfit for such an office.[72]

What seems clear, in light of these similarities and discrepancies, is that Ibn Rajā', like others before and after him (e.g. compilers of legendary Bāḥīrā material or Bar Ṣalībī), was drawing from Islamic traditions about Paradise and using them to assail the sanctity and prophetic viability of Muḥammad. The places in which the translator strayed from Ibn Rajā' further suggest that he was either working from a manuscript of the *Kitāb al-Wāḍiḥ bi-l-Ḥaqq* for which we no longer have access or, perhaps more likely, that he was interpolating information known to him from other sources, either Muslim ones or Christian ones, at the same time he was translating and abridging the *Kitāb al-Wāḍiḥ bi-l-Ḥaqq*. These particular passages would seem ripe opportunities to add graphic details in order to bolster the desired effect of repulsion. Intriguingly, since the translator's interpolations are also drawn from Islamic traditions (even if Eastern Christian sources were a link between the traditions and the translator), the speculation that he was an Arabized Christian familiar with sources in Arabic seems all the more sound.

Both Ibn Rajā' and the translator, in their own ways as there are discrepancies in how this passage was concluded, are clearly shocked and repulsed, not only by what they have found intimated in the Qur'ān but especially by what they have understood from the literature meant to interpret it. The literature in question is, of course, attributed to al-Ḥasan al-Baṣrī, and many traditions, especially those pertaining to the afterlife, are attributed to him. Nevertheless, I have not been able to find any tradition from al-Ḥasan al-Baṣrī or related to him that reports the exact details that Ibn Rajā' and the translator of the *Liber denudationis* shared in this passage.[73] What is certain, as we have seen in connection with the legend of Sergius Baḥīrā, a figure mentioned by Ibn Rajā' and in the *Liber denudationis*,[74] and the treatise of Bar Ṣalībī,[75] is that Islamic descriptions of Paradise – particularly its special features and measurements, as well as the physical descriptions and sexual stamina of its occupants – are bountiful. As I have mentioned, many of these descriptions are offered using numbers like seventy, which are suggestive of cosmological perfection.[76] In a similar light, and also noteworthy, Muslim descriptions of those in Paradise are often given in exaggerated terms. The houris, for example, are large and luminous, a 'rhetorical allegory', Maher Jarrar suggests, 'built around a sensuously embellished spatiality and luminosity'.[77] In such literary contexts, figures 'lose their substance in order to hint at a reality that transcends worldly existence and is greater than it'.[78] It would not be surprising, with this in mind, to find in *ḥadīth* or *tafsīr* literature the description that Ibn Rajā' and the *Liber denudationis* refer to above. In their case, however, the tradition is disconnected, perhaps even unintentionally, from its eschatological interpretive framework and offered at face value where the description surely struck Ibn Rajā', the translator and their readers as both shocking and demeaning.

Equally intriguing is the language employed to refer to the length of genitalia in Paradise. It will be '*berid imberid*', according to the *Liber denudationis*. Thomas Burman, before he was aware of the connection between the *Liber denudationis* and Ibn Rajā', suggested that the translator may have mistakenly read what would have been *mazīd al-mazīd*, an idiom meaning, generically, 'the greatest possible extent or length' and one that fits the text's context. Indeed, the notion of 'surplus' (*mazīd*) is also an expected one in commentary on relevant qur'anic passages pertaining to visions of the afterlife.[79] One can imagine a scribe mistaking the Arabic *mīm*s for *bā*'s and the *zāy*s for *rā*'s (making *barīd* *al-barīd*). Further scribal corruption or negligent misreading could then yield '*berid imberid*'.[80]

Burman's speculation is certainly plausible as far as it goes, but it may only be a red herring in light of the *Kitāb al-Wāḍiḥ bi-l-Ḥaqq*. In fact, '*berid imberid*' follows Ibn Rajā', though '*imberid*' and its 'm' are unusual. Has the translator misread a *hamzah* beneath the *alif* as a *mīm*? This would be an odd mistake for someone who knew Arabic, just as it is odd that the phrase is left untranslated and reduced to a clumsy transliteration. It may be that the terms related to size suffered from the passage being abridged. Indeed, Ibn Rajā''s three references to size are reduced to a single reference in the *Liber denudationis*. And so *ibarīd fī ibarīd*, *barīdā* and *barīd* are conflated by the translator. With continued deterioration under a copyist's misreading, by the time the text found its way to the scribe who produced the manuscript we have of the *Latin denudationis*, a poor transliteration representing an amalgamation of terms or even a simple haplography was all that could be produced.

Whatever its origin, the odd Latin transliteration nevertheless reveals the consistency in which these texts reflected Islamic traditions. *Ḥadīth* literature is full of similarly generic references with respect to size and shape. For example, Abū Hurayrah (d. 681), one of the Prophet's companions, reported Muḥammad stating that the scent of Paradise could be detected from 'such and such' (*kadhā wa-kadhā*) a distance, clearly indicating a very great length.[81] Similarly, the long Arabic recension of the Baḥīrā legend described the physical dimensions of the houris as 'so-and-so much' (*kadhā wa-kadhā*), indicating that its author was not censoring his descriptions but likely following his Islamic source, which, like so many references, employ such generic phrases like *kadhā wa-kadhā*.[82] So, too, with Ibn Rajā' and the *Liber denudationis* who, as I pointed out above, drew upon a *ḥadīth* in order to explain the origins of Muḥammad's revelations, quoting an answer given to the Prophet by Gabriel as 'such and such' (*talis et talis* in the *Liber denudationis* and *kadhā wa-kadhā* in the *Kitāb al-Wāḍiḥ bi-l-Ḥaqq*).[83] *Ḥadīth* literature also employs vocabulary like *barīdā* and *barīd* with respect to units of measurement[84] and so their use by Ibn Rajā' and, however clumsily, in the *Liber denudationis* continues to suggest their recollection of *ḥadīth* and *tafsīr*.

The use of Islamic sources by Ibn Rajā' and in the *Liber denudationis* is significant. To begin with, it indicates that they were not necessarily or haphazardly firing wildly invented accusations at Muslims in order to malign their Prophet. Instead, they appear to have had Islamic sources close to hand as they wrote or translated and were using the information they found within them. But also significant are the ways in which their use of these sources is often disconnected from the ways Muslims used them. As a result, references to descriptions of Paradise, for example, are not linked to Muslim eschatological hermeneutics and rhetoric, but instead skim the surface of their meaning and were subsequently made available as examples in which Muḥammad was nothing more than a pervert whose licentiousness during life on earth was carried forward to life in the hereafter. For this reason, Ibn Rajā' and the translator rhetorically questioned whether St John the Baptist or any of the Hebrew Prophets ever longed for a carnal eternity.[85] Muḥammad's perversion, once it was exposed and put on display for others to see, fell far short of a truly prophet-like ideal.

Muḥammad versus Christ

Muḥammad fell short of more than just prophets like St John the Baptist. In fact, one of the main features that is especially apparent in the more succinct *Liber denudationis* is the way in which Muḥammad is pitted against Christ in a comparative match, a strategy we have already seen with references to Christ's miracles, prophetic lineage and the Apostles' universal mission. Adding to this competition is the examination of Muḥammad's uniquely indecorous qualities that I consider above. As a result, when Muḥammad did compete against Christ in a focused manner, he is already well behind. The goal of such a match was to demonstrate in a conclusive manner the ways that Muḥammad was infinitely inferior to Christ.[86]

The chapter's comparative match began with a rather garbled paraphrase of the Qur'ān (2:134, 141), offered as 'God said, "do not inquire regarding those who are in hell"' (the Qur'ān has 'who have passed away'). Those in hell were identified as the 'forefathers of the first Muslims'. With respect to these, Muḥammad purportedly responded, 'Would that I knew what their work is.'[87] There is an important implication here about the eternal destiny of Muḥammad's parents that will become important later on in the text.

But early on, both Ibn Rajā' and the translator refer to Muḥammad's parents as a means of scrutinizing his past. 'For they do not dare to say', the texts say of Muslims, 'that he prophesied until after forty years. What, therefore, was he doing for those forty years?'[88] The texts provide their own answer along with further quotations from the Qur'ān, explaining that prior to his first revelation Muḥammad was an infidel who taught idolatry to others. What, for Muslims, was evidence of a shift from polytheism to monotheism is used in the texts to highlight Muḥammad's idolatrous, and therefore ultimately damning, beginnings.

From here the texts go on at length with direct comparisons between Muḥammad and Christ, many of which were based upon quotations from the Qur'ān. Accordingly, Christ's mother, Mary, was a pure and holy virgin; Muḥammad's parents – and here the texts were able to return to the opening claim – were unclean idolaters.[89] Christ was sinless; Muḥammad was not since he required forgiveness.[90] Christ produced innumerable miracles; Muḥammad performed none.[91] Christ cast out demons; Muḥammad, had he tried an exorcism, the translator of the *Liber denudationis* interpolated with an almost palpably malevolent grin, would invariably have only succeeded in casting a demon from himself.[92] Christ had a miraculous virgin birth and was the culmination of Abraham's inheritance through Isaac; Muḥammad was allegedly the descendent of Ishmael who was only related to Abraham by the maidservant, Hagar. Through Christ, Abraham's blessing would spread to all the nations; Muḥammad would only carry on Ishmael's legacy as a warring wild man.[93] In the end, it was through Christ that his followers had 'the certain promise of the kingdom of God, if we continue as worshippers of Him'.[94] They would not be like Muḥammad who, though he acknowledged that Christ was the Spirit and Word of God, nevertheless did not worship him as such. Instead, for Muḥammad, Christ was nothing more than 'clay' (*limum*) and so he worshipped 'a god without a word and a spirit'.[95] With this, the comparison between Christ and Muḥammad is complete, but one wonders if the implication of this final remark was that Muḥammad and his followers, in light of their false worship of created matter, were destined for hell very much like their pre-Islamic, idolatrous forebears with whom the comparison began. In any case, the result of the comparative match was a horrible loss for Muḥammad who was exposed as simply and utterly inferior.

An anti-hero defeated on the field of prophets

In the *Liber denudationis* and the *Kitāb al-Wāḍiḥ bi-l-Ḥaqq* Christ was the ultimate victor. He was not, like Muḥammad, an imposter on the field of prophets for he had scriptures to foretell his arrival. He had no need for violence or trickery in order to obtain followers. Like a true prophet, his message was universal and unrestricted by language or geography. His lineage was as pure as his life on earth and in the hereafter. In this comparative match Christ was the victorious hero. That made Muḥammad a vanquished anti-hero. More than just inferior to Christ and authentic prophets, for Ibn Rajā' and the translator of the *Liber denudationis* Muḥammad lacked all of the necessary characteristics of the champion.[96]

The *Kitāb al-Wāḍiḥ bi-l-Ḥaqq* and the *Liber denudationis*, on their own, remain relatively obscure texts. Brought together, however, we can see how widely the text by Ibn Rajā' travelled and that it had profound influence as a source for Christian information about Islam. In fact, as I mentioned above, it had tremendous, though indirect, influence upon the thirteenth-century Dominican monk, Riccoldo da Monte di Croce, who used the *Liber denudationis* as one of the central sources for his *Contra legem Saracenorum*, an attack upon the Qur'ān and Islam. In fact, Riccoldo quoted or paraphrased the *Liber denudationis* fifty times in his work.[97] Riccoldo's text went on to become one of the most influential Latin treatises devoted to Islam in the medieval period.[98] It was translated into other languages including, in the fourteenth century, Greek. This Greek translation was later retranslated back into Latin, a version that saw several reprintings. Notably, it was this Latin version that formed the basis for Martin Luther's (d. 1546) translation of *Contra legem Saracenorum* into German in the middle of the sixteenth century.[99] And, at the beginning of the twenty-first century, Luther's German translation of the *Contra legem Saracenorum* was translated into English by Thomas Pfotenhauer.[100] In this way, the *Kitāb al-Wāḍiḥ bi-l-Ḥaqq* and the *Liber denudationis* had influence far beyond their original audiences.

8

Muḥammad as a powerless Prophet to the Arabs

Paul of Antioch and letters written to Muslims

It is not unreasonable to suggest that when it comes to the texts considered thus far their authors' chief intention was for them to be useful to Christian communities. They likely wrote, in other words, for fellow Christians. Of course, Muslims may well have been listening in, too, as it were, but the texts functioned primarily in order to say something to specific Christian communities and their concerns about life vis-à-vis Islam and the Prophet Muḥammad.

It is intriguing, therefore, to consider Christian texts that purported to be, or actually were, delivered to Muslims. One of the most significant examples is the correspondence that emerged around the *Letter to a Muslim Friend* and *The Letter from the People of Cyprus*. Taken together, these two letters form one of the most provocative and fascinating exchanges in the history of Christian–Muslim relations and the figure of Muḥammad was fixed front and centre in them.

Paul of Antioch and his *Letter to a Muslim Friend*

It must have been in the early thirteenth century when Paul of Antioch, Melkite bishop of Sidon in what is today Lebanon, undertook a western journey around the Mediterranean. He wrote about his travels in a letter to an unnamed Muslim friend. In it, he shared about his visit to Constantinople, south-eastern Italy and Rome. Apparently his Muslim friend, being fully aware of the bishop's journey, wanted him to inquire among the people he met about what they thought of Muḥammad.[1] What remains of the letter – the bulk of it, in fact – is comprised of the opinions and discussions the bishop encountered.

Little else is known about Paul or his alleged journey. From his own writings it would seem that he was active in the first half of the thirteenth century. While it was certainly possible for him to undertake an expedition around the Mediterranean basin and seek opinions about Islam from local intellectuals, it seems much more likely that the journey was a rhetorical device wherein the intellectuals were used as mouthpieces for Paul's own arguments. These arguments are far too closely linked to the topics that Arabic-speaking Christians and Muslims discussed and the adept use of the Qur'ān reflects a familiarity better suited, in this period, to an Arabic-speaking Christian as opposed to a European.[2] So Paul may or may not have actually went on his journey. He may not have actually consulted with intellectuals in Constantinople, Rome and other Mediterranean cities. So did he actually send his letter to a Muslim friend? It is, of course, entirely possible and the contents of the letter make such an occasion very provocative.[3] It is equally possible, however, that framing the text as a correspondence with a Muslim and inventing a panel of Christian intellectuals with whom he could dialogue only helped to lend creative credence to what was otherwise a religious treatise.

Paul wrote early on in the letter that his Muslim friend 'asked me to give you a clear account of what the people I met, and with whom I spoke, thought of Muḥammad, peace be upon him'.[4] The intellectuals he encountered claimed, 'When we heard that a man whose name was Muḥammad had appeared among the Arabs saying that he was God's messenger and that he brought a book, mentioning that it was sent down to him from God … we set about getting possession of the book for ourselves'.[5] So they heard that a prophet had been sent with a book from God. Offering their due diligence, then, they acquired a copy of the Qur'ān in order to see what it had to say. This would surely suggest to readers that the judgements they were about to read were given with authority and after having considered the primary source in its own words.

Paul responded to the intellectuals' claim by asking, 'Since you have heard of this messenger (*rasūl*) and you have made an effort to get for yourselves the book which he brought, what is the reason why you have not followed him?' After all, Paul went on to quote directly from the Qur'ān, 'Whoever wants a religion other than Islam, it will not be accepted from him; in the hereafter he will be among the losers' (Q 3:85).[6] There follows in the letter seven reasons, each one based on qur'anic text, why the intellectuals, even after having read the Qur'ān and considered Muḥammad, did not become Muslims. First, they said that the Qur'ān was in Arabic and not in their own language (Q 12:2; 20:113). Second, they noted that God only sent messengers to people of specific language groups (Q 14:4). In other words, to Greek speakers God sent Greek-speaking prophets; to Arabic speakers, he sent an Arabic-speaking prophet. Third, Muḥammad was raised up for a scripture-less people in order to purify them (Q 62:2). Fourth,

Muḥammad was sent to those for whom no one had previously been sent (Q 32:3). Fifth, Muḥammad was sent with an Arabic Qur'ān specifically for those in Mecca (Q 42:7). Sixth, Muḥammad was sent to those whose forebears had not previously been given divine revelation (Q 36:6). And finally, the seventh reason the intellectuals considered and declined Islam was that Muḥammad was specifically sent to preach to those related to him, that is, the Arabs (Q 26:214).[7]

In sum, God sent Muḥammad and his message specifically to Arabic speakers who had no previous knowledge of the one, true God. As the intellectuals concluded based upon their reading of the Qur'ān,

> When we considered [these quotations from the Qur'ān], we knew that he was not sent (*yursal*) to us, but to the pagan Arabs (*al-jāhiliyyah min al-'Arab*) … . We are not bound to follow him because messengers had already come to us before him, addressing us in our own languages. They warned us and they handed over to us the Torah and the Gospel in our own vernacular languages.[8]

Intriguingly, though the emphasis in the intellectuals' conclusion was that Christians were excused from following Muḥammad, the statement logically implied that Muḥammad was actually sent by God. Paul even employed here the verb *arsala* – and one thinks here of *rusul*, the Messengers sent by God with his revelation – which seemingly suggests a conscious nod by Paul to the validity of Muḥammad's role as prophet.[9] He may not have been sent to *Christians*, but Muḥammad was, nevertheless, sent in some authentic way. There was a place, then, for Muḥammad in God's eternal plan.[10]

This recognition of Muḥammad as a prophet, though it stops well short of the way Muslims describe him,[11] is notable. In Paul's estimation, Muḥammad's ministry may have been limited, but he was a prophet nonetheless. As significant as such an assessment must have been, it was not without precedent. It must have had some currency in contexts where Jews, Christians and Muslims encountered one another because it appeared in Andalusī Muslim juridical (*fiqh*) discussions concerning punishments for blaspheming the Prophet. The Mālikī *qāḍī* Ibn Sahl (d. 1093), citing the opinion of Malik ibn Anas (d. 795) and his companions, said that if a *dhimmī*[12] proclaimed 'Muḥammad was not sent to us but to you; our Prophet is Moses or Jesus' or other claims along those lines, then the *dhimmī* should not be executed, a typical punishment for blasphemy. If, however, a *dhimmī* blasphemed the Prophet in the usual way, such as denying him prophethood entirely or slandering his name, then the customary penalty applied.[13]

An entire sea and more than a century separated eleventh-century al-Andalus and Mālikī jurisprudence from Paul of Antioch. Was he aware of these kinds of legal discussions in his own surroundings? Did he know if his view of Muḥammad could be a legally acceptable one to Muslims? We can only speculate, but the legal discussion nevertheless suggests a context in which non-Muslim views of the Prophet were shared. It further suggests that these views could impact intercommunal relations, and possibly to control those relations, Muslims considered the extent to which blasphemy could be punished. Granting that Muḥammad was a prophet to some extent was, according to some rulings, an acceptable position for a Jew or a Christian to hold, for it honoured the commitments they had to their revelations and made space for a new one intended for another monotheistic community.

This new revelation was, of course, the Qur'ān, a text that Paul treated with as much provocation as he did Muḥammad. On the one hand, Paul's use of the Qur'ān reflects, even if indirectly, a subtle nod to its authenticity as an authoritative text because he – or, perhaps, the intellectuals to whom he spoke on his journey – used the Qur'ān in order to substantiate nearly every claim made about Muḥammad and Islam and in efforts to excuse Christians from following Muḥammad. The key to the Qur'ān's authority, on the other hand, was correct interpretation. By allowing the Qur'ān to have a claim on authority, Paul made a way for proving Christian truth. So, after the conclusion the intellectuals offered that I quote above comes what would be the first of a litany of Christian interpretations of the Qur'ān. Referring back to their use of Q 3:85, Paul recounted their reading of it:

> So, according to the demand of justice, the quotation 'Whoever wants a religion other than Islam, it will not be accepted from him; in the hereafter he will be among the losers' would mean, the book's own people to whom it came in their own vernacular language, and not anyone to whom it did not come – and this according to its own testimony.[14]

What the Qur'ān really meant, then, was that eschatological condemnation was not for just anyone who rejected Islam but specifically for pagan Arabs who rejected Muḥammad's message. This hermeneutic typifies the approach taken throughout the *Letter to a Muslim Friend*. Passages from the Qur'ān are either used to support Christian claims, irrespective of their context or history of Muslim interpretation, or qur'anic material is veritably pressed through a Christian sieve, stripping it of its Muslim meaning so that it might yield Christian truth. It is a shrewd Christianization of the Muslim text.[15]

As I have mentioned, Paul's letter consists almost entirely of these Christian interpretations of the Qur'ān. Some are more complex than others; some interpretations are very literal and simplistic. But they are all used in order to prove Paul's arguments that Christianity was given favour by God in the Qur'ān, that its doctrines can be found in the Qur'ān or that Christians are somehow excused from the explicit claims made in it about Muḥammad. I will highlight here one example that deals specifically with the claim that Muḥammad was sent as a messenger. In this argument, the intellectuals quoted a portion of Q 57:25, which Paul recounted, accurately, as, 'We have sent Our messengers with clear signs, and the Book was with them, so that people might stand up for fairness.' Muslims understand the verse to indicate that God sent his messengers – those like Moses, Jesus and Muḥammad – with a revelation for the sake of just guidance. But the *correct* understanding of this verse, as Paul revealed it, was that God sent the Apostles – they were the 'messengers' (Paul highlighted the shared plural grammar between 'Apostles' and 'messengers') of whom the Qur'ān spoke – and he sent them with 'the Book', that is, the Gospel (Paul highlighted the shared singularity). Had God intended to indicate messengers like Abraham, Moses, David or Muḥammad, then he would have referred to 'books'.[16] In this way, the notion of Muḥammad's universal prophethood is deflected onto Christ's apostles.

In a few places, Paul attempted to anticipate the difficulty Muslims might have in response to this kind of reading of the Qur'ān. For example, Paul wrote that he counselled the intellectuals, 'If we argue based on what is in their scripture, Muslims will say, "If you are going to argue based on part of it, you must accept all of it".'[17] In other words, verses from the Qur'ān should not be plucked at will here and there in support of claims that are not native to its context. In response, the intellectuals demurred. 'This is not the case', they said, and then they introduced a short parable. Suppose a man had a bill of debt, which he paid and for which he possessed a receipt of payment. If a creditor produced the bill and demanded a payment, would not the man show him his receipt? And in response, would it be reasonable for the creditor to say that, just as the man acknowledged his receipt, so also he should continue to acknowledge the bill and pay it again? This would of course not be the case. In a similar way, the intellectuals asserted, 'because of the arguments on our behalf we find in the Qur'ān, we reject what ever else is said in it and urged against us'. Essentially, the bits of the Qur'ān that are supportive of Christians and their faith are given precedence over bits that contradict them; the passages of the Qur'ān that support Christian truth are the receipt of payment. One might even see in the parable an argument that some verses abrogate others.[18] But which ones? Paul does not address this and it is difficult not to view the parable as ultimately (and unintentionally) illustrating his cherry-picking of the Qur'ān.[19]

In any case, the resounding assessment is that Muḥammad was a prophet only for the Arabs. Was Islam, by implication, a religion only for the Arabs? Paul's answer to such a question is placed near the end of the letter when the intellectuals asserted that a new religion (*sharīʿah*) after Christianity was unnecessary and superfluous.

> Whereas everything that preceded [Christianity] demanded it, there would be no need for anything to come after it, because nothing could come after perfection and be superior in grace. Rather, it would be beneath it or derived from it; and the derivative is a kind of grace for which there is no need.[20]

Islam, then, was no more than derivative of Christianity. With this conclusion, the authenticity granted to Muḥammad's prophethood and the validity offered to the Qur'ān are both limited by their relative impotency. Muḥammad may have been sent with a message from God, but that message, insofar as it was derivative of Christianity, was unneeded. The best the Qur'ān could do, when it was correctly understood, was to confirm Christian truth. In this way, Muḥammad's role as a prophet, though Paul did not say so explicitly, seems to have been to reveal to Arabs what they had as yet been unable to see. And this was only made plain in the light of Paul's qur'anic exegesis. This made of Muḥammad a very small prophet. He could only be said to underwrite Christianity when his message was properly interpreted – or, better, Christianized – and so his prophethood was, in the view of Paul of Antioch, rather powerless.

A softened reprisal in *The Letter from the People of Cyprus*

In the early fourteenth century, perhaps one hundred years after Paul of Antioch wrote his *Letter to a Muslim Friend*, the bishop's letter, or at least a form of it, re-appeared in a very unique way. An anonymous author based in the Mediterranean island of Cyprus somehow came across the letter and, editing some portions of it and revising many other parts, sent a very similar letter to two notable Muslim intellectuals in Damascus: the Ḥanbalī scholar Ibn Taymiyya (d. 1328) was sent a copy in 1316 and the intellectual Muḥammad ibn Abī Ṭālib al-Dimashqī (d. 1327) received one on 11 March 1321. Ibn Taymiyya was easily one of the most prominent Muslim scholars of the period, so sending a version of the letter to him is noteworthy. Al-Dimashqī was much less widely known, but renowned in the city of Damascus and its surroundings. This indicates the anonymous Christian author likely had connections to Damascus, perhaps even being from there, and further suggests that his strategy for the letter had something to do with engaging both well-known Muslims and those with clout in Damascus. Ibn Taymiyya and al-Dimashqī wrote lengthy texts in response to the letters they received, the nature of which I address a bit further on below.[21] It is also noteworthy that, though there is some speculation as to whether or not the *Letter to a Muslim Friend* was authentic correspondence, there is no doubt that *The Letter from the People of Cyprus* was truly intended for Muslim eyes.

The Letter from the People of Cyprus is closely structured around the *Letter to a Muslim Friend* and incorporates a great deal of its content. As a result, there are numerous similarities between the two letters. Both incorporated the concept of a journey, though the Cypriot letter only included travel to Cyprus, in order to inquire with European intellectuals about their knowledge of Muḥammad. Both letters made ample use of the Qur'an and employed a similar hermeneutic whereby a Christian interpretation of the Muslim text helped to reveal its authentic meaning. In particular, both letters conceived of Muḥammad and his prophethood in similar ways, contending that he was a local, parochial prophet sent only to the Arabs with a message that, when adequately understood, endorsed Christianity.

As in Paul's letter, the author of the letter from Cyprus also wondered why the intellectuals he consulted did not follow after Muḥammad even though they had heard of him and acquired a copy of the Qur'ān. The answer provided in the Cypriot letter came with different and more precise quotations from the Qur'ān – a revision to which I will return – but the message was, overall, very similar. Muḥammad had been sent to the pagan Arabs (*al-jāhiliyyah min al-'Arab*), a people for whom there had not yet been a prophet, with a message in Arabic that they had not yet received.[22] In this way, the same kind of recognition Paul granted to Muḥammad and the Qur'ān is also granted by the author of the letter from Cyprus. Similarly, much of the author's reasoning for why Muḥammad is restricted to the Arabs and not applied to Christians is derived from the Qur'ān.[23] And both letters concluded that, since Christ represented the apex of revelation (*al-kamāl*), no further revelation was required; it would only be derivative of perfection.[24] Like Paul, the author writing from Cyprus proclaimed that his letter should draw Christians and Muslims together in agreement.[25]

Despite the ways in which *The Letter from the People of Cyprus* closely followed the overall design of Paul's letter, even pulling in much of Paul's content, it is much more than a lightly edited edition. The anonymous author altered Paul's letter in significant ways.[26] The main divergences in terms of content can be seen even at the very beginning of the Cypriot letter. There, the anonymous author wrote:

> You have asked me to make a full inquiry for you of what the Christians, followers of Christ, who are diverse in languages and scattered over the four corners of the earth from east to west, south to north, inhabiting the islands of the sea and established on the dry land stretching as far as the setting sun, believe.[27]

The author seems eager to highlight here at the very beginning, both in detail and in eloquence, the universality of Christianity. Its followers covered the earth – both the islands of the sea and the expanse of dry land – and spoke a multitude of languages. Readers unfamiliar with Paul's letter would not fully appreciate the Cypriot letter's introductory remarks. But for those aware of how both letters limited Muḥammad's prophethood to Arabia and Arabic speakers, these comments come as an early, potent jab. And the jabs continued throughout the letter, in between remarks about Muḥammad being sent only to the Arabs; Christians are those 'scattered over all the world and in all their languages, as they received [biblical prophecies] from the pure Apostles (*al-rusul al-ʾaṭhār*), to this day a single message'.[28]

Many other revisions, however, when compared to Paul's letter, surface as attempts to soften arguments and perhaps make them more palatable to Muslims. For example, it was the question of what intellectuals thought of Muḥammad that focused Paul's journey. In the Cypriot letter, the unnamed scholar – he is called *shaykh* and *sayyid*, a hint that perhaps the Cypriot letter aimed to make its protagonist into a more sympathetic figure than a Christian bishop[29] – inquired, much more generally, about what Christians believed.[30] All of the same information about Muḥammad followed, but the Cypriot letter came with a much more gentle and less pointed intent, or so, at least, it might have seemed.

More significantly, the qur'anic evidence the intellectuals used in order to rationalize their decision not to follow Muḥammad is altered in the Cypriot letter. In Paul's letter, seven passages from the Qur'ān are offered, each one without reference and sometimes not given in full. Some, as can be noted in my description of them above, are repetitive of each other. The Cypriot letter also listed seven verses from the Qur'ān. The first followed Paul's letter directly and the rest were, like Paul's, repetitive in their reasoning. But they are a different selection of verses that are given with the names of their *suwar* intact.[31] The intellectual's defence does not change – they did not follow Muḥammad because, according to their reading of the Qur'ān, he was sent only to Arabs who had not yet had a prophet – but the result of the anonymous author's alteration is a much more polished and presentable response.[32] It is almost as if he was making a more sincere appeal, a more irenic gesture, to Muslims with the hope that they might give serious consideration to his letter.

Other divergences reinforce this observation. For example, in Paul's letter he summarized the qur'anic account of Jesus's childhood miracle, writing that 'He made clay into the shape of a bird and breathed into it and it flew away, by God's permission' (Q 3:49; 5:110). Jesus was, therefore, 'God's Spirit and His Word'.[33] Paul followed the general qur'anic description of the miracle, but in his retelling he wrote that Christ 'made (*'amala*) clay into the shape of the bird' instead of the Qur'ān's 'create (*ākhluqu* or *takhluqu*) clay into the shape of a bird'. The shift in vocabulary for the operative verb is significant. In the Qur'ān, creation is reserved only for God and so we see *khalaqa*. In Paul's letter, this is demoted to *'amala* – Christ simply made the clay into a bird, an act that God allowed. One senses in Paul's revision an attempt to provide a qur'anic image of Christ's two natures at work in unison – the human that made the clay and the divine that allowed it to come to life.[34] The Cypriot letter reproduced the summary of the miracle, but the vocabulary followed the Qur'ān where Christ 'created (*khalaqa*) from clay the likeness of a bird'[35] and the Christological implication disappeared. The Cypriot letter marked in this way a return to the Qur'ān that, in turn, indicated at least some hesitancy to meddle with the Muslim text.[36]

There are also a number of significant additions and omissions that the Cypriot letter introduced. Some of the additions comprised quotations from the Hebrew Bible, many of which the author used in order to add more biblical credence to Paul's argument about the Jews stumbling into idolatry or ignoring their prophecies.[37] The author also added extra and more precise quotations from the Qur'ān. The longest revision shows the author omitting large chunks of Paul's letter and replacing them with scriptural additions. Here we see the author hard at work, once again, smoothing out the pointedness of Paul's letter in order to offer an argument that was softer and more inviting to consider. Similarly, in his letter, Paul devoted several paragraphs to discussion of God having a Son and the Incarnation. These passages consisted largely of theological propositions that are offered with relatively brief explanation.[38] The author of the Cypriot letter omitted these passages almost entirely and replaced them with a series of biblical quotations.[39] These added quotations worked to demonstrate that Christ's coming was the culmination of Hebrew prophecy and had, therefore, been anticipated for quite some time.[40] In place of a complex theological exposition, then, readers found a scriptural account drawn from the prophets that attempted to demonstrate the steadfast commitment Christians showed to their doctrine. The narrative is still used to explain why Christians did not need to pay heed to a new prophet with a new message,[41] but the argument was, nevertheless, relaxed in comparison to the original brusque presentation.[42]

All of these elements made *The Letter from the People of Cyprus* more than a simple reworking of Paul's *Letter to a Muslim Friend*. The Cypriot letter was, instead, heavily edited. Even with all of its omissions, additions and revisions, however, Muḥammad was to the author of the Cypriot letter, as he was to Paul, a prophet. In this way, both authors managed to find a place for Muḥammad in the grand scheme of God's plan. It was just that Muḥammad did not have a unique function, instead only serving to confirm Christian truth. In this, validation of his prophethood did not pose a problem to the claims Christians attached to religious superiority because, according to *The Letter from the People of Cyprus*, and to Paul of Antioch, Muḥammad actually represented the finality of Christianity.[43] This kind of recognition of Muḥammad essentially made him redundant. And because Christianity had no need for him, he was a powerless prophet.

Most intriguingly, then, it would appear that the anonymous author's heavy-handed revisions for the Cypriot letter had most impact on the letter's function. For as David Thomas surmises, 'Paul was writing to force Muslim readers to acknowledge the compelling truth of his arguments and bow to his rational and scriptural proofs that Christianity is the true religion, the anonymous Cypriot was making the gentler attempt to invite Muslims to see the truth of Christianity by persuasive quotations from scripture and rational arguments.'[44] And, in particular, the author from Cyprus used the letter in order to invite Muslims into a discussion, which was itself based upon sacred text.[45] Building from here, it may not be unreasonable to suggest that the author, having granted to Muḥammad what he thought at least met a legally acceptable threshold – that 'Muḥammad was not sent to us but to you; our Prophet is Jesus', as Paul had acknowledged – considered himself to have come a certain ways towards Muslims. In turn, he could perhaps hope for some reciprocal recognition of Christianity beyond what Muslims were normally prepared to grant.[46]

Interreligious and intergenerational correspondence about a powerless Prophet

Taken together, the letters from Paul and the anonymous author in Cyprus are at once provocative and puzzling. It is difficult to imagine that either of the authors could have hoped to accomplish anything more than to needle Muslim readers. This is surely the case with Paul's 'deceptively reasonable Qur'anic re-interpretations', as David Thomas calls them, and his seemingly diplomatic evaluation of Muḥammad.[47] As we now know, the Cypriot letter was more restrained, but the status of the Qur'ān and Muḥammad remains much the same in it. How could these Christians have reasonably expected Muslims to sincerely consider their petitions since one of the essential premises of their letters was that they could tell Muslims how to understand their own Prophet and sacred text? It is difficult to imagine either author expecting anything less from Muslims than a scandal even with the concessions they allowed for Muḥammad.[48]

To consider first the case of Paul, he left open the possibility that his Muslim friend might not be satisfied with his letter. He was open to sharing the Muslim's disfavour with the intellectuals he met in order to solicit their feedback.[49] This may simply be a rhetorical flourish, especially if Paul invented the intellectuals and Muslim friend, but we know that one Muslim in particular came across the letter, read it and was as provoked by its contents in the ways we might expect. Shihāb al-Dīn Aḥmad ibn Idrīs al-Qarāfī (d. 1285), the Egyptian Mālikī jurist, responded to the letter and spared very little in his disapproval in the first chapter of his *al-Ajwiba al-fākhira 'an al-as'ila al-fājira* ('Splendid Replies to Insolent Questions'). He dismantled each of Paul's arguments in a devastating reply that sought to reorder a proper, Islamic understanding of the universality of the Prophet and his message.[50] One of his overall assessments was that Christians were 'a blind nation and an ignorant sect, which servile conformism has overcome'.[51]

What, then, are we to do with the letter's function and Paul's deceptively generous approval of Muḥammad? Paul went much further in his view of Muḥammad than many other Christians. Patriarch Timothy I, for example, argued that Muḥammad only functioned *like* the prophets; Paul concluded that he *was* a prophet with a message from God. It was just that Muḥammad's prophethood was very parochial – he was only sent to the Arabs with a book in Arabic – and he was only meant to confirm the truth of Christianity, inasmuch as the Qur'ān could do, for it was Christianity that boasted the fullness of universal truth. This layering of provocation beneath Paul's irenic tone seems to obscure any indication of the letter's function. But perhaps a clue is discernible in this layering as well. At the outset of the letter, Paul wrote to his Muslim friend, 'May God grant us and you the benefit of reflection (*i'tibār*) and may He make it conducive for you and for us to gain insight in the works that lead to Paradise and deliver one from Hell-fire'.[52] Again, a measure of courtesy seems clear on the surface, but beneath this is also what seems to be an admonition that proper and rational deliberation will lead to salvific knowledge of God (*i'tibār*). Salvation and the Paradise that follows, in other words, will be found by those who understand correctly.[53] And it was Paul's intention to demonstrate a precise understanding of relevant qur'anic text and the nature of Muḥammad's prophethood. This was all for the benefit of his Muslim friend who might, as a result, find the truth of Christian teachings come into focus.[54]

So this explanatory function formed the provocative layer of Paul's letter, for he was surely aware that any Muslims who read what he wrote would not accept his interpretation of the Qur'ān or his assessment of the Prophet. The layer of irenic, much like the intellectuals who Paul doubtless invented, helped to give his letter an air of certainty to Christian readers. Paul even confidently declared at the end of his letter that, as a result of what he wrote, God 'will have made quarrelling cease between His servants the Christians and the Muslims'.[55] Polemicizing Muḥammad made him into a threat from which to keep distance. A seemingly irenic approach, though, neutralized such a threat by explaining to Christians why Islam had come into the world – to confirm Christian beliefs – and convincing them that Muḥammad and his message were not things about which they needed to be concerned.[56] And so Paul's closing sentiment leaves one with the impression that he considered the question of Muḥammad's efficacy, at least as far as any Christian readers might be concerned, closed. Muḥammad was simply not sent to non-Muslims. Armed with proof from the Qur'ān itself, Christians need not bother with his message and, with a satisfactory sigh of relief, could move on to other concerns. It would seem, then, that Christian readers might have benefitted most from Paul's letter, despite the 'deceptively reasonable' way in which it reached out to Muslims.

What about the anonymous author who wrote from Cyprus? In this case, the author *intended* for specific Muslims to read what he wrote because, as I mentioned above, the letter was actually sent to Ibn Taymiyya and al-Dimashqī in Damascus. The letter was, in this sense, an invitation for interreligious consideration.[57] Could it be that the author was attempting to create a space for innovative thinking that he hoped the Muslim recipients of his letter would enter as well? He had found space for Muḥammad in Christianity. Would Muslims reciprocate in some way, too? Such questions are as provocative as the letter and the author's creative revisions to it, but what kind of discussion could he possibly have hoped to initiate when Muḥammad was, in his estimation, a parochial prophet completely subservient to the finality of Christian truth?

We know from the lengthy responses written by Ibn Taymiyya and al-Dimashqī that *The Letter from the People of Cyprus* stirred up two of the most antagonistic responses from Muslims to Christian treatises in existence. They were neither moved by the Cypriot's appeal nor inspired to rethink how they might conceive of Islam vis-à-vis Christianity. Instead, the treatises they wrote in reply shattered the Cypriot letter and its attempt to place Muḥammad within a Christian frame of view. For them, Muḥammad was a universal prophet with a final, universal revelation. On this point there could be no room for flexibility.[58]

In this light, another possibility emerges for the function of the deceptively interreligious letter. Could it be that the author sent the letter to two well-known, even famous, Muslim intellectuals, hoping to provoke a response and to ensure that his letter would circulate and draw attention? Doing so would ensure that, besides Muslims noticing his text, Christian communities would hear word of it, too. Having done so they could read a very polished text that might help them make sense of their faith with respect to Islam and to understand how someone as effective as Muḥammad fit into their religious world view where Christianity was supreme. In such a case, Muḥammad's prophetic function, particularly his powerless limitations, could be thrown into its proper subservience to Christianity.

That the letter was meant to function in this way is not at all unimaginable. After all, we know that al-Qarāfī came into possession of a version of Paul's letter. The anonymous author in Cyprus was also able to obtain a copy. So it would not be impossible for the Cypriot letter to circulate widely, beyond Ibn Taymiyya and al-Dimashqī, across different religions, generations and geographies. In fact, Ibn Taymiyya mentioned in reference to Paul's letter that 'Their scholars hand it down among themselves, and old copies still exist.'[59] So sending the letter in such a way that it garnered notice may have been the most effective strategy for an author in Cyprus to speak to issues of concern for Christian communities in Damascus where they might benefit from the kind of triumphalist nourishment that the notion of a powerless Prophet Muḥammad offered.[60]

9

Muḥammad as a Prophet and colonial goad for persecutors

Mary Fisher and a notorious encounter with a Sultan

It was not just Paul of Antioch and *The Letter from the People of Cyprus* travelling around the Mediterranean basin considering the prophethood of Muḥammad. There was also Mary Fisher, an English Quaker from Yorkshire. Her life in England and her travels in Europe are not what interest me here, but instead the travels she took much further afield. In 1658 Fisher made her way to the Ottoman Empire in order to preach to the Turks she encountered there. Along with five other Quakers, she travelled through southern Europe and into Adrianople, present-day Edirne in northwest Turkey. In Adrianople she met a sixteen-year-old Sultan Mehmed IV (d. 1693) whereupon they discussed not only her Quaker message but the Prophet Muḥammad as well. Her encounter became the stuff of legend, which made its way, along with Fisher herself, to Colonial New England.[1] There, it took on new life in support of the Society of Friends as a marginal, oftentimes persecuted religious community.[2]

Mary Fisher and the context of Quakerism

The details of Fisher's encounter and the claims that she made before the Sultan are best understood within the context of seventeenth-century Quaker particularities. This takes us from Adrianople where she met Mehmed in 1658 back to England where Fisher was born and where Quakerism, or the Society of Friends as Quakers called themselves, began. In the seventeenth century, England endured a civil war during which time a number of religious dissenting groups emerged. Dissatisfied with the Christian establishment, the Church of England in particular, many of these dissenters sought to reaffirm what they thought was a true form of Christianity. Among these seventeenth-century dissenters was a young man named George Fox (d. 1691). Like other religious dissenters, Fox became convinced of religious ideas that put his Christian faith in a new light. He regularly preached these ideas that cut across the grain of established Christianity and was imprisoned on several occasions as a direct result of what he preached. The charge against Fox and others like him was usually blasphemy, an umbrella term for a wide variety of claims that contradicted recognized dogma. One such case came for Fox in 1650 when he travelled to Derby in central England to visit a few other Friends, as his sympathizers were known. When a lecture convened in the town, Fox attended and 'spoke to [those in attendance] what the Lord commanded me'.[3] The details of Fox's message are not given in his autobiographical account, but an officer who heard Fox's remarks asked that Fox accompany him to the local magistrate. Under examination, Fox denounced 'their preaching, baptism and sacrifices [that] would never sanctify them' and admonished his examiners to 'look unto Christ within them, and not unto men; for it is Christ that sanctifies'.[4] Fox's testimony triggered pandemonium among those who listened to him and he was subsequently imprisoned. According to Fox's own account, it was in this Derby prison where one of the justices first 'called us Quakers, because I bade them tremble at the word of the Lord'.[5]

Rufus Jones, the editor of Fox's autobiographical journal, made the note that this reference from Fox about the name 'Quakers' constitutes the extent of what is known about the origins of the term and its application to members of the Society of Friends. Yet the manner in which the term is applied suggests that it may have already been in use as a pejorative reference. If this was indeed the case, then the term would have been readily available to the justice who dismissed Fox and his followers as such.[6] Those who disapproved of religious dissenters along with their beliefs and their actions could thus call them collectively, regardless of their specific identities, 'quakers'. In fact, other religious sects known for their literal trembling in response to their alleged divine encounters were already being called 'quakers'. There was, accordingly, 'a sect of women (they are from Southwark) come from beyond the sea, called Quakers, and these swell, shiver and shake, and, when they come to themselves – for in all this fitt Mahomet's Holy Ghost hath been conversing with them – they begin to preach what hath been delivered to them by the Spirit'.[7]

Several things emerge from the description of Fox's imprisonment in Derby and the origins of the term 'Quaker'. Perhaps most intriguing is the connection made between supposed direct encounters with God (or divine revelation), subsequent physical shaking and Muḥammad. Those who claimed to have a direct encounter with God were accused of conversing with 'Mahomet's Holy

Ghost'. Likely in view here was not only the apparent doubt that one might hear directly from God, such as Muḥammad claimed to have done (though this was facilitated by the angel Gabriel), but also the descriptions of Muḥammad's physical response to revelation, perhaps even the accusation that what he really experienced was epilepsy.[8] The entire description, neatly packaged in the phrase 'Mahomet's Holy Ghost', cut down the claim that Muḥammad had a divine encounter – he was really just mentally unstable – but this assessment of Muḥammad's claim to prophethood was also used in order to discredit other religious dissenters who claimed to hear something directly from God. In this way, the Society of Friends were considered 'quakers', whether because they literally trembled in response to an alleged word from God, exhorted others to tremble (literally or figuratively) in response to God's presence or were simply dismissed as spiritually and religiously suspect.[9]

More generally, the description of Fox's time in Derby also reveals something of the Society of Friends' basic beliefs and practices, some of which are significant to what follows with respect to Mary Fisher. To begin with, we see Fox seeking out an opportunity for verbal, or perhaps prophetic, confrontation. This was not uncommon in the Society of Friends,[10] but it had less to do with a proclivity for verbal hostility than it did with an emphasis upon prophetic preaching. It was the basic belief among Friends that, reflecting the book of Joel in the Hebrew Bible, the Spirit had in their time been poured out on all men and women.[11] In turn, any individual could be a prophet because God taught everyone directly. This made Quaker thought and practice highly experiential and very individualistic. As a result, the Friends eschewed any kind of mediation, such as ordained clergy, organized ecclesial hierarchy, religious rituals or sacraments. For them, anyone could experience God's presence by simply responding to what they called the Seed or Light of Christ within them.

This view meant that Quakers did not need a priest, for example, to mediate God's presence through sacraments in the context of a religious gathering. Further, although the Bible was a sacred text incorporated into the Friends' religious life and spirituality, it nevertheless remained inferior to the living Word of God within individuals.[12] As a result, Friends ought to wait upon the Lord in order to experience direct inspiration from him.[13] When such inspiration occurred, it became incumbent that they proclaim the message they were given, do so in the context in which they were given it and then simply depart. It was in this light that Fox set himself to address a group of people who had gathered in Derby in 1650 to hear a lecture that was otherwise unrelated to the Society of Friends or Quaker thought and practice.

Besides the emphasis upon a personal, unmediated encounter with God, there was a variety of other practices in which the Friends engaged that marked them out as peculiar. Together, these practices are what Richard Bauman calls a 'rhetoric of impoliteness' that distinguished the Friends from wider society.[14] This peculiarity was intentional, for the Friends wished to be seen as deliberately set apart. Their 'rhetoric of impoliteness' included the refusal to swear oaths or observe holidays such as Sunday and Christian feast days like Christmas. They insisted on plain clothing and speech, especially resisting language that conformed to social class norms.[15] They also refused to use normal greetings, honorific titles or customs of social politeness like the tipping of a hat. They were not, as we have seen with Fox, deterred from publicly denouncing what they saw as egregious religious and spiritual behaviour. These kinds of social and religious norms, for the Society of Friends, were considered vain, a mark of idolatry (they gave too much deference to humans instead of God) and lent themselves to the kind of social and ecclesial hierarchy that they found distasteful, sinful and a departure from the true Church.[16]

Undergirding these characteristics was the Society of Friends' particular eschatology. As I have already mentioned, the heart of Quaker thought was the view that the Holy Spirit had been poured out on all people in their day and age. The time was ripe in the mid-seventeenth century, then, for proclaiming the messages God was giving those who were attentive to his voice. To do so would be to finally worship in spirit and in truth.[17] And absolutely anyone could receive this revelation from God, this Divine Light, as the Friends called it. As a result, the Friends were not shy of confronting others with their beliefs and condemning what they saw as spiritual affronts. Further, if the Divine Light was truly universal in this age – available to anyone regardless of gender, social class, religious hierarchy or spiritual persuasion – then the notion of social class or custom was meaningless. The Friends, then, did not need to conform to custom or class. Instead, it was more important in the context of this eschatological levelling of society to proclaim the messages they received directly from God.[18]

Of course, one of the results of this eschatological view of the world was that Quakers were frequently ridiculed and persecuted for their beliefs. But the Friends' confrontations with civil and religious authorities and their subsequent torture and imprisonment only fuelled their eschatological expectation, for what lay on the line for them was martyrdom.[19] And so, driven by their eschatological urgency, the Friends threw aside caution and class and made their way throughout England, Europe, beyond the Mediterranean Sea and even across the Atlantic Ocean in order to proclaim the message of the Divine Light's wide accessibility. As Fox wrote to his fellow Friends: 'walk cheerfully over the world, answering to that of God in every one; whereby in them ye may be a blessing and make the witness of God in them to bless you'.[20]

Mary Fisher and the possibility of prophethood for Muḥammad

It was this context to which Mary Fisher converted and that which she helped to shape when she became a Quaker in the early 1650s. Fisher was born sometime around 1623 in Yorkshire. At about the age of thirty she lived in Selby, just to the south of York, where she worked as a servant in the household of Richard and Elizabeth Tomlinson. All three of them became Quakers. In 1652, not long after Fisher's conversion, she was imprisoned in York Castle after having interrupted the sermon of a Selby priest and shouting, 'Come downe, come downe, thou painted beast, come downe. Thou art but an hireling, and deludes the people with thy lyes.'[21] Fisher pleaded guilty for her crime. A fine was imposed, which she likely could not pay, and so she was imprisoned.

Fisher met other Quakers while serving her sentence and composed along with them a small tract. The Friends gave it the title *False prophets and false teachers described*. The tract outlined for its readers the means by which they could discern a true prophet from a false one. English ministers typified the latter category and the Quaker authors equated them to the Scribes and Pharisees described in the Gospels:

> Do they not sit in the same Seats that the Scribes and Pharisees had? They had the chiefest place in Assemblies, have not your Priests so now? They had the uppermost rooms at Feasts, have not your Priests so now? They went in long Robes, do not your Priests so? They were called of men Masters, are not your Priests so now, do they not hold the same things that they did, and yet they are sent of Christ?[22]

Drawing upon St Paul's epistles, the imprisoned Quakers noted the qualities of true ministers of Christ. Such authentic prophets,

> gave no occasion of offence in any thing, that their Ministerie should not be blamed … . But in all things approved themselves as Ministers of God, in much patience, in afflictions, in necessities, in distresses, in stripes, in prisons, in tumults, in watchings, by fastings, by puritie, by knowledge, by long suffering,

by kindesse, by the Holy Ghost, by love unfeigned, by the word of truth, by the Power of God.[23]

After her imprisonment in York, Fisher continued to travel throughout England, confronting priests and facing imprisonment for her message. In 1655, she travelled across the Atlantic to the island of Barbados where she preached. By the summer of 1656 she arrived in Boston, Massachusetts, likely one of the first Quakers to visit New England.[24] Her arrival in Boston was at first refused. Her luggage was confiscated and her books were seized and burned. She was again imprisoned and subjected to an aggressive search for witch marks. After five weeks in prison she was sent back to Barbados. Her reception there was more positive, but she nevertheless returned to London in 1657. From there she wrote to Friends who remained in Barbados, 'Dear hearts go on in the power and might of our God, that you may conquer the whole earth, and rule over the inhabitants thereof, go on, look not back, press forwards.'[25]

Such an exhortation certainly reflected Fisher's Quaker eschatological sensibilities in which the Divine Light, poured out upon all, should go out over all the earth. But her exhortation also surely informed her own transatlantic journeys and, significantly, the trip she took with five other Friends to the Levant in July 1657. The original intent of the journey may have been to preach to Jews and Muslims in Jerusalem, but the group altered its plans in Leghorn, present-day Livorno in northwest Italy. In Leghorn, the Friends planned to redirect their efforts from Jerusalem to Rome. There, they would confront the Pope and eventually move on to the Ottoman Empire. Once in Constantinople they would also preach to Sultan Mehmed IV. But from Leghorn Fisher and the others travelled to an island off the western coast of Greece where they split up. Fisher made her way with three others to Turkey, arriving in Smyrna, present-day Izmir, in the later months of 1657. The original group of six eventually reunited in Turkey where they caused enough of a disturbance with their preaching and their intention to convert the Sultan, or at least to meet with him, that the English ambassador had them sent to Venice. With their original plans deterred, they aimed to preach to Jews in Venice.[26] Before they reached northeast Italy, however, the group split up once again with Fisher and another woman, Beatrice Beckley, heading for Adrianople. As it happened, the Sultan was encamped there with his army.

In Adrianople, according to one account, Fisher,

acquainted some of the citizens with her intent [to meet with the Sultan], and desired some of them to go with her; but, when none of them dared to go,

> fearing his displeasure, she passed alone, and coming near the camp, procured a man to inform at the tent of the Great Vizier, or chief general of the army, that there was an English woman who had something to declare from the Great God to the Great Turk, who soon sent her word that she should speak with him the next morning.[27]

The scene has, so far, all the patterns of an encounter that we might expect from Fisher and the Friends: she dismissed hierarchy and traditional etiquette by presenting herself to an authority that, according to the norms of the time, far outmatched her social standing. All this was done so that she could deliver a word given to her directly from the Lord.

The following day, Fisher returned to the Sultan's camp and waited. Eventually, Mehmed sent word for her and when she arrived he asked, 'Whether it was so as he had heard, that she had something to say to him from the Lord?'[28] She said that it was true and the Sultan, with three interpreters by his side, urged her to speak, a gesture we are not accustomed to when it comes to Fisher's meetings with authorities. Fisher stood before Mehmed in silence, 'waiting on the Lord as to when to speak', the account relates in typical Quaker fashion. Assuming she was afraid, the Sultan inquired whether she might want anyone to leave so she would feel more comfortable. When Fisher said no, he urged her to 'speak the Word of the Lord to them, and not to fear, for they had good hearts, and could hear it'.[29] One senses that the Sultan and his entourage were not necessarily bracing themselves for whatever religious onslaught that might be coming their way, but that they were customarily prepared to graciously tolerate whatever it was that Fisher felt so compelled to share. In fact, the Sultan and his entourage listened, according to the account, to what Fisher had to say and she asked Mehmed whether he had understood her. 'Yes, every word', came the reply. So there could be no doubt, from Fisher or from those reading the account of her meeting, that the Sultan's response came in light of his complete comprehension of what she had said, not a misunderstanding or a half-hearted interest.

We are not told the contents of Fisher's message. If she said anything similar to what she normally preached to others then it certainly did not meet with the same ferocious response and punishment. Instead, the Sultan responded and said that what Fisher had to offer ' "was the truth", and [he] desired her to stay in that country, saying "That they could not but respect such an one as should take so much pains to come to them, so far as from England, with a message from the Lord" '.[30] He then proposed to have a guard accompany her to Constantinople. Fisher declined and assured the Sultan that the Lord's protection would be sufficient. Nevertheless, Mehmed promised that she would not be hurt for as long as she remained in Ottoman territory, 'a worthy expression', the account tells us, 'of so great a prince'.[31]

Sultan Mehmed and his entourage were apparently eager to hear more from Fisher and so 'they asked her, "What she thought of their prophet, Mahomet?"' The question hints at what Fisher may have previously said to the Sultan in order to prompt an inquiry about Muḥammad. She must surely have had something to say about the divine revelation God intended for all people and their resulting obligation to proclaim God's word. What else might have prompted a question about a figure who, for the Sultan, was *the* Prophet? Thinking of Muḥammad, Fisher replied:

> 'That she knew him not; but the Christ, the True Prophet, the Son of God, who was the Light of the world, and enlighteneth every man that cometh into the world, Him she knew'; and further said, concerning Mahomet, 'That they might judge of him to be true or false, according as the words and prophecies he spoke were either true or false'; saying 'If the word that the prophet [Mahomet] speaketh come to pass, then shall ye know that the Lord hath sent that prophet; but, if come not to pass, then shall ye know that the Lord never sent him'; to which they confessed and said, 'It was truth'.[32]

Here, the scene departs dramatically from what we have come to expect from Fisher and Quaker religious encounters with others in the seventeenth century. Unlike many of Fisher's other confrontations – even some in Constantinople that resulted in the ire of the English ambassador – the meeting with the Sultan was remarkably amicable. She did not seem to have shouted the Sultan down from what she likely saw as his perch of usurped, artificial authority. The result of the meeting was also extraordinary. After other encounters, Fisher was publicly ridiculed, tortured and imprisoned. The Sultan and his entourage, on the contrary, received Fisher peacefully, listened to her message in its entirety, found her responses to their questions satisfactory and, though they may have been unmoved by her message, sent her on her way with the promise of safety.

I will return a bit further on to the marked differences in how Fisher was treated by the Sultan and the manner in which Quakers were traditionally handled. But first, is it reasonable to imagine that when it came to Muḥammad Fisher really 'knew him not'? What about the availability of information concerning Islam in English during the period, the time she had already spent in the Ottoman Empire before her meeting with the Sultan or even Fox's interaction with Muslims and the topic of Islam of which she might have been familiar?[33] Perhaps she was masking her knowledge for the sake of congenial diplomacy. But this seems unlikely given what we know of unwavering Quaker boldness in the face of authority. It would not be impossible to have some awareness of Muslims and Islam but still lack sufficiently detailed knowledge of Muḥammad. And yet one of the most basic and oft-repeated Muslim claims was that Muḥammad's central identity came to life as God's Final Messenger. Was Fisher really unacquainted with these details?

In fact, Fisher's response conforms in its entirety to the Quaker context as I have outlined it above. This is more apparent in the latter portion of her reply. It was possible, in Fisher's assessment, that Muḥammad was a prophet. One needed only to examine what he said and consider whether or not it had come to pass. If it had, then he was from God; if not, then he was not from God. Of course, Mary had spent a great deal of time considering the marks of a true prophet. She had helped to write the tract *False prophets and false teachers described* and, like most Quakers, she had ample opportunity to defend her own claims to being a messenger of God when she stood before examiners and judges preparing to imprison her for her audacious preaching. John Perrot, a fellow Quaker and one of Fisher's companions on the journey to Turkey (though he was in Venice by the time Fisher met with the Sultan) addressed the matter of prophetic criteria in his *A visitation of love and a gentle greeting of the Turk*. He wrote the tract in 1657 from Venice while awaiting entry into the Ottoman Empire, so Fisher was surely aware of it, perhaps even contributing her thoughts to it as well.[34] Therein, Perrot employed many of the stock biblical texts Quakers used to defend their prophetic claims and to discriminate among true and false prophets within the Society of Friends.[35] Among the texts, Perrot quoted Deut. 18.18-19 in which the promise of a prophet is foretold and he singled out Jesus, though he only named him as 'the Prophet', as the one to come. The Quaker understanding was that later prophets would come in the same spirit as those discussed in Deuteronomy who would minister in the light of the Prophet, Jesus. He also asserted, in a nearly veiled reference to Deut. 18.18-19, that a true prophet can be distinguished from a false one by the outcome of his or her prophecies.[36]

Fisher's response to Sultan Mehmed essentially matched what Perrot outlined in *A visitation of love*. She, too, referred to Deut. 18 and paraphrased verses 21-22 in which a true prophet is distinguished by his or her prophecies actually coming to pass. Curiously, 18.20, in which a prophet who proclaims something not from God or speaks in the name of other gods is condemned, was seemingly glossed. This would seem to have been a pertinent consideration for Fisher, but it went unmentioned. What she did note was that Christ was the 'True Prophet, the Son of God, who was the Light of the World',[37] a phrase very reminiscent of Perrot in *A visitation of love*,[38] but in the end, the possibility that there might be other prophets seems relatively unguarded for Fisher. The basis for such a conclusion came down to Fisher's Quaker views in which the Spirit of God had been poured out on everyone, including Muḥammad. The possibility for prophethood was as much available to him as it was to Fisher or to anyone else.

The same Quaker frame applies to Fisher's claim to not know Muḥammad. She may or may not have heard about him; she may or may not have been aware of the Muslim claim that he was a prophet. What mattered most were the things Muḥammad said and did as a prophet. If those stood up to the Quaker test, then that is what mattered most. And these were the things of which Fisher was apparently unaware. The only clarification was that Christ, the Light of the world and the True Prophet, to use Fisher's words, informed one's prophethood. Taken on face value, this might not be unacceptable to Muslim ears, though her acknowledgement that Christ was the Son of God would be problematic. But this apparently did not bother the Sultan and his entourage, perhaps because they expected it from what they may have known about Christian beliefs. In the end, Fisher's curious remarks about Muḥammad were enough for them to affirm that what she said was true.[39]

In all of this, there is a sense in which the Quakers' harshest criticism was reserved for their co-religionists, fellow Christians who had lost the way of the true Church. In a time of heightened eschatological awareness, however, there was perhaps room to reconsider the place of non-Christians.[40] Perhaps it was in this light that Fisher felt there was a possibility that Muḥammad was a prophet. She simply needed to consider him in more detail, but for the time being, in the presence of Sultan Mehmed, it just might be the case that Muḥammad was who Muslims said he was.

Mary Fisher, the Sultan and Muḥammad against colonial persecutors

As Fisher made her way from Adrianople back to England and eventually to Charleston in present-day South Carolina where she died in 1698, so the story of her meeting with the Sultan made its way around the world.[41] More than just a famous story of an unlikely encounter, however, Fisher's meeting with the Sultan became noteworthy for its contrast with the ways in which Quakers were normally viewed and treated. Intriguingly, this difference was noted and later Quaker authors were able to use Fisher's encounter with the Sultan and the contents of their discussion as a goad against their persecutors, hoping to alter the treatment of Quakers as a religious minority in Colonial America.

This use of Fisher's story is especially apparent in the account provided by George Bishop (d. 1668) in his *New England Judged*. Bishop's text is a veritable *testimonia* of evidence, showing how Quakers had been treated around the world and in New England. In fact, it was written in response to the execution of four Quakers in Boston. By 1661, when Bishop's text was originally published, the profession of Quakerism had been deemed a capital offence in New England. Famously, the Quaker Mary Dyer, who was repeatedly sent away from Boston by authorities, was hanged in 1660 for her beliefs and for disregarding the laws that restricted her presence in the area.[42] Thus, Fisher's experience with Sultan Mehmed in Adrianople stood in stark contrast to what Quakers might experience with officials in Boston. In Adrianople, Fisher was warmly received. She was treated well. She was given space to say what she thought was necessary.

The story also upended the many traditional conceptions of Muslims as stereotypically violent and lascivious. On the contrary, the Sultan and his companions were generous and kind. They welcomed her in their midst and helped her to feel safe, quite the opposite of the invasive search to which she was subjected in Boston. They listened to Fisher – a single woman travelling with only one other woman and in the presence of the Sultan by herself – and made sure she had communicated everything that she felt she had to say. They told her that they were satisfied with her replies to their questions. They recognized the Word of the Lord was with her, unlike some of her Christian examiners who, in one instance, had mockingly probed her and asked, 'how many Gods there were?'[43] Both their demeanour and their treatment of Fisher were markedly different than the descriptions used to relate other Quaker experiences with authorities in all different parts of the world. In this way, the entire event is employed as a foil for the ways in which Quakers were received generally and for their treatment in Colonial New England in particular. In New England Quakers were persecuted and the Puritans who rejected them were brutal and dishonourable, quite the opposite in the Ottoman Empire under the noble Sultan Mehmed IV.

Can the same be said of Fisher's assessment of Muḥammad? Was it, too, used by later Quakers as a kind of foil? It is possible to tell Fisher's story of her meeting with the Sultan and recount the details of her treatment without referencing the Sultan's follow-up question to Fisher about Muḥammad or her corresponding reply. This part of Fisher's story seems relatively tangential to the task of employing the Sultan's tolerance as a foil to New England persecution. Even so, all of the main accounts of Fisher's encounter include reference to the Sultan's question and her answer. Could it be that Fisher's assessment also said something about her as a Quaker that might nudge authorities to refashion their policies concerning the legal status and treatment of those like Fisher? In fact, Fisher appeared calm in her reply to the Sultan. Her response seems measured. It drew upon the Bible as a means for evaluating prophets and prophetic claims and she framed the nature of prophecy with Christ as the 'True Prophet', acknowledging him as the 'Son of God'.[44] Perhaps, readers might think, Fisher was not all that different from them after all. And, if such an amicable encounter and peaceful exchange over a delicate topic was possible with the so-called Great Turk and his entourage, then surely Christians could do the same, perhaps even better, in their own realms when discussing matters about which they ought to have more room to agree. Thus, the question of Muḥammad, much like the encounter itself, became a point from which to draw a comparison. Though it could have been the cause for Fisher's downfall, it became a sign of religious tolerance. In turn, Fisher, the Sultan and Muḥammad are used to push back against harsh religious policies.[45]

10

Muḥammad as a redundant Gabriel and missionary conscript

Samuel Ajayi Crowther and West African mission to Muslims

Having traversed the eastern Mediterranean and crossed the Atlantic Ocean to Colonial New England, we now return eastward but this time to the continent of Africa. The story of Islam in sub-Saharan Africa, well south of better-known centres like Egypt and the Maghreb, is often given less attention in the literature concerning Islam and the Prophet Muḥammad. One story, of course, is well known: the first *hijrah*, or seventh-century migration to Axum in present-day Ethiopia. When the early Muslim community faced persecution in Mecca, Muḥammad advised them to go to Axum for protection.[1] Islamic sources even record an encounter in 615 between an envoy from Mecca and the Christian king who ruled the area where the Muslim migrants lived. The king reportedly wept when he heard one from the envoy recite a passage from *Sūrah Maryam* (Q 19) that sounded to him so very much like the Gospel.[2]

But beyond the encounter of this early Muslim community and the Christians of Axum, the development of Muslim communities in sub-Saharan Africa is paid relatively less attention. Subsequent to the conversion of Berber communities, Islam spread from northern and eastern Africa alongside trade and Muslim missionary networks. Muslims were present in West Africa as early as the eighth century. By the thirteenth century and into the sixteenth century great empires like the Mali Empire, the Kingdom of Kanem and the Mande Songhay Empire emerged. While these states were multi-ethnic and multireligious, and while Muslim rulers often incorporated indigenous religious practices, Islam was considered the state religion. Reform and colonial movements in the nineteenth century pushed a wider awareness of Islam throughout West Africa, and slave trade, long present on the continent, meant that people, Muslim and non-Muslim alike, were displaced throughout the region as well as across the Atlantic Ocean. Sufi orders also worked to spread Islam throughout the region.[3]

The great movement of Islam on the continent of Africa and the introduction and spread of Christianity southward, away from its historic centres in the north, did relatively little to engender notable interaction between Christian and Muslim communities. By the nineteenth century, however, West Africa in particular exhibited a period of noteworthy engagement, in large part due to the work of one individual: a Yoruba convert to Christianity and former slave, Samuel Ajayi[4] Crowther (d. 1891).[5]

Samuel Ajayi Crowther and the making of a missionary bishop and linguist

Crowther, according to Andrew Walls, was 'probably the most widely known African Christian of the nineteenth century'.[6] Ajayi, Crowther's Yoruba birth name, was born around the year 1807 in the town of Ośogun in Yorubaland, present-day western Nigeria.[7] Crowther's youth marked a period of transition and violence in the Yoruba states as the Muslim Fulani empire expanded. Yoruba communities were often victims of raids and were, in turn, subjected to slave trade. The slave trade was, by this time, illegal, but was nevertheless maintained by those who continued to seek a profit from it.

In Crowther's early teenage years, Fulani and other Muslim groups raided his town of Ośogun. They surrounded the town with relatively little resistance from the otherwise surprised inhabitants. Despite attempts to flee, many were captured and Crowther was taken along with his mother, two sisters and a cousin.[8] Many other family members were taken and separated.[9] After a day of marching with a rope wrapped around his neck, Crowther was separated from his family and traded for a horse. Over the following months, Crowther was sold to others and moved to various locations until he was finally purchased by Portuguese slave traders.[10] In order to avoid this finality, Crowther made several suicide attempts, but was never able to complete the task.[11]

Crowther's Portuguese owners tried to leave the West African coast on several occasions, but the British, who opposed the slave trade, were patrolling the coast. On 7 April 1822, a British naval squadron intercepted and commandeered Crowther's vessel. All 187 slaves were brought up from the vessel's hold, distributed among the British and given clothing. The Portuguese crew was arrested and bound, except for the cook who prepared the now-former slaves' breakfast.[12] When Crowther encountered his former Portuguese owner on a ship, he 'had the boldness to strike him on the head, while he was shaving by his son'.[13] After cruising for nearly two months, enduring storms and the loss of several ships, crew and former slaves, Crowther landed at Sierra Leone on 17 June 1822.[14]

Sierra Leone, on the western coast of Africa, was a colony founded by those with anti-slavery interests, many of whom were evangelical Anglican Christians connected to the Clapham Sect, a group that included William Wilberforce and concerned itself with social reform and the abolition of slavery. Members of their group established Sierra Leone in 1787 as a settlement for freed slaves. As a result, the colony became a centre for 'thousands of … uprooted, disoriented people from inland Africa'.[15] Some of its inhabitants, like Crowther, had never actually left the continent, but many returned as free people from places across the Atlantic Ocean where they had been sent to live and work as slaves.[16] Sierra Leone became the 'Province of Freedom' and its emphasis on freed slaves was linked inseparably to Christian mission both on the coast and further inland.[17]

In Sierra Leone, Crowther came under the care of the Church Missionary Society (CMS). He learned to read the New Testament and was baptized on 11 December 1825, at which point he took the name Samuel Crowther after a member of the CMS.[18] Crowther received an English education in Sierra Leone and later became one of the first students at the new Fourah Bay College. He eventually entered the service of the CMS as a schoolmaster, missionary to inland West Africa and was sent to England for further study and ordination. He was eventually consecrated Anglican bishop of 'the countries of Western Africa beyond the limits of the Queen's dominions'.[19]

One of the unique features of Crowther's ministry was his aptitude for and use of languages. Not only did he speak Yoruba and English, but he was also convinced that the use of indigenous languages, as opposed to emphasizing English, was key to engaging non-Christians on his missionary expeditions. Many of his encounters include his use of multiple languages in his effort to communicate and he worked tirelessly to learn new languages and to produce written versions of languages he already knew, like Yoruba. Crowther's linguistic work was used not only in his missionary engagement with others but also in his effort to help produce Bible translations.[20]

Crowther's view of the importance of language was especially apparent when it came to his engagement with Muslims. 'I believe in this part of Africa,' Crowther wrote in a journal entry during an expedition on the Niger River, 'where the knowledge of Arabic is so imperfectly known, the use of the Arabic character, combined with teaching in Roman or Italic characters in the native tongues, would be the means of counterbalancing the rapid spread of Mohammedanism among the rising generation'.[21] He continued with a lament, warning that, despite the warmth and hospitality of the Muslims they encountered,

> as long as the use of the Arabic character is excluded from our schools, and left to the use of the ignorant followers of Mohammed alone, [Muslims] will take advantage of this to continue their deception upon the ignorant heathen by holding these letters as more holy than any others in the world; but by these letters being brought into common use, their artful cheat would be laid open.[22]

Crowther's observations about Islam, Arabic and Muslims in West Africa are revealing for several reasons. On a practical level, they reflect the sanctity Muslims ascribe to the Arabic language. At times, especially in Crowther's context where Arabic was not always known or well known among Muslims, this meant that prayers were memorized and, as I look at more extensively below, many Muslims with whom Crowther interacted were impressed with the holy books he had in their indigenous languages. On another level, it would seem that Crowther missed a theological distinctive between Islam and Christianity, whereby the former places value on the fixed sanctity of God's holy language and the latter subscribes to a translatable sanctity in which the sacred can be made to speak different languages. For Crowther, the appearance of Arabic marked the spread of Islam and a ruse that Muslims used to hold non-Arabic speakers in the grip of a religion with which they were not sufficiently familiar. If he could harness the use of Arabic, not restricting it to Muslim usage, then he might be able to use it to his advantage. More positively, Crowther also knew that by appealing to 'Islam's admirable bookishness' – a phrase Stephen Ney uses to describe Islam's emphasis upon the sanctity of a revealed word, or book, and the resulting emphasis that literature had in the West African Islamic milieu – he could assert the primacy of his own sacred text, the Bible.[23] And so, time and time again in his journals and published texts, Crowther appeals to the Bible and never strays from it in his engagement with Muslims.

With respect to Muḥammad, one catches a glimpse in the spaces between Crowther's view of Islam and Arabic of a prophet who might be parochial and linguistically restricted to his own people. Crowther's effort to unlink Arabic from Islam and make it useful for conversion to Christianity makes one wonder about how he saw language impinging upon Muḥammad's role as a prophet and messenger. Did he consider him hampered by linguistic restrictions and, in this way, somehow inferior in his claims to prophethood?

Crowther and a West African approach to Islam and its Prophet

Crowther did not answer this question directly, nor did he address the notion of Muḥammad's alleged particularity as other Christian authors did. Nevertheless, Crowther's views of Muḥammad can be seen in both his more systematic treatment of Islam as well as in the offhand remarks he recorded in his journals. It is difficult to say which of these sources provides a more accurate view of what Crowther thought, though it must be said that the comments found in his journals are much more severe and reflect views not at all uncommon among Christian communities throughout history.[24] They suggest that when it came to articulating views on Islam and Muḥammad there could be a tendency to resort to fixed language as opposed to fresh perspective. For example, in a journal entry from January 1853, Crowther related the story of a girl 'who was born to a Mohamedan when the mother was in slavery'. It was intended that the girl be 'brought up in the religion of Mahomed', but the mother, whom Crowther described as a 'heathen', the term he reserved for adherents of traditional religions, refused. As a result, the girl was sent to a Christian school where both she and her mother converted to Christianity. Crowther marked this shift with gratitude and described the serendipity of the girl's conversion from Islam as the moment 'when the Lord is pleased to administer the antidote of his saving health to the soul poisoning doctrine of this great imposter of mankind', a reference clearly meant to describe Islam and Muḥammad.[25]

In another example, this one from 1855, Crowther described his experience of being near a market where those observing his group looked on with curiosity as they spoke English. Crowther took advantage of the moment and called the onlookers together and told them that Jesus, the one whom he preached as saviour and judge of the world, would call all the multitudes, just like the crowd gathered near the market, to account for their works. 'A priest of Shango came forth,' Crowther wrote, 'in defence of his god as being the most powerful among the gods.' After some shouting and debate, Crowther repeated his claims about the authority of Christ. 'I only preached Christ and made no personal attack', Crowther recorded.[26] At that point,

> A Mohammedan priest also stepped forward in defence of his religion, as it was of no manner of use to argue with either me or the others in the marketplace, I repeated my short sermon, that Christ whom we preach … before whom both Mohammed and all his followers also shall fall and render account to him, that

> every one may receive according to his works. At this the Mohammedans were indignant and went away in contempt, shouting the praises and power of their false prophet.[27]

In these examples, Muḥammad appears as an imposter, a recalcitrant peddler of a poisonous doctrine and as, quite simply, a false prophet. None of these descriptions represent anything new in the history of Christian views of Muḥammad. Crowther does not relate whether he inherited such views from other Christians, though he could have done in either Britain or among CMS missionaries in West Africa, or if they represent his own logic. In any case, we glean very little from them beyond the reminder that these perspectives connect Crowther the missionary with his intention to assert the uniqueness of Christ in a context where Islam and traditional religions predominated.[28] In this sense, the comments are unlikely to denote Crowther's considered appraisal of Muḥammad and his prophethood.

Far more intriguing, especially in light of the paucity of remarks about Muḥammad in Crowther's journal entries, is the more focused commentary that comes from Crowther's published work that focuses on Islam and his engagement with Muslims. The remarks found here, while some of them reflect customary views, are situated within a framework of fresh perspective. This is most apparent in Crowther's booklet *Experiences with Heathens and Mohammedans in West Africa*, published posthumously in 1892.[29] Completing this work was something Crowther resisted, especially since some of the experiences already appear in published journals. But he persisted and eventually wrote the material for the booklet so that it might be offered as a guide for West African teachers, particularly those dealing with older Muslims and traditional religionists who were already predisposed against Christianity and despised young Christians.[30] When it came to Muslims, Crowther pinpointed this anti-Christian predisposition as a certainty that Christ was not the Son of God as Christians claimed, a view derived directly from the Qur'ān. This made Muslims, in Crowther's estimation, not only especially resistant to Christians but also adherents of a 'poisonous doctrine'; dependent upon their own merits for salvation, Muslims were essentially impervious to Christianity, the only 'true religion'.[31] And so Crowther set out to offer a guide for successfully engaging Muslims that was derived from his experiences. The result is a tract-like booklet of related stories, wisdom and missionary strategy.

Crowther began relating some of his failures, which he used in order to generate what he thought, and what he experienced as, a more successful approach to engaging Muslims. These experiences also shaped his response to the prophethood of Muḥammad. One story concerned his experience as a schoolmaster. A Muslim student was sent to school 'with a charm sewn in a piece of leather tied to his neck as a protective'. Crowther cut the charm off from the boy's neck and sent him home with it along with instructions to relate to his father that such superstition was not welcome 'in any Christian school'.[32] This naturally upset the boy's father who found Crowther at his home and demanded an explanation for 'meddling with his religious belief'. Crowther's response was to forestall a discussion for a time in which the father was more composed, and so a meeting was arranged between Crowther and 'the elders of [the father's] profession'.[33]

The following evening Crowther met with the elders and discussed Islam and Christianity in an anger-free environment. 'I tried to convince my opponents by arguments from the Bible, and from the translations of [George] Sale's Koran', Crowther wrote.[34] In particular, he argued that the Bible was internally consistent and did not contradict itself, a point that 'Mohammed could not have denied … if he had carefully studied, and compared one passage to another'.[35] But Crowther's Muslim listeners were impenetrable and they were steadfast in their affirmation of the Qur'ān's denial that God could have a son. 'We had to separate,' Crowther admitted, 'when they said no human being was able to settle the matter in this world till the day of *Alkiama* (*al-qiyāmah*), judgment'.[36] This encounter affected Crowther who suspected that 'a more friendly and persuasive' approach might be more fruitful.[37]

His suspicions were confirmed when he observed the actions of a Wesleyan missionary who preached the Gospel to Muslims every Sunday in Freetown, Sierra Leone. Each Sunday the missionary and members from his church would go to a Muslim village and enter the mosque. They would hold a Christian service and the missionary would preach a sermon, focusing on 'the errors of Mohammedanism'. Thinking of one such Sunday in particular, Crowther recalled that the Muslims listened to the sermon and remained quiet until the Christian group returned to their homes. The following Sunday, the Christians returned and found that the 'Mohammedans, who would not be converted to Christianity by storm, had secured the sacred precincts of their mosque by a strong fence, to exclude the zealous missionary and his followers from further profanation of their holy ground'. The missionary and his group eventually gave up attempting to preach at the Muslim village and considered the endeavour a failure.[38]

Crowther concluded that the approach to Muslims to which he was accustomed and the ways in which Christians known to him framed their response to Islam were insufficient. Clearly, part of this insufficiency reflected a weakness in the mechanism for Christian mission – a focused Gospel presentation or, at times, heated apologetic was not successful – but for Crowther, it also had something to do with the West African Muslim disposition. 'One cannot reason effectually with these uneducated people,' he concluded, 'because Mohammedanism, according to their belief, is superior to all other existing religions.'[39] In this way, Crowther faced not only what he perceived to be the shortcomings of previous Christian approaches to Muslims but also the Muslim intransigent commitment to their faith, in particular that God could not have a son and that, in turn, their religion was superior. This particular belief Crowther considered a 'fatal weapon' by which Muslims came 'to regard Christianity with abhorrence as blasphemy'.[40] Christians were powerless against this Islamic belief, even though, in Crowther's estimation, it was 'contrary to the doctrine of the Koran, which teaches, "There is no God but God, and Mohammed is his prophet" '.[41] Crowther felt that in the *shahādah* there was an implicit recognition of Christ's divinity – if there is only one God and Christ can be shown to be his Son via Scripture, then he must be the one God – but Christians without training in how to use the Bible were left powerless before Muslims.

In Crowther's experiences with Muslims and traditional religionists, he also faced a challenge of theological mediation. For him, Christ alone was a mediator between God and humankind and his divine sonship, the basis of his mediatory role, was uncreated, not granted to him by an external source. Many others around him, however, saw things differently. For many traditional religionists, material objects could work to protect against evil. Both Christian and Muslim communities drew upon this tradition of superstition and incorporated it into their own piety. So Crowther's Muslim student, as we have seen, wore a charm, possibly with a passage from the Qur'ān embedded inside, around his neck. Christians, too, had similar practices but Crowther honed in on the 'Roman Catholics … with their erroneous doctrine of Mariolatry'.[42] This was problematic for Crowther, not only because such an elevation of Mary, in his mind, suggested that Muslims were correct in their accusation that Christians worshiped multiple gods[43] but because it seemed to function as a substitute for Christ.

With this in mind, Crowther was convinced that a new missionary approach was required that would more adequately respond to the challenges of previous missionary shortcomings and the dogged nature of Muslim belief. Crowther summarized his new approach as 'employ[ing] the Scriptural examples for their information and instruction, without *rudely* and *contemptuously* attacking their superstitious objects of worship or their erroneous creed'.[44] In other words,

Crowther would make sole use of the Bible to make his claims and he would rely completely upon the Holy Spirit, not apologetic debate, to convince Muslims of his claims. Intriguingly, the distinctive element of this strategy, especially for our concerns, was Crowther's foregrounding of the Bible's descriptions of the angel Gabriel when it came to discussions of scriptural revelation and the prophethood of Muḥammad.

Crowther provided personal illustrations in his booklet that showed what this new strategy looked like in practice. Two of them are especially relevant for what they reveal about his assessment of Muḥammad. Before relating the first personal experience, Crowther noted that the Qur'ān made Muslims a special challenge, especially when compared to tradition religionists. It was, he observed, 'the last revelation from God through the ministry of the Angel Gabriel to Mohammed his messenger'. For this reason, Crowther reasoned, 'the Mohammedans … can only be argued with upon the ground of what the Koran admits … . Islamism admits the miraculous conception of Christ, and that he was a great prophet; also that the Angel Gabriel was God's faithful messenger to this world from time to time'. He concluded, 'well, we must build upon this foundation'.[45]

With this caveat in mind, Crowther related his encounter in 1872 with a Muslim king in Ilorin, western Nigeria. The king invited Crowther to meet with him and to answer a series of questions, before which Crowther 'got them to acknowledge that they believed in the Koran of the Angel Gabriel (Yibirila), who was always the faithful messenger of God to this world, and was sent to the prophet Mohammed with portions of the Koran from time to time; all this they readily admitted'.[46] Armed with this recognition – and here Crowther slipped into the kind of extra-biblical apologetic technique from which he seemed to want to distance himself – Crowther asked the king and his entourage, which included a chief imam, or Lemamu,[47] 'whether Gabriel was capable of making a mistake, and whether having delivered one message in the morning, and another in the evening he could deny his having done so in the morning?'[48] The king replied, 'It was impossible for him to do so.'[49] On this basis, Crowther opened up a discussion of Islamic and Christian doctrines, 'commencing with the miraculous conception of Christ, and in consequence his Sonship of God, declared by the Angel Gabriel, more than six hundred years before Mohammed commenced his mission'.[50] The implication was that Gabriel had been sent with a message from God long before Muḥammad claimed to have received one from him; since Gabriel would not contradict himself, it would be prudent to inquire about his earlier message in order to see what he said. This was found in the Bible.

Having made this assertion, Crowther opened his bag and took out several books: an English Bible with Yoruba translations, an English prayer book (presumably the *Book of Common Prayer*) with Yoruba translations, a pocket English dictionary and a book of Yoruba vocabulary. Using these, Crowther read several passages from the Bible, first in English and then in Yoruba. The first several passages concerned the sonship of Christ, all of which 'had been so before the era of Mohammed'.[51] This prompted the Muslim king to ask 'whether Anabi Isa (Jesus the Prophet) was not to be the Judge of the world?'[52] Crowther's response was that his answer would come directly from the Bible. And so he read several more passages, first in English and then in Yoruba. These readings prompted other questions and more passages from the Bible in response until a contemplative silence fell upon the group. After a while 'some one near the king suggested the question: what does your (Litafi) Bible say of Mohammed?'[53] Crowther's response to this came without derision but was nevertheless dismissive, almost as if he offered it with a shrug: 'I replied that, as it was not till six hundred and twenty-two years after Christ that Mohammed established his doctrine, our Bible is quite silent about his name.'[54]

Crowther's listeners then inquired 'which was the fuller, our (Litafi) Bible, or the Koran?'[55] Crowther responded, telling them 'our Bible is very full' and then he detailed its contents, even showing them the various sections in the English Bible he had on hand and telling them that the Qur'ān drew upon these various sections. He went on, saying that Muslims in places like Constantinople, Egypt and Smyrna examined the Bible and desired to know it. Christian missionaries were also in these places, and in many more locations, in response to Christ's command to 'Go ye therefore, and teach all nations'.[56] The implication seems very much to be that Christ, his message and his followers were universal in nature and that even Muslims found further afield were interested in their message.

With this in mind, it is difficult not to make a comparison to accusations in which Islam and Muḥammad appear as parochial and geographically restricted, especially since Crowther has already set Christianity out has having historical primacy, which reduced Islam to an erroneous afterthought. So it was with Muḥammad. When asked directly about the Prophet, Crowther had very little to say, not because he had not given him any thought but because Muḥammad did not figure, either chronologically or theologically, in his missionary approach. In other words, the Bible did not have anything to say about Muḥammad and so Crowther did not have anything to say about him either. In Crowther's experience, as far as can be known from his own reflections on the matter, Muslims offered no rejoinder to the notion of Muḥammad's scriptural absence.[57] In all of this,

Muḥammad seems rather unworthy of much consideration. Crowther's was very much an argument from silence that nevertheless spoke rather loudly about the status of Muḥammad.

A redundant Gabriel and missionary conscript

Aside from the Bible, which Crowther used as his main source – much of his *Experiences with Heathens and Mohammedans in West Africa* is essentially *testimonia* of verses supporting Christ's divine sonship[58] – the centrepiece of Crowther's approach to Islam and response to Muḥammad was the angel Gabriel. As 'Protestant Christianity on the West Coast of Africa' was poised to engage Muslims in the region, Crowther proclaimed, 'This is the time to bring in the Angel Gabriel, who stands in the presence of God, as a faithful messenger from God to the Virgin Mary.'[59] In Crowther's context, where traditional religions and Islam had long been predominant, it was paramount to assert one messenger over and against others. As one man commented at one of Crowther's services, 'Truly Jesus Christ came first, and Mahomet last, but wherever one goes throughout this country, whether to a large town or to a small village, one finds more or less Mahommedans in each of them … the messengers whom Jesus Christ sent at first were too slow so the messengers of Mahomet have taken the country'.[60] These remarks certainly help to frame Crowther's view of Islam as a 'soul poisoning doctrine' and Muḥammad as a 'great imposter', but they also shed light on Crowther's determined insistence that the angel Gabriel was the key to sorting out the true religion and that revelation's true messenger. In Crowther's estimation it was the angel Gabriel who was sent first. His message, when understood correctly, positioned Jesus as the divine Son of God. What Gabriel was said to have brought Muḥammad could be little more than misconstruals. And so we encounter Muḥammad in Crowther's accounts as a distraction to a focused missionary endeavour in which the Prophet did in a much poorer way what the angel Gabriel had already done well. In this way, Muḥammad was merely redundant to Gabriel, and rather poorly so.

Curiously, there was yet one achievement that could be granted to Muḥammad in West Africa. Crowther noted that 'Mohammedanism … is superior to the religion of the heathens'. For this reason, traditional religionists converted to Islam.[61] In one sense, then, Islam represented a source of competition for souls, but in another sense, the successful spread of Islam in West Africa also represented a progression of religious thought due not only, as I have pointed out, to the emphasis it put upon the centrality of a book but also to its monotheism.[62] As Crowther admitted, Muslims 'abolished the worship of idols and offering of human sacrifices'.[63] In turn, Islam could be conceived as a means for preparing a way in West Africa for Christianity, which was considered by proponents of such a view as 'the pinnacle of human development and religious truth'.[64] For Crowther, this meant correcting and honing local traditions, not abolishing them, so that they conformed and submitted to Christian truth, the flowering and perfection of religious truth.[65]

Crowther's view was made even more explicit in a tract written by one of his sons. In it, the younger Crowther illustrated the variations of religions in Yorubaland in a way that suggested an evolutionary progression of religious thought and development. In the first image appeared 'the heathen bowing down to his god of thunder and lightning called Shango', a rather primitive depiction. The second sketch portrayed 'the Mahomedan sitting in the street praying and counting his beads in the midst of numerous spectators'; this was more refined, but the Muslim still reflected the self-centredness of his religion. The third and final illustration showed 'the Christian praying to God in penitence and humility'; here we see the refinement of religion.[66] This was essentially a transplantation of a very old idea in which, as we have seen, Muḥammad preached against idolatry, drew his listeners towards monotheism and unknowingly prepared them to hear about the divine Christ. In the West African context, then, Muḥammad, even if he was sidelined and redundant, could be conscripted into service for Christian missionaries, supporting those like Samuel Ajayi Crowther in their efforts to preach Christianity.

11

Muḥammad as a signpost for fellow pilgrims

Lamin Sanneh and Christian appreciation for the Prophet's biography

Well to the west of Nigeria, where Samuel Ajayi Crowther was born, and north of Sierra Leone where Crowther was baptized a Christian, lay the small, sliver-shaped country of The Gambia. There, in 1942, on a small island in the River Gambie, Lamin Sanneh was born to a Muslim family with a royal lineage. Sanneh eventually became a convert to Christianity, first as a Methodist and then a Roman Catholic. A scholar of both Islam and Christianity, especially in West Africa, he went on to become one of the world's most renowned experts in the field of World Christianity. He held academic posts in West Africa, the UK and the United States and, on the occasion of his untimely death on 6 January 2019, he was a professor at Yale Divinity School.

Religion was a part of nearly every aspect of Sanneh's life and certainly took centre stage in his infancy.[1] On the eighth day after his birth, a kettle drum, usually used to call worshippers to prayer on Fridays, was beaten in order to announce a ceremony for infants and mothers. In the presence of the local imām, Sanneh's head was shaved and water was poured over it. Facing east, all those present recited the *Fātiḥah*, the first chapter of the Qur'ān, after which the imām recited the *shahādah*. Then the imām spit into each of Sanneh's ears, pronounced a blessing on him and announced the name given to him by his parents: 'Ma-Lamin'. Sanneh's name was a variant of Muḥammad al-Amīn, one of the names given to the Prophet Muḥammad in recognition for his trustworthy and upright character, but it was simply 'Lamin' that stuck.[2]

With Sanneh's name announced to the gathered community, the imām raised him in the air and offered a prayer for his safety. A feast followed the name-giving ceremony, with men and women dressing in their finest clothes. Reflecting on the entire event, Sanneh commented,

> The birth of this Muḥammad as another Ma-Lamin was occasion for communal jollification as much as for honouring anew God's exalted Envoy whose own birth brought glad tidings to the world. In that way, the Prophet's *barakah*, his grace and virtue, was celebrated on the numerous occasions when firstborn sons received his name in public collective ceremonies. Thus Muḥammad became the established rule of social conduct, the rule that made first claim on the pride of the tribe. The Prophet's grand historical mission of bringing God's message to humanity was thus affirmed on the numerous occasions when families and communities dedicated to him male children to obtain his *barakah* and to express their gratitude.[3]

In this way, religion permeated most aspects of Sanneh's life in general, but his birth and identity were intrinsically connected to the Prophet Muḥammad in particular, a link that extended to Sanneh's family and community. Since the Prophet earned the title al-Amīn, the trusted one, those who came after him could draw upon his *barakah*, his virtue, as a defining characteristic of their lives. The Prophet, then, was an archetype whose virtue was re-embodied in Ma-Lamin Sanneh of The Gambia who, in turn, would be a blessing for his community.

With religion imbuing his life, religious questions naturally surrounded Sanneh as well. He eventually took up religious studies as an academic pursuit, but his religious identity became a more primary dilemma. Sanneh was irretrievably drawn to Christian claims and wrestled early on with the notion of Christ's crucifixion. Ingrained in his Muslim psyche was an adamant denial of Christian beliefs about Christ's death on a cross. But a Christian friend of Sanneh's circumvented the challenges presented by the crucifixion and asked questions about Christ's resurrection. These questions and the notion of resurrection deeply provoked Sanneh. Grappling with the possibility of Jesus's resurrection and the implications that lay ahead of it, Sanneh eventually relented and, as he put it, surrendered to God in the same way that Jesus did.[4] This decision did not mean that Sanneh was subsequently welcomed with open arms into the Christian community. Protestants and Catholics who knew him were pleased with the new way in which Sanneh had devoted his life to Jesus but were seemingly ambivalent about receiving him into the Church. In the end, Sanneh's entry came by way of the Methodists but he was later received as a Roman Catholic.[5]

The trajectory of Sanneh's life – beginning as Ma-Lamin and continuing as a religious inquirer and Christian scholar – gave his work a particular concern when it came to Christians and World Christianity, on the one hand,

and the intersection these had with Muslims and Islam on the other. There is a sense in which his scholarship, much like his life, was dialogical. His attention to Islam, more than just a nod to his childhood, carried with it a concern for the ways in which Christians saw Muslims and their faith. But more than mere dialogue, which he saw as a 'word game … tantamount to nothing more than a monologue', Sanneh sought to cultivate the company of Muslims as fellow pilgrims.[6] Seeing one another as companions who walked a path together was, to Sanneh, authentic, meaningful dialogue. In turn, his scholarship, specifically when it came to Muḥammad, was devoted to helping Christians see aspects of Muḥammad's life that many Christians would not otherwise be able to discern.

Seeing *barakah* live in Muslim devotional life

Sanneh's most focused treatment of the Prophet Muḥammad and his meaning for Christians appear in two essays: 'Muḥammad, Prophet of Islam, and Jesus Christ, Image of God',[7] which was published in 1984, and 'Muḥammad's Significance for Christians',[8] which appeared in 1996. In both essays, Sanneh used his personal biography as a foundation upon which to build a Christian reflection upon the Prophet's biography. This was surely a natural strategy given the nature of Sanneh's birth and the choice of his name, but Sanneh's biography also linked to his awareness of how Muḥammad functions in Muslim devotional life and the ways in which biography as an oral, intellectual and literary genre could inform a Christian appreciation for the Prophet's life.

Looking back to his childhood, Sanneh acknowledged early on that it was 'through Muḥammad that we (i.e. his Muslim community in The Gambia) came to God as a moral, ethical and eschatological reality'.[9] Teetering on the edge of exalting Muḥammad to a divine status by making him a kind of mediator, 'God the abstract being [nevertheless] arrived by the agency of the Prophet as the judge, the avenger and the benefactor of humans. The Prophet was the human measure of an otherwise unapproachable transcendence, the unerring beacon in the vast sea of divine infinitude.'[10] It was through Muḥammad that the Qur'ān came to the rest of humanity. His name even appeared in the *shahādah*, fusing his identity with God's and ensconcing him, not as the revelation of God but as the one who pointed to the revelation of divine reality. Even in the call to worship God (*adhān*), one heard the name of Muḥammad as God's 'human instrument', as Sanneh put it.[11]

This awareness in Sanneh's life, and his acknowledgement that Muḥammad functions in this way for many Muslims, flirted, Sanneh admitted, with *shirk* for it threatened to ascribe a divine quality to Muḥammad. But this threat, and the Islamic jurisprudence that worked to dampen it, actually only served to underscore its reality. And in reality, Muslims, at least in Sanneh's observations and experience, saw Muḥammad as standing in between them and God, not only pointing the way to him but also signifying the ways in which God's message came down to them. In response, the *fuqahā* reminded the *ummah* that Muḥammad was not God and the latter should not be personified, which only emphasized that, mortal human though he was, Muḥammad remained a very special kind of human. In fact, he may indeed have died, but he was venerated nonetheless, almost as a consequence of his death.[12]

Naturally, then, Muḥammad became a fixture in Muslim devotional life and his followers developed a rich devotional literature centred upon him. Muḥammad was, as Sanneh described, the '*primus mobile*' of *Ḥadīth* literature. His name was encircled with elevated titles, including not only the oft-uttered epithets like *ṣallā llāhu ʿalayhi wa-sallama* but also mystical titles like 'the Perfect Man' (*al-Insān al-Kāmil*). Invocations of blessing upon the Prophet were also offered in addition to obligatory prayers, a practice even commanded in the Qur'ān (33:56). And there were the annual *mawlid al-nabī* celebrations in which the Prophet's name was a special theme of devotion. 'Consequently,' Sanneh inferred, 'God's statesman,' the instrument chosen by God for his revelation, 'became our spiritual pioneer as well. By concentrating on him, Muslims have been able to carve themselves devotional niches in the obligatory duties (*wājibāt*) of the faith.'[13]

In this way, Muḥammad 'was more than a juridical figure', Sanneh reflected, and his importance 'exceeds that of a mechanical transmission of the religious code'. Those who worshipped a God who was ultimately beyond them could also find in Muḥammad a 'sense of Muslim identity' that bridged the distance between them and God and engendered a spiritual devotion.[14] And so the Prophet became for Sanneh more than the passive, unlettered recipient of revelation; Muḥammad became the means by which he followed God. Sanneh prayed to him for help in his daily life. Parents held up the Prophet before their children as the 'accessible model of moral, religious and ethical conduct'.[15] Naturally, then, Sanneh imitated the Prophet's example by respecting his parents and by being courteous, generous, honest, loyal, courageous and modest. All of this provided the frame in which Muḥammad was viewed and understood. It justified emulation of the Prophet and made him a fixture in Muslim devotional life. It was the impetus for the ceremony that gave Sanneh his name and activated Muḥammad's biography as a resource and blessing for Muslim communities. And most importantly, all of this meant that, for Sanneh, Muḥammad 'made *barakah* live'.[16] He was the embodiment of virtue and the means by which virtue came alive in his followers.

Embodied *barakah* and appreciating Muḥammad as a signpost

The realities that Muḥammad's biography had for Muslims also had, in Sanneh's mind, important implications for Christians. One of these implications was that Christians ought to rethink the division they inserted between biography and history in light of the Muslim attitude towards Muḥammad. Sanneh's remarks in this regard were chiefly aimed at Western Christians. This is especially apparent in his comments about the favouritism shown towards historical-critical methods in the West and the ways in which these divide history and biography. Sanneh saw in this favouritism a certain ambivalence about the kind of mysticism that would fuse the virtue of someone in the past with a community in the present. As a result of such ambivalence, Sanneh reasoned, saints' lives were reduced to simple moral tales.

According to Sanneh, then, when it came to the Prophet's biography, especially as it is preserved in the traditions attributed to him in *Ḥadīth* literature, Christians dismissed what was to them an unfamiliar source. They found its details repetitive, 'tedious and monotonous'. Where Muslims found 'reason for confidence', Christians merely located foreign irrelevance. Looking for the logical coherence they often found in historical-critical readings of sources, they could not see in Muḥammad the product of 'logical demonstration'. They could not discern, as Muslims like Sanneh had done, that Muḥammad's 'voice vibrates throughout the range of Muslim life and action, his outward manner and demeanour the very meaning of inward *barakah*'. Missing this, Christians could not see that it was the things Muḥammad was reported to have said and done that demonstrated the validity of what he claimed. In turn, all the seemingly mundane descriptions of his life and words were ways of bringing Muḥammad into the lives of his followers. But for Christians who were keen to analyse a source, Muḥammad seemed to only fall further and further away, beyond the divide that separated reality from myth.[17]

But for Sanneh, the conflict 'between history and myth' did not exist.[18] 'Even as a child,' he wrote, 'I saw how a community's symbols, the object and subject of its history, could shape and motivate, and in turn be shaped and motivated by its actions and reflection, by its conduct and intention, its deeds and aspirations.' Muḥammad was that symbol for Sanneh and so the stories of the Prophet's past formed the identity of a community in a different time and space. 'The qualities of the Prophet that we admired as children … had attached to them the ring and dust of actual events.' Muḥammad may have lived in a period far removed from Sanneh and his community, but he was near to them metaphysically.[19] Separating history and biography in the ways Sanneh perceived among Western Christians prevented them from appreciating the ways in which Muḥammad functioned for Muslims. And so part of Sanneh's project was to help Western minds appreciate the place biography had in understanding important figures and the role it took in situating figures in spiritual and devotional life. 'It would thus bring matters to a precise point,' he wrote, 'to say that Christians have first to overcome their condescending attitude toward biography as such in order to see Muḥammad as Muslims see him.'[20] Not only would this help Christians to see aspects of Muḥammad that were often ignored, misunderstood and overlooked, but it would also help to shift the Christian focus on Muḥammad from a merely theological assessment to the ways in which he functioned in devotional life.

In the course of Sanneh's commentary, one thinks quite readily of Christian hagiography and the predominance these kinds of sources have, especially in Eastern Christian traditions and for Eastern Christian devotional lives. Sanneh did give a passing nod to Christian hagiography, but this gesture was only towards two Western sources: *Butler's Lives of the Saints* (eighteenth century) and *The Golden Legend: Readings of the Saints* (thirteenth century).[21] This gap in Sanneh's analysis seems to affirm that he had modern, Western Christians in mind when he wrote and that his encounters in Western academia loomed large in the backdrop of his perspective. We have seen, however, that quite a few Christians for whom hagiography was a central feature of their devotion nevertheless persisted in lampooning Muḥammad. Perhaps it was not merely a truncated view of biography that prevented Christians from appreciating Muḥammad but an inability or an unwillingness to see in him the life of a saint. At the very least, the devotional implications generated by a Muslim view of Muḥammad consistently failed to appear in theological analysis of the Prophet.

Thinking, then, of the Christian tendency to ridicule Muḥammad, Sanneh advocated an end to the continual repudiation of the Prophet, as if Muslims might be convinced by such attacks anyway. In place of repudiation, he argued that Christians ought to acknowledge how Muḥammad functioned in Muslim spiritual devotion. It would be unrealistic, Sanneh accepted, to ask Christians to adopt the same attitude towards Muḥammad that Muslims enjoyed. Nevertheless, appreciating the Muslim view would require a new Christian imagination and the acknowledgement that intolerance only breeds reciprocal intolerance, a risky exchange in an age of not only religious proximity between Christians and Muslims but physical coexistence as well.[22] It would be more advantageous, Sanneh argued, if Christians (and he has Western Christians in mind here) allowed the challenges posed by Muḥammad and biography to reshape the ways they divide certain spheres that may actually have different kinds of relationships with one another. How, for example, does the private impinge upon the public, or the church upon the state or religion upon politics?[23] An imagination that might reconsider these relationships might also, for Sanneh, reconsider the divides that exist between Christianity and Islam insofar as each religion's adherents might learn something from the other's strengths and weaknesses.[24]

Sanneh turned once again to his own biography in order to illustrate the nature of this interreligious learning. 'When I was a child,' he recalled, 'I learned that when you travelled to visit a relative elsewhere, you took with you a gift and that when you returned home you also brought a gift, so that, speaking symbolically, life gave you in return what you put into it, perhaps seventy times seven.' This giving and receiving, Sanneh suggested, had 'relevance for interfaith relations'.[25] On one level, the nature of this exchange could mean appreciating the translatable qualities of Christianity as it found its way into a multiplicity of indigenous vernaculars, even as one could honour the untranslatability of the Qur'ān as a means by which language and culture could assign to a sacred source an 'unalterable primacy'.[26] These views were things Islam and Christianity could offer one another as long as their respective adherents saw them as gifts to be understood and appreciated.

On a deeper level, though, Sanneh saw the Muslim view of Muḥammad's biography as a gift. Muḥammad himself was a gift that unfolded over time for Sanneh, but it began in the context of his childhood community where he focused on the Prophet's intercessory role. As I mentioned above, Sanneh was fully aware of the problems with turning to Muḥammad as an intermediary, the ways in which this kind of move flirted with *shirk* and the fences *fuqahā* erected in order to protect Muslims from going too far in this direction. Nevertheless, by making Muḥammad the instrument of divine revelation, by positioning him as the pre-eminent example of what it means to be human and by investing in his life the embodiment of *barakah*, Islamic sources invariably situated the Prophet in between God and Muslims. In turn, 'for most of us,' Sanneh wrote, 'it was his intercessory role that we cherished'.[27]

Sanneh was aware of the qur'anic warnings about seeing an intercessor in anyone but God.[28] And yet he was also familiar with passages that seemed to nod towards figures that functioned in this way. What was his community to do with revelations such as, 'And no one misguided us except the criminals. So now we have no intercessors and not a devoted friend' (Q 26:99–101); or 'Whoever intercedes for a good cause will have a reward therefrom; and whoever intercedes for an evil cause will have a burden therefrom' (Q 4:85); or 'Who is it that can intercede with [God] except by His permission' (Q 2:255)?[29] Sanneh was aware that there were authoritative ways of interpreting passages like these. Yet he read them and concluded that

> You would need exceptionally delicate maneuvers to march through these and other verses under juridical command. Most ordinary people would not be able to avoid getting entangled by the intercessory mesh so deliberately spread over the field. The Qur'ān itself appears to be sanctioning intercession as the ultimate criterion of a loyal friend. Who can blame us if our hearts tell us that God's leave is ours to invoke in our need for an intercessor?[30]

Sanneh admitted that the next logical step from this conception of intercession to the one in which Muḥammad met the need of a loyal friend was a natural progression.

So Sanneh and his community 'yielded [their] hearts to [Muḥammad] as a meek and lowly mount'.[31] For in reality, Sanneh wrote, Muḥammad 'bore our infirmities. He became by that means our ally, friend and intercessor, and in his saddle he placed us', pointing them, even carrying them, to God.[32] Again, Sanneh found qur'anic support, leaning on Q 3:81:

> And when God took the covenant of the Prophets, [saying,] 'Whatever I give you of the Scripture and wisdom and then there comes to a messenger confirming what is with you, you believe in him and support him'. [God] said, 'Have you acknowledged and taken upon that My commitment?' They said, 'We have acknowledged it'. He said, 'Then bear witness, and I am with you among the witnesses'.

In this revelation, Sanneh saw God using messengers to convey his revelation and prophets to confirm the truth of what the messengers said. God even joined his people as a witness to their call. In this way, at least in Sanneh's mind, to follow God's prophets was to follow God. To be close to God's prophets was to be close to God. And here the gift of Islam in presenting Muḥammad as a friend and exemplar also became a hinge that swung Sanneh towards another view of Christ. For to view Muḥammad in the way that Sanneh had come to understand him was to 'provoke the question about an equally personal God accessible by his nature and his action'.[33]

For Sanneh, Muḥammad had become so deeply personal that he had 'brought personal religion within range of the ordinary worshiper'.[34] In this way, Muḥammad had 'brought God within range'.[35] Reading the Islamic sources and hearing about a view of Muḥammad as a devotional figure standing in between humanity and God, not only pointing the former towards the latter but also drawing the two together, had a remarkable Christian ring to it. And so the notion of Christ as a suffering servant, come down in human form in order to draw humanity closer to God, made sense to Sanneh and questions about Christ's crucifixion and resurrection provoked him. In fact, Sanneh came to see in Christ the flowering of a divine project, a project to which Muḥammad pointed. He concluded that 'redemptive suffering is at the very core of moral truth, and the prophets were all touched by its fearsome power. But only One embodied it as a historical experience, although all, including the Prophet of Islam, walked in its shadow'.[36] This was a decidedly Christian view of Christ, but it made Muḥammad a prophet and placed him alongside the ranks of prophets who preceded him. And, like the other prophets before him, Muḥammad was, according to Sanneh, a signpost for 'God's ineffable grace'.[37]

Sanneh's conclusions seem to offer space for Muḥammad among God's prophets, but he did not clarify how the phrase 'Prophet of Islam' may have been for him a way of fencing off the extent of what Muḥammad did. Was Muḥammad, as in Paul of Antioch's estimation, a prophet for Muslims only, serving as a sign of God's grace within the context of Islam but not necessarily outside of its boundaries? Was Muḥammad, as in Patriarch Timothy I's assessment, a figure who was *like* the prophets before him in preparing the way for Christ?

Sanneh offered no clarifications in his essays that might have helped to answer questions like these. But what can be clearly inferred is that, for Sanneh, Muḥammad was a signpost for God. In Sanneh's devotion to Muḥammad, he followed the way in which Muḥammad pointed and, in so doing, found his way to Christ. The fact that Muḥammad played a role in pointing Sanneh to Christ may only be a feature of Sanneh's own biography. Many other Muslims would certainly not follow him in this trajectory, but for Sanneh, appreciating the way Muḥammad functioned in the devotional life of many Muslims drew other Christians onto a path in which they, too, could be fellow pilgrims. And so Muḥammad, the embodiment of *barakah* for Muslims, could also be appreciated by Christians as a figure drawing them together, not forcing them apart. Muḥammad could turn monologue into true dialogue, which was really the walking of a path together.

Conclusion

In eleven chapters we have traversed early-medieval Iraq and Syria, travelled around the Mediterranean basin, sailed across the Atlantic to the New World and Colonial New England, returned across the ocean to West Africa in the twentieth century and returned to North America in the twenty-first century. What I attempted along the way was to introduce a set of authors who could represent, in a sustained and coherent manner, the kinds of things Christian authors said when they encountered the claims Muslims made about the Prophet Muḥammad. What were the main ways they interpreted Muḥammad when they considered his life and ministry? How did they deal with the theological implications of his status as a Prophet and Final Messenger in Islam?

'Is there not to be found in my Prophet anything praiseworthy?'

In this dizzying journey, do you remember Jirjī, the old Melkite monk and his Muslim interlocutors who smelled of musk? In their two-day debate they covered a wide array of theological topics, frequently coming to light upon the subject of Muḥammad's prophethood. One *ʿalīm* asked Jirjī, 'Do we not know, oh monk, that Muḥammad is the apostle and prophet of God, that he guided the people of Ishmael and converted them from idolatry to the knowledge of the living God like Christ and the apostles?'[1] Jirjī disagreed. In fact, the monk declared, Muḥammad 'usurped authority over the Arabians, the sons of Ishmael'.[2] He may have guided the Arabs, converting them from idolatry to knowledge of the one, true God, but that knowledge was incomplete. Muḥammad only taught what would elicit his followers' obedience. In turn, Jirjī neither regarded nor called Muḥammad a prophet or an apostle.[3] On the contrary, discovering the true and complete knowledge of God could be drawn directly from the Qur'ān and

Muḥammad himself. Such sources need only be interpreted correctly, something Jirjī was happy to disclose.[4]

Towards the end of the exchange, after a veritable onslaught of argumentation and denunciation of Muḥammad and the Qur'ān, one Muslim's exasperation becomes palpable in the text. He complained to Jirjī, 'You pass judgment, oh Christian, and decide for yourself; you assert the truth of your own religion, and say that you are in the right, and all others in error. You are both the accuser and the judge.'[5] Jirjī casually swept this complaint away; reason and common sense were the judge, not him, he responded. 'Is there not to be found in my book and prophet', the Muslim finally questioned with an almost audible sigh of desperation, 'any virtue, or anything praiseworthy?' Surely not *all* virtue or laudable character was limited to Christ and the Gospels. Might there not be something – *anything* – that one might attribute to Muḥammad?

Jirjī's response to the Muslim's distressed question is dismissive. 'I find one thing to praise in your prophet; and this is, when someone said, "What do you love best in the world, oh apostle of God?" He replied, "Prayer and women, and next, sweet odour".'[6] One wonders if the *'ulamā'* instinctively bowed to smell the musk exhaling from their robes as they considered Jirjī's back-handed reply. But then the monk continued. '[Muḥammad] possesses also virtue', Jirjī allowed and one senses the *'ulamā'* lifting their heads from their robes and leaning in with anticipation. 'When one of his relations once visited him, Muḥammad asked him if he had a wife; he replied, "No". Muḥammad then said, "If you be a presbyter or a Christian monk, adhere to [Christian marriage stipulations], and do as they do; but if you be of us, we ordain marriage".' So Jirjī admitted that Muḥammad respected the regulations governing marriage for respective religious communities. Was there anything else? The *'ulamā'* must have wondered and then surely breathed a sigh of relief when the monk kept talking. 'I know of many other virtues of your prophet and could easily enumerate them.'[7] But the enumeration of Muḥammad's supposedly lengthy list of virtues never came, at least not in the account of the debate.

Graciousness with respect to community ethics, an allegiance to monotheism and a love of prayer—these were the morally admirable virtues Jirjī ascribed to Muḥammad in the course of the debate. Even these, however, came with clarifications: Muḥammad's monotheism may have led Arabs away from idolatry, but he only took them so far as an incomplete knowledge of God. The Prophet may have loved prayer, but he adored women and luxury just as much. And so the ease with which Jirjī laid claim when it came to listing Muḥammad's résumé of virtuous character lands as little more than a dull plunk of literary flourish. The damage had been done with the monk's careful dismantling of Muḥammad and the Qur'ān throughout the debate. He showed how Islam, rightly interpreted, actually supported Christian truth. There was little need to enumerate Muḥammad's virtues, however easy such a task may have been.

The goal of this book has not been to merely locate Christians saying positive things about Muḥammad. Even so, having come this far, readers may wonder, very much like Jirjī's *ʿālim*, 'Is there not to be found in Muḥammad any virtue, or anything praiseworthy?' It is clear from our journey that Christians did not find a great deal in Muḥammad that was admirable. Nevertheless, a few authors observed some noteworthy characteristics. In the Baḥīrā legend, Muḥammad appeared as a humble, simply boy who was a willing student. The monk from Bēt Ḥālē described him as wise and god-fearing, responsible for drawing his followers away from idolatry and towards monotheism. Patriarch Timothy I echoed much of the Bēt Ḥālē monk's remarks and spoke eloquently about Muḥammad's prophet-like qualities. Paul of Antioch as well as the author of *The Letter from the People of Cyprus* lauded Muḥammad as a prophet for the Arabs. Mary Fisher was willing to say that Muḥammad might have actually been a prophet. Samuel Ajayi Crowther credited Muḥammad for his monotheism, too, and saw in Islam a movement towards the flowering of human development. Lamin Sanneh, going further than perhaps anyone else in our study, acknowledged that, for Muslims, Muḥammad made virtue come alive, a characteristic worthy of Christian appreciation.

But each of these observations stands out in high relief because the greater backdrop behind them is one of overall disdain and limitation. Muḥammad may have been an able student in the Baḥīrā legend, but he was really exploited by the monk Sergius-Baḥīrā. The monk could only use him so much, given the boy's overall intellectual limitations, and, in the end, their message was corrupted. John of Damascus found Muḥammad completely lacking and rather sordid. For all Timothy I had to say about the Prophet, he really only achieved what previous prophets before him had done with respect to monotheism. ʿAbd al-Masīḥ ibn Isḥāq al-Kindī, along with Dionysius bar Ṣalībī, gave some of the greatest focus to Muḥammad's allegedly unseemly personal qualities and lack of prophetic characteristics. The same can be said about Būluṣ ibn Rajāʾ and the translator of the *Liber denudationis* for whom Muḥammad the anti-hero inevitably fell short of Christ. And many of the same repugnant features were memorialized in a biography written in Spain where Muḥammad was fashioned as an anti-saint. For all the possibility that Muḥammad had in Fisher's Quaker view of prophethood, he would only have been seen as a prophet just like anyone else might be seen, including Fisher. Even then, all prophets would still be subordinate to Christ. For whatever Islam achieved in West Africa, Muḥammad remained, as ever, the founder of a poisonous doctrine in Crowther's mind. And, though Sanneh called for a reprisal of Christian denunciation of the Prophet, Muḥammad ultimately functioned in the shadow of Christ as one of his signposts, a signification that no matter how laudable, most Muslims would look towards and demur. In this way, while each of these observations certainly lays 'beyond aversion'[8] and helps to problematize simplistic historical views that only see Christians condemning the Prophet, they also demonstrate that Christians could only go so far in their estimation of Muḥammad and even those willing to ascribe some aspect of prophethood to him would fall short of the Muslim ideal.

Finally, an oversight exhibited by nearly all of the authors in this book was their failure, not necessarily to identify the ways in which Muḥammad might have been virtuous but to perceive how the Prophet existed in Muslim spirituality and devotion as an archetype of virtue, outlining what it meant for his followers to live well in the contexts they inhabited.[9] Lamin Sanneh saw this shortcoming and used his analysis to focus on it directly. He had personal knowledge of the ways Muslims viewed Muḥammad in terms of virtue and how they centred this feature in their piety. And Sanneh used this experience as the basis upon which to advocate a new way for Christians to appreciate Muḥammad.

Two additional Christian authors came close in this regard. The monk from Bēt Ḥālē and Timothy I, both East Syrian Christians, recognized that Muḥammad, for all he did religiously with respect to monotheism, was also responsible for a shift in ethics. For the monk from Bēt Ḥālē, Muslims might spend eternity near the gates of Paradise as a direct result of their good deeds. Of course, this inclusion would also seem to apply to others besides Muslims. And anyways, being near the gates of heaven was not as good as entering through them. Even so, inherent in the monk's use of the Syrian tradition here was tacit recognition of Muslim virtue. The monk did not make an explicit connection between Muslim good deeds and Muḥammad's influence, but as we have seen, the similarity of what he said about Muḥammad with what Timothy I said suggests he might possibly have had such a connection in mind. After all, Timothy conceded that, like other prophetic figures before him, Muḥammad drove his people away from evil and guided them nearer to good works. There can be seen here a nod towards Muḥammad's virtue and the ways it transferred to those who followed him.

But, again, the clarifications are ever near, for Muḥammad's good deeds were not, for Timothy, so much reflected in his followers as they were a reflection of the manner in which Muḥammad did in prophet-like fashion what biblical prophets before him had already done. The imprint of virtue lay not with Muḥammad but in a prophetic lineage that began with the Hebrew prophets and traced its way towards Christ. In this way, Timothy found a way of connecting the Prophet's praiseworthy traits to pre-Islamic faith. Any virtue that could be attributed to Muḥammad was not really his. It had a different source that only Christians, so it seemed, were capable of disentangling from Islam. Not unlike Timothy I, Sanneh rooted Muḥammad in a long prophetic lineage with a trajectory that arced towards Christ. But for Sanneh, Muḥammad was still able to make virtue come alive for his followers. It was simply that his inevitably intermediary role, a function that made him an archetype of virtue, also made him a signpost for Christ.

The same ground, retraced?

Stepping aside from any of Muḥammad's potentially praiseworthy traits, it is important to note that many of the ways in which Christian authors interpreted Muḥammad often sounded very much alike. In fact, many of the same types of things are repeated about the Prophet. His alleged violence and promiscuity, the way he usurped and manipulated his way towards political authority, his shortcomings as a so-called prophet without any miracles and his connections to monotheism are highlighted by Christian authors again and again. A significant amount of continuity can be detected in this observation. Part of this continuity is surely due to the common reactions upon which one might depend when evaluating the life of a significant figure. Used to evaluating religious claims, these Christian authors deployed a common stock of interpretive tools in order to make sense of Muḥammad. More important, however, is the degree to which knowledge was shared, either within traditions as might be the case for East Syrians like the monk of Bēt Ḥālē and Timothy I or across traditions and geography as is likely the case between Būluṣ ibn Rajā' and the translator of the *Liber denudationis*. In either case, despite covering a wide swath of geography, chronology and ecclesiology, a red thread can be traced through most of the texts. That red thread suggested that Muḥammad was, at best, prophetic in nature but certainly not the Final Messenger and, at worst, completely unworthy of consideration as a prophet.

But for all the continuity tied together by this red thread, it also throws into high relief a number of notable disparities when it comes to how Christians interpreted Prophet Muḥammad. To begin with, our journey demonstrates that there was never a single Christian vision of Muḥammad. While he was a despot for many, for others he was a signpost that pointed the way towards monotheism and even Christ. There were even those like the monk from Bēt Ḥālē who, following alongside St Ephrem the Syrian, were able to find a place for Muḥammad and his followers very near to them in the vicinity of Paradise. A gate may still have separated them, but a notable distance is removed by the monk's remarks when compared to others. In this, harsh comments condemning Muslims and Muḥammad wholesale were not broadly characteristic of Christian assessments of his life.

Besides the relative diversity of Christian interpretations, another notable feature in the landscape is that no one kind of assessment can be fixed to a single region, time period, language, Christian tradition or literary genre. What can be more firmly tethered to an author and his or her assessment of Muḥammad's prophethood is instead a given context, which formed the occasion, purpose and goal of an author's writing or the record of his or her encounter. Al-Kindī's epistolary exchange with al-Hāshimī can serve as a case in point. The polemical text, likely written entirely by al-Kindī himself, was a wide-ranging 'summa' discussing pertinent theological details related to the Trinity and Christology. Al-Kindī also addressed matters pertaining to Christian practice and contesting claims of Muslim faith and practice. And, of course, he railed against Islam and Muḥammad in particular. The result was a nearly comprehensive text for Christians living in an Islamic milieu.[10]

The effect, to the extent that al-Kindī's letter was successful, was to render Islam an unattractive set of beliefs, especially when compared to Christianity, and Muḥammad an unseemly character to follow. Hence, al-Kindī shattered any validity al-Hāshimī claimed for Islam and Muḥammad and he firmly rejected the Muslim's invitation to convert. Christian readers who were convinced of the arguments in the likely imagined epistolary exchange would, in theory, have reason to distrust Muḥammad and his message. As a result, al-Kindī's *Risāla* can be seen as a pastoral tool intended to guide Christians living in contexts with increasing Muslim influence away from Islam. They should not follow Muḥammad despite the growing temptations to do so. In this way, a Christian assessment of prophethood may, more than anything else, most accurately reflect a Christian author's context, not necessarily the identity of Muḥammad. An author's text might therefore best be understood, not as a window through which to understand the Prophet but as a mirror by which to see reflected the concerns of a particular person and community.[11]

Despite this relatively inward-focused approach, many authors did not hesitate to look outside their traditions and search Muslim sources for information that could support their interpretations of Muḥammad. A number of authors made extensive use of the Qur'ān and Islamic traditions in their attempts to impugn the character of Muḥammad and the claims he made. Such was the case for Ibn Rajā' and the translator of the *Liber denudationis*. Both the *Kitāb al-Wāḍiḥ bi-l-Ḥaqq* and the *Liber denudationis* relentlessly attacked the Qur'ān and *ḥadīth* literature in order to disclose the invalidity of Muslim scripture and Muḥammad's lacking prophetic credentials. In other cases, however, seemingly wild accusations were made by some of our authors. But as we have seen, their observations were not completely frivolous but often represented engagement with Muslim interlocutors or Islamic traditions. Where such Christian authors strayed was in their use of these sources since they often plucked Muslim traditions from their native Islamic contexts where they ceased to be understood adequately and were instead put into service for use in the authors' polemical agendas. Such was the case for authors like John of Damascus and Eulogius. John seemed aware of Muslim debates regarding the meaning of Q 2:223 and was able to reflect Muslim disagreement about how the verse ought to be understood. But his critical engagement with this portion of the Qur'ān was not meant to shed light on how Muslims wrestled with the difficulty of various revelations but instead to draw attention to potential scandal in the Qur'ān and, in turn, to cast doubt on the authenticity of Muḥammad's claims. What is intriguing is that in order to understand John's strategy here, one must be able to discern the extent to which he was familiar with his Muslim sources.

Similarly, Eulogius made, on the surface, one of the most madly salacious accusations we have seen in the texts: did Muḥammad really claim to deflower the Holy Mother in Paradise? For Eulogius' readers, the mere thought of such an assertion was enough to disregard Muḥammad and his followers entirely. For scholars studying Eulogius along with the martyrs of Córdoba and their supporters, the accusation could be proof that Eulogius' polemic was not only vehemently anti-Islamic but rabidly unhinged as well. And yet I have shown that Eulogius did not invent the information about Muḥammad in the afterlife. Instead, he seemed to have been familiar with or made aware of a Muslim tradition regarding the Prophet and the rank of his wives in Paradise. Eulogius simply misconstrued that tradition, mismatched the names of Muḥammad's wives and misapplied what was being discussed. When he did that, the now-garbled tradition became a ready-made dart for a Christian to fling at Muḥammad. Very much like the example from John of Damascus, what is intriguing is not

Christian unfamiliarity with Muslims or Islam but the ways in which Islamic traditions were, often unknowingly, uprooted from their contexts, resituated into new Christian frameworks and used to support a Christian author's agenda to interpret Muḥammad for his or her community.

In all of this, there are many times in which authors retraced the same ground that had been covered before them. In just as many instances, however, authors struck out into new territory, considering different angles of view or drawing upon different Christian and Muslim sources in their effort to interpret the prophethood of Muḥammad. And, because it was usually the case that Muḥammad was being interpreted for *particular* readers and communities, the ground being covered was always, in some senses, new.

A Christian Muḥammad?

Perhaps the most important conclusion to make from our journey brings us back to the idea that Timothy I attempted to disentangle Muḥammad from Islam by linking his virtue and prophet-like acts to non-Muslim sources. For Timothy, and other authors who wrote similarly, the good that Muḥammad did reflected what the Hebrew prophets had already done. In this way, the source of Muḥammad's virtue was not his book or religion but pre-Islamic monotheism. Likewise, the *telos* of Muḥammad's ministry was not Islam but Christ. Of course, one could discern spaces of overlap between the things done by Christ, the Hebrew prophets and Muḥammad, especially when it came to proclamations about monotheism. At the very least, such spaces were what made Muḥammad a *final* messenger for Muslims and prophet-like for those such as Timothy. But more significantly, loosening the connections between Islam and Muḥammad effectively placed the Prophet on different footing for it began to alter his very identity.

Put another way, in their attempts to understand or account for Muḥammad many of the authors we have considered made him into an unwitting Christian. This feature is not present in all Christian texts devoted, wholly or in part, to Muḥammad, but it is the case in many of them. For example, in the Baḥīrā legend, the story of the young Muḥammad is used in order to launch a Christian understanding of history, distil the Christian meaning from the Qur'ān and draw a community of pagans towards monotheism. In the *Disputation between a Muslim and a Monk from Bēt Ḥālē*, Muḥammad became a crypto-Trinitarian who gently massaged his followers towards monotheism by making them more receptive to the fullness that was Christian truth. Theodore bar Konī concluded that Muslims were Jew-like in their beliefs because, even though they were monotheists, they denied the Trinity. This made Muslims almost-Christians, which by implication made Muḥammad very nearly Christian in his beliefs. For the author of the 'Tultusceptru de libro domni Metobii', Muḥammad was a vessel of Christ. He was given a Christian message to proclaim. This message, like Muḥammad himself, was eventually tainted by an evil angel, but in their original forms the message and the messenger were Christians meant to draw an errant people towards the one God. Paul of Antioch and the later author of *The Letter from the People of Cyprus* distilled the Qur'ān down to a Christian text. Interpreting Muslim scripture correctly allowed readers to see that Muḥammad could be a prophet, but only for the Arabs since what he brought were things Christians already knew. This could only be seen when the Qur'ān and Muḥammad were seen in their properly Christian frame. In a surprisingly similar way, Mary Fisher was open to the possibility of Muḥammad's prophethood because she saw him through a Quaker frame in which all people could be prophets, though they would inevitably be subordinate to Christ. In this way, if Muḥammad was a prophet, and one would only know by discerning the quality of his fruits, then he would have been one in the service of Christ. Samuel Ajayi Crowther could see the good in Muḥammad insofar as he helped to draw pagans closer to the flowering of human development. This latter vision was realized in Christian truth, and so Muḥammad only really did in a poorer way what Christians were doing, which was to draw people closer to Christ. While Lamin Sanneh saw Muḥammad, like other prophets before him, standing in the shadow of Christ and acting as a signpost for God's grace, his position seems distinct from the sources mentioned. Instead of Christianizing Muḥammad, Sanneh took the Prophet's position in spiritual devotion, understood that role on its own Islamic terms and then turned in a decidedly Christian direction. Even so, Christian meaning was not far from an interpretation of Muḥammad.

And so one of the predominant ways in which many Christian authors attempted to interpret the Prophet's life and ministry was to make him one of their own by dressing him in Christian clothes and making his way of speaking conform to Christian speech. Conscripting Muḥammad into Christian service like this risked pulling him beyond his Islamic context, scrubbing the Muslim character from the Qur'ān and twisting his mission into one that could be contained within the frameworks of Christianity. But it was a way in which Christians could offer an interpretation of the Prophet that fit in their theological purview and helped him make sense to their Christian communities.

Notes

Introduction

1 The term 'Melkite' originates from the Syriac *malkāyā* and the Arabic *malakī*, meaning 'royal' and thereby pejoratively implying that Melkites were 'imperialists' who joined with the Byzantine emperor and the Christology formulated at the Council of Chalcedon (451). Otherwise known as Greek Orthodox Christians, the medieval Melkites are to be distinguished from present-day Melkite communities who, after 1729, came from the Greek Orthodox Patriarchate of Antioch into communion with the Roman Catholic Church and are presently known as Melkite Greek Catholics. See Joshua Blau, 'A Melkite Arabic Literary *Lingua Franca* from the Second Half of the First Millennium', *Bulletin of the School of Oriental and African Studies* 57/1 (1994), 14–16. See also Sidney Griffith, '"Melkites", "Jacobites" and the Christological Controversies in Arabic in Third/Ninth-Century Syria', in D. Thomas (ed.), *Syrian Christians under Islam* (Leiden, 2001); Sidney Griffith, 'The Church of Jerusalem and the "Melkites"', in O. Limor and G. G. Stroumsa (eds), *Christians and Christianity in the Holy Land* (Turnhout, 2006), 175–204.

2 Constantine Bacha (Qusṭanṭīn Bāshā), *Mujādalat al-anbā Jirjī l-rāhib al-Simʿānī maʿthalāthat shuyūkh min fuqahāʾ al-Muslimīn bi-ḥaḍrat al-amīr Mushammar al-Ayyūbī* (Beirut, 1932), 12; Alex Nicoll, 'Account of a Disputation between a Christian Monk and Three Learned Mohammedans on the Subject of Religion', *Edinburgh Annual Register ad annum 1816* 9 (1820), 407. For the textual issues related to the account of Jirjī's debate, see Mark N. Swanson, 'The Disputation of Jirjī the Monk', in D. Thomas and A. Mallett (eds), *Christian-Muslim Relations: A Bibliographical History* (heretofore, *CMR*) 4 (Leiden, 2012), 166–72; Charles Tieszen, '"Can You Find Anything Praiseworthy in My Religion?"', in D. Pratt, J. Hoover, J. Davies and J. Chesworth (eds), *The Character of Christian-Muslim Encounter* (Leiden, 2015), 127–32.

3 Bacha, *Mujādalat al-anbā Jirjī l-rāhib al-Simʿānī maʿthalāthat shuyūkh min fuqahāʾ al-Muslimīn bi-ḥaḍrat al-amīr Mushammar al-Ayyūbī*, 12; Nicoll, 'Account of a Disputation between a Christian Monk and Three Learned Mohammedans on the Subject of Religion', 407.

4 Bacha, *Mujādalat al-anbā Jirjī l-rāhib al-Simʿānī maʿthalāthat shuyūkh min fuqahāʾ al-Muslimīn bi-ḥaḍrat al-amīr Mushammar al-Ayyūbī*, 12; Nicoll, 'Account of a

Disputation between a Christian Monk and Three Learned Mohammedans on the Subject of Religion', 407–8.

5 Bacha, *Mujādalat al-anbā Jirjī l-rāhib al-Simʿānī maʿthalāthat shuyūkh min fuqahā' al-Muslimīn bi-ḥaḍrat al-amīr Mushammar al-Ayyūbī*, 23; Nicoll, 'Account of a Disputation between a Christian Monk and Three Learned Mohammedans on the Subject of Religion', 411.

6 Bacha, *Mujādalat al-anbā Jirjī l-rāhib al-Simʿānī maʿthalāthat shuyūkh min fuqahā' al-Muslimīn bi-ḥaḍrat al-amīr Mushammar al-Ayyūbī*, 23–4; Nicoll, 'Account of a Disputation between a Christian Monk and Three Learned Mohammedans on the Subject of Religion', 411.

7 The most recent studies include, for example: Mahmut Aydin, *Modern Western Christian Theological Understandings of Muslims since the Second Vatican Council* (Washington, DC, 2002); Mark Beaumont, 'Christians, Prophethood, and Muḥammad', in C. Tieszen (ed.), *Theological Issues in Christian-Muslim Dialogue* (Eugene, 2018); Clinton Bennett, *In Search of Muḥammad* (London, 1998); Clinton Bennett, 'Christian Perceptions of Muḥammad', in D. Pratt and C. Tieszen (eds), *CMR* 15 (Leiden, 2020); Anna Bonta Moreland, *Muḥammad Reconsidered* (South Bend, 2020); Jabal Muhammad Buaben, *The Image of the Prophet Muḥammad in the West* (Leicester, 1996); Daniel Cyranka, *Mahomet* (Göttingen, 2018); Michelina De Cesare, *The Pseudo-Historical Image of the Prophet Muḥammad in Medieval Latin Literature* (Berlin, 2012); Christiane Gruber and Avinoam Shalem, eds, *The Image of the Prophet between Ideal and Ideology* (Berlin, 2014); David Kerr, 'Toward Christian Theological Recognition of the Prophethood of Muhammad', in Y. Y. Haddad and W. Z. Haddad (eds), *Christian-Muslim Encounters* (Gainesville, 1995); Christian Lange, *Mohammed* (Amsterdam, 2017); Daniel Madigan, 'Jesus and Muḥammad, the Sufficiency of Prophecy', in M. Ipgrave (ed.), *Bearing the Word* (New York, 2005); David Marshall, 'Muḥammad in Contemporary Christian Theological Reflection', *Islam and Christian-Muslim Relations* 24/2 (2013), 161–72; Minou Reeves, *Muhammad in Europe* (New York, 2000); Avinoam Shalem, *Constructing the Image of Muhammad in Europe* (Berlin, 2013); John V. Tolan, *Faces of Muhammad* (Princeton, 2019).

1 Muḥammad as a Christian catechumen

1 Barbara Roggema, 'A Christian Reading of the Qur'an', in D. Thomas (ed.), *Syrian Christians under Islam* (Leiden, 2001), 57–8.

2 See *The Life of Muhammad*, trans. A. Guillaume (Karachi, 2007), 79–81.

3 It is unlikely that the Muslim versions of the legend informed the Christian versions, though there are some similarities. See Krisztina Szilágyi, 'Muḥammad and the Monk', *Jerusalem Studies in Arabic and Islam* 34 (2008), 192–202.

4 Ibid., 170; Sidney H. Griffith, 'Muḥammad and the Monk Baḥīrā', *Oriens Christianus* 79 (1995), 147. The story was even known among Jewish readers. For Jewish versions of the story, see Moshe Gil, 'The Story of Baḥīrā and its Jewish Versions', in H. Ben-Shammai (ed.), *Hebrew and Arabic Studies in Honour of Joshua Blau* (Tel Aviv, 1993), 193–210.

5 Barbara Roggema, 'The Legend of Sergius Baḥīrā', in D. Thomas and B. Roggema (eds), *CMR* 1 (Leiden, 2006), 600–3.

6 Editions and translations of the legend, this one from the East Syrian recension written in Syriac, come from Barbara Roggema, *The Legend of Sergius Baḥīrā* (Leiden, 2009), 254–527. Roggema's work is also the most extensive study of the legend, but see also Szilágyi, 'Muḥammad and the Monk', 169–214; Richard Gottheil, 'A Christian Bahira Legend', *Zeitschrift für Assyriologie* 13 (1898), 189–242, 14 (1899), 203–68, 15 (1900), 56–102, 17 (1903), 125–66; Griffith, 'Muḥammad and the Monk Baḥīrā', 146–74.

7 Roggema, *The Legend of Sergius Baḥīrā*, 330–1.

8 Ibid., 330–3.

9 On Muslim traditions for the Prophet's death and the Christian use (and, at times, adaptation) of these traditions, see Krisztina Szilágyi, 'A Prophet like Jesus?', *Jerusalem Studies in Arabic and Islam* 36 (2009), 131–71.

10 Roggema, *The Legend of Sergius Baḥīrā*, 334–5.

11 Ibid., 340–1.

12 Ibid., 348–9.

13 Ibid., 284–5. See also ibid., 354–5.

14 Ibid., 402–3.

15 Ibid., 408–9.

16 Griffith, 'Muḥammad and the Monk Baḥīrā', 173. For Armenian versions, see Robert W. Thomson, 'Armenian Variations on the Bahira Legend', *Harvard Ukrainian Studies* 3-4/2 (1979–80), 884–95.

17 See Szilágyi, 'Muḥammad and the Monk', 171–84 for the most accessible breakdown of the legend's synoptic versions and the passages that are unique to certain recensions.

18 Ibid., 185–92.

19 See Jn 14.16, 15.26 and 16.7. Cf. Q 61:6, which Muslims take as confirmation that Muḥammad fulfilled this role. For the Muḥammad–Paraclete theme as a topos of Christian–Muslim literature, see Charles Tieszen, *A Textual History of Christian-Muslim Relations* (Minneapolis, 2015), 239–51; Sandra Toenies Keating, 'The Paraclete and the Integrity of Scripture', in C. Tieszen (ed.), *Theological Issues in Christian-Muslim Dialogue* (Eugene, 2018). See also, Charles Tieszen, *Christian Identity amid Islam in Medieval Spain* (Leiden, 2013), 152, n. 22.

20 On the legend's use of the Qur'ān, see Roggema, 'A Christian Reading of the Qur'ān'.

21 Roggema, *The Legend of Sergius Baḥīrā*, 418–19.
22 See Roggema's comments in *The Legend of Sergius Baḥīrā*, 513, n. 136.
23 For more on the marriage and its use in Christian literature, see Tieszen, *Christian Identity amid Islam*, 255; Norman Daniel, *Islam and the West* (Oxford, 2000), 119–21.
24 Roggema, *The Legend of Sergius Baḥīrā*, 426–7.
25 E.g. ibid., 484–5, 492–3.
26 See Roggema's comments in *The Legend of Sergius Baḥīrā*, 453, n. 29.
27 Ibid., 466–7. For the biblical text to which Sergius alluded, see Mt. 3.16-17, Mk 1.9-11, Lk. 3.21-22 and Jn 1.29-34.
28 Roggema, *The Legend of Sergius Baḥīrā*, 488–9.
29 Maher Jarrar, 'Houris', in J. D. McAuliffe (ed.), *Encyclopaedia of the Qur'an*, vol. 2 (Leiden, 2002), 456–7. See also, Ṣoubḥī El-Ṣaleḥ, *La vie future selon le Coran* (Paris, 1986); Jane Idleman Smith and Yvonne Yazbeck Haddad, *The Islamic Understanding of Death and Resurrection* (Oxford, 2002), 158–68.
30 See Daniel, *Islam and the West,* 158–85; Tieszen, *A Textual History*, 245–8.
31 Roggema, *The Legend of Sergius Baḥīrā*, 482–3.
32 E.g. see Ṣaḥīḥ Muslim 53.63.
33 Alexandra Cuffel, *Gendering Disgust in Medieval Religious Polemic* (Notre Dame, 2007), 118–19; Tieszen, *Christian Identity amid Islam*, 135.
34 Roggema, *The Legend of Sergius Baḥīrā*, 390–1.
35 These passages begin in Roggema, *The Legend of Sergius Baḥīrā*, 416–17.
36 On the evidence here, see Roggema's comments in *The Legend of Sergius Baḥīrā*, 401, n. 25.
37 Each of the recensions discusses Christian waywardness as a source of blame. The result of this, however, is not Islam but God sending a ferocious lion that heavily persecutes Christians. In the monk's vision, the lion represented 'the Mahdī', the son of Fāṭima in the West Syrian and short Arabic recensions and the son of 'Ā'isha in the long Arabic recension. See Roggema, *The Legend of Sergius Baḥīrā*, 292–5, 364–7, 412–13, and 504–5.
38 Ibid., 514–15.
39 Ibid., 520–1. The short Arabic recension says that Muḥammad is not 'a prophet or an apostle' (*wa-laisa huwa nabī wa-lā rasūl*), which, in qur'anic language (cf. Q 33:40), not only denies the Muslim claim that Muḥammad was a prophet but also rejects the claim that he was a Messenger (*rasūl*) sent with a revelation. See Roggema, *The Legend of Sergius Baḥīrā*, 426–7. In the East Syrian recension, Muḥammad is called a prophet – 'You are destined to become a master and a king and a prophet and a leader and a head of your people' (Roggema, *The Legend of Sergius Baḥīrā*, 272–3; cf. the West Syrian recension, Roggema, *The Legend of Sergius Baḥīrā*, 340, where the phrase about being a prophet does not appear). In context, however, Muḥammad is really only Baḥīrā's prophet – the mouthpiece for his Qur'ān – instead of a prophet of God.

40 Ibid., 526–7. A similar remark appears at the end of the short Arabic recension (Roggema, *The Legend of Sergius Baḥīrā*, 428–9).
41 Ibid., 258–9, 322–3, 380–1, 436–7.
42 Ibid., 450–1.
43 Ibid., 452–3. See Roggema's comments on these redactions in Roggema, *The Legend of Sergius Baḥīrā*, 206–7.
44 Szilágyi, 'Muḥammad and the Monk', 203; Griffith, 'Muḥammad and the Monk Baḥīrā', 147.
45 Ibid., 152.
46 Szilágyi, 'Muḥammad and the Monk', 169.
47 Ibid.
48 Roggema, *The Legend of Sergius Baḥīrā*, 30.
49 Ibid., 31. Roggema is quoting Amos Funkenstein, 'History, Counterhistory, and Narrative', in S. Friedlander (ed.), *Probing the Limits of Representation* (Cambridge, 1992).
50 As Roggema points out, the most extensive example is the *Tathbīt dalā'il al-nubuwwa* written by 'Abd al-Jabbār in 995. Roggema, *The Legend of Sergius Baḥīrā*, 31. See also Gabriel Said Reynolds, 'Tathbīt dalā'il al-nubuwwa', in D. Thomas and A. Mallett (eds), *CMR* 2 (Leiden, 2010), 604–9. Of particular interest in this work is the chapter *Critique of Christian Origins*, ed. and trans. G. S. Reynolds and S. K. Samir (Provo, 2010).
51 Roggema, *The Legend of Sergius Baḥīrā*, 33. The phrase 'subterranean tradition' comes from David Biale, 'Counter-History and Jewish Polemics Against Christianity', *Jewish Social Studies* 6 (1999), 131. In this article, Biale attempts to expand the concept of counterhistory as Funkenstein defined it.
52 Ibid., 130–1; Roggema, *The Legend of Sergius Baḥīrā*, 207–8.
53 Ibid., 208.
54 For example, see the direct response to such claims in the early fourteenth century by one of the most renowned Muslim intellectuals, Ibn Taymiyya, in his *Al-jawāb al-ṣaḥīḥ li-man baddala dīn al-Masīḥ*. See Jon Hoover, 'Al-jawāb al-ṣaḥīḥ li-man baddala dīn al-Masīḥ', in D. Thomas and A. Mallett (eds), *CMR* 4 (Leiden, 2009), 834–44. His response is to a Christian letter, the *Risāla min ahl jazīrat Qubruṣ*. See David Thomas, 'The Letter from the People of Cyprus', in D. Thomas and A. Mallett (eds), *CMR* 4 (Leiden, 2012), 769–72. I analyse this letter in Chapter 8.

2 Muḥammad as a prophet of inferior monotheism

1 Quoted in Daniel J. Sahas, *John of Damascus on Islam* (Leiden, 1972), 4.
2 On George of Cyprus, see Kenneth Parry, *Depicting the Word* (Leiden, 1996), 136.

3 It is possible that John was not a monk but a priest ordained by Patriarch John V who remained in his service among the monks of the Church of the Holy Sepulchre (Church of the Anastasis) in Jerusalem. See Sidney Griffith, 'The Manṣūr Family and Saint John of Damascus', in A. Borrut and F. M. Donner (eds), *Christians and Others in the Umayyad State* (Chicago, 2016), 35. See also Peter Schadler, *John of Damascus and Islam* (Leiden, 2018), 4, 100–1.

4 Sean W. Anthony, 'Fixing John Damascene's Biography', *Journal of Early Christian Studies* 23/4 (2015), 619. See also Sidney H. Griffith, 'The Qur'an in Christian Arabic Literature', in M. Beaumont (ed.), *Arab Christians and the Qur'an from the Origins of Islam to the Medieval Period* (Leiden, 2018), 4.

5 Andrew Louth, 'John of Damascus and the Making of the Byzantine Theological Synthesis', in J. Patrich (ed.), *The Sabaite Heritage in the Orthodox Church from the Fifth Century to the Present* (Leuven, 2001), 301.

6 Anthony, 'Fixing John Damascene's Biography', 610–13.

7 Ibid., 618–22.

8 Ibid., 5; Louth, 'John of Damascus and the Making of the Byzantine Theological Synthesis', 301. 'John' was his monastic name. Sean Anthony speculates that his pre-monastic name was 'Cyrene son of Manṣūr'. See Anthony, 'Fixing John Damascene's Biography', 625–6.

9 See John's *Three Treatises on the Divine Images*, ed. and trans. A. Louth (Crestwood, 2003).

10 Anthony, 'Fixing John Damascene's Biography', 626.

11 Sidney Griffith, 'John of Damascus and the Church in Syria in the Umayyad Era', *Hugoye* 11/2 (Summer 2008), 208.

12 On the process of claiming public space, see Charles Tieszen, *Cross Veneration in the Medieval Islamic World* (London, 2017), 32–7; Sidney Griffith, 'Images, Islam and Christian Icons', in P. Canivet and J.-P. Rey-Coquais (eds), *La Syrie de Byzance à l'Islam VIIe–VIIIe siècles* (Damascus, 1992), 121–38.

13 Tieszen, *Cross Veneration*, 34; Griffith, 'John of Damascus and the Church in Syria', 209–10.

14 Anthony, 'Fixing John Damascene's Biography', 617–18.

15 Griffith, 'John of Damascus and the Church in Syria', 210–11.

16 See the edition in J. P. Migne (ed.), *Patrologia Graeca* (Paris, 1864), XCIV.521–1228.

17 Some studies give a count of 101 (or more) chapters/heresies, but as Reinhold Glei points out, these 'must be rejected for reasons of uniformity and traditional use of the "century" number'. See Reinhold F. Glei, 'John of Damascus', in D. Thomas and B. Roggema (eds), *CMR* 1 (Leiden, 2006), 297–8.

18 Sahas, *John of Damascus on Islam*, 58.

19 John of Damascus, as quoted in Frederic H. Chase, trans., *St. John of Damascus* (Washington, DC, 1958), 5.

20 Schadler, *John of Damascus and Islam*, 20–1.
21 Ibid., 6, 201–2.
22 Fergus Millar, 'Hagar, Ishmael, Josephus, and the Origins of Islam', *Journal of Jewish Studies* 44 (1993), 23–45.
23 Ibid., 39.
24 Ibid., 42.
25 Ibid., 42–6.
26 Ibid., 50–1.
27 John of Damascus, as quoted in Chase, 10. See also Schadler, *John of Damascus and Islam*, 55–6.
28 Schadler, *John of Damascus and Islam*, 53.
29 Ibid., 64.
30 Ibid., 62.
31 Ibid., 57, 60.
32 Ibid., 60–1.
33 Ibid., 93, 96.
34 Ibid., 62.
35 John B. Henderson, 'The Multiplicity, Duality, and Unity of Heresies', in W. J. van Bekkum and P. M. Cobb (eds), *Strategies of Medieval Communal Identity* (Leuven, 2004), 18–21. See also Schadler, *John of Damascus and Islam*, 47.
36 Henderson, 'The Multiplicity, Duality, and Unity of Heresies', 18.
37 John of Damascus, *Peri haireseōn*, ch. 100, ed. and trans. P. Schadler (Leiden, 2018), 218 (Greek)/219 (English translation); and D. Sahas (Leiden, 1972), 132 (Greek)/133 (English translation). Henceforth cited as John of Damascus, *Peri haireseōn*, ch. 100, 218/219 (Schadler); 132/133 (Sahas). On the reading of '*thrēskia*', see Schadler, *John of Damascus and Islam*, 89–93. It is interesting to note that chapter 100 of the *Peri haireseōn*, which begins by describing the Ishmaelites as the forerunner of the Antichrist, begins in very much the same way John ends the third and final section of the *Pēgē gnōseōs*, by addressing the Antichrist and the everlasting fire of judgement that he awaits. See John of Damascus in Chase, 406; Schadler, *John of Damascus and Islam*, 61.
38 Andrew Louth, *St John Damascene* (Oxford, 2002), 77.
39 John of Damascus, *Peri haireseōn*, ch. 100, 218/219 (Schadler); 132/133 (Sahas). For a discussion of the identity of 'Habar' and its meaning and connection to Aphrodite, see Barbara Roggema, 'Muslims as Crypto-Idolaters', in D. Thomas (ed.), *Christians at the Heart of Islamic Rule* (Leiden, 2003), 6–11.
40 John of Damascus, *Peri haireseōn*, ch. 100, 218/219 (Schadler); 132/133 (Sahas).
41 Ibid. The notion that a monk taught Muḥammad was repeated in numerous Christian sources and even appears, though for different reasons, in Muslim biographical accounts of the Prophet. John, however, is unique in labelling the

monk Arian (or 'supposedly Arian', *homoiōs areianō*). The Melkite Theodore Abū Qurrah, whose birth in the mid-eighth century would have been very near to John's death, borrowed the idea, among others, from John. Abū Qurrah was more explicit in his text about the monk's tradition and even ascribed demonic influence to Muḥammad's revelations. See his 'Refutations of the Saracens', in J. C. Lamoreaux (trans.), *Theodore Abū Qurrah* (Provo, 2005), 224–5. It may be that John and Abū Qurrah labelled the monk an Arian for rhetorical reasons, but evidence exists that they believed this to literally be the case. See Schadler, *John of Damascus and Islam*, 166–73, 197–9; Radko Popov, 'Speaking His Mind in a Multi-Cultural and Multi-Religious Society', in G. C. Papademetriou (ed.), *Two Traditions, One Space* (Boston, 2011), 119.

42 Ibid.

43 E.g. Q 20:2.

44 John of Damascus, *Peri haireseōn*, ch. 100, 218/219 (Schadler); 132/133 (Sahas).

45 Ibid., 220/221, 224/225, 226/227 (Schadler); 134/135, 136/137 (Sahas).

46 E.g. ibid., 228/229, 232/233 (Schadler); 138/139, 140/141 (Sahas).

47 Ibid., 218/219, 220/221, 232/233 (Schadler); 132/133, 134/135, 140/141 (Sahas).

48 Ibid., 228/229 (Schadler); 138/139 (Sahas).

49 'Jabir (Allah be pleased with him) declared that the Jews used to say, When a man has intercourse with his wife through the vagina but being on her back [meaning from behind her], the child will have squint, so the verse came down.' See Ṣaḥīḥ Muslim 16.138–40 (and a similar discussion with respect to menstruation in Ṣaḥīḥ Muslim 3.16). For traditions related to the wider debate, see Christopher Melchert, 'Bukhārī's *Kitāb tafsīr al-Qur'ān*', *Journal of the International Qur'anic Studies Association* 1 (2016), 161–3.

50 Ṣaḥīḥ al-Bukhārī 65.4526.

51 Melchert, 162. Cf. Ṣaḥīḥ al-Bukhārī 65.4528.

52 Radko Popov suggests that John's obscure generalization 'possibly created a critical opinion about Islam by knowing and using the Christian readers' Pauline idea of sexual sins'. See Popov, 'Speaking His Mind in a Multi-Cultural and Multi-Religious Society', 132.

53 John of Damascus, *Peri haireseōn*, ch. 100, 220/221 (Schadler); 134/135 (Sahas).

54 Ibid., 220/221–222/223 (Schadler); 134/135 (Sahas).

55 Ibid., 222/223–224/225; 134/135 (Sahas).

56 See Alfred Guillaume, trans., *The Life of Muhammad* (Karachi, 2007), 106. According to Islamic tradition, Muḥammad received his first revelation alone in the Cave of Ḥira. See Ṣaḥīḥ al-Bukhārī 1.3.

57 John of Damascus, *Peri haireseōn*, ch. 100, 222/223, 224/225 (Schadler); 134/135 (Sahas).

58 Ibid., 230/231 (Schadler); 140/141 (Sahas).

59 Schadler, *John of Damascus and Islam*, 101.
60 Sidney H. Griffith, 'Anastasios of Sinai, the *Hodegos*, and the Muslims', *Greek Orthodox Theological Review* 32/4 (1987), 341–58.
61 Griffith, 'The Qur'an in Christian Arabic Literature', 2.
62 Popov, 'Speaking His Mind in a Multi-Cultural and Multi-Religious Society', 129–34. This is a more likely explanation for the information John shares than the possibility that he simply mishandled or invented details not found in the Qur'ān. See Schadler, *John of Damascus and Islam*, 149.
63 See, e.g. John of Damascus, *Peri haireseōn*, ch. 100, 222/223–224/225 (Schadler); 134/135–136/137 (Sahas).
64 Cf. Griffith, 'The Qur'an in Christian Arabic Literature', 4.
65 Sahas, *John of Damascus on Islam*, 71–2.
66 Schadler, *John of Damascus and Islam*, 57, 212. See also David Thomas, 'With the Qur'an in Mind', in M. Beaumont (ed.), *Arab Christians and the Qur'an from the Origins of Islam to the Medieval Period* (Leiden, 2018), 148–9.
67 Schadler, *John of Damascus and Islam*, 49–50.
68 Reinhold F. Glei, 'John of Damascus', in D. Thomas and B. Roggema (eds), *CMR* 1 (Leiden, 2009), 299.

3 Muḥammad as a retrograde Moses of minimal significance

1 Recent, notable exceptions include Michael Philip Penn, *Envisioning Islam* (Philadelphia, 2015), the bibliography of which also points to further important studies. See also Penn's *When Christians First Met Muslims* (Berkeley, 2015).
2 On the genres of Christian literature originating in Islamic milieus, see Sidney Griffith, *The Church in the Shadow of the Mosque* (Princeton, 2008), 75–105.
3 The Arab is referred to in the text as a *ṭayāyā*, a term that, in the Islamic period, had come to indicate the religion of the Arabs, that is, Muslims. See David Taylor's comments in 'The Disputation between a Muslim and a Monk of Bēt Ḥālē: Syriac Text and Annotated English Translation', in S. Griffith and S. Grebenstein (eds), *Christsein in der islamischen Welt* (Wiesbaden, 2015), 204, n. 67. On the likely location of the monastery, see Taylor, 'The Disputation between a Muslim and a Monk of Bēt Ḥālē', 190.
4 The issues are summarized in Barbara Roggema, 'The Monk and the Arab Notable', in D. Thomas and B. Roggema (eds), *CMR* 1 (Leiden, 2006), 269.
5 David Taylor comes to the same conclusion (Taylor, 'The Disputation between a Muslim and a Monk of Bēt Ḥālē', 189).
6 Gerrit J. Reinink, 'Political Power and Right Religion in the East Syrian Disputation between a Monk of Bēt Ḥālē and an Arab Notable', in E. Grypeou, M. Swanson and

D. Thomas (eds), *The Encounter of Eastern Christianity with Early Islam* (Leiden, 2006), 160. The Muslim began the questioning by asserting that Islam is 'better than all the (other) religions on earth'. See Diyarbekir MS 95, fol. 267v; Taylor, 'The Disputation between a Muslim and a Monk of Bēt Ḥālē', 208.

7 Diyarbekir MS 95, fol. 267v; Taylor, 'The Disputation between a Muslim and a Monk of Bēt Ḥālē', 208.

8 Diyarbekir MS 95, fol. 274r; Taylor, 'The Disputation between a Muslim and a Monk of Bēt Ḥālē', 238.

9 Sidney Griffith, 'Disputing with Islam in Syriac', *Hugoye* 3/1 (2000), 33–5. In the account of the debate the Muslim asked why, despite their superior religion, God delivered the Christians into Muslim hands and allowed their subsequent suffering. The monk responded that it was the result of Christian wickedness. See Diyarbekir MS 95, fol. 274r; Taylor, 'The Disputation between a Muslim and a Monk of Bēt Ḥālē', 238.

10 Diyarbekir MS 95, fol. 267v; Taylor, 'The Disputation between a Muslim and a Monk of Bēt Ḥālē', 208.

11 Diyarbekir MS 95, fol. 271r; Taylor, 'The Disputation between a Muslim and a Monk of Bēt Ḥālē', 223.

12 Diyarbekir MS 95, fol. 274r; Taylor, 'The Disputation between a Muslim and a Monk of Bēt Ḥālē', 237. This is perhaps a reference by the author to Q 5:82, though the Qur'an only states that among the Christians, those nearest in affection to the believers (i.e. Muslims) are priests and monks. Later on we also learn from the monk that some of Muḥammad's teachings were found in the Qur'ān while others were found 'in the Sūrah of the Cow, and in (that of) the Spider, and in (that of) Repentance' (see Diyarbekir MS 95, fol. 272r; Taylor, 'The Disputation between a Muslim and a Monk of Bēt Ḥālē', 229). Here, the monk has either mistakenly separated what is now known as chapters 2, 29 and 9 from the Qur'ān or we have early evidence for how the chapters of the Qur'ān were collected. In addition, it may also be the case that a textual corruption, the result of many years of transmission, has obscured the fact that the monk was referring to 'the Sūrah of the Cow, and in the Gospel, and in the Torah'. See Robert G. Hoyland, *Seeing Islam as Others Saw It* (Princeton, 1997), 471–2, Griffith, 'Disputing with Islam in Syriac', 47–8. In such a case, the monk suggested that Muḥammad had taken some of his teachings from Jewish and Christian sources. For more on this, see below.

13 Diyarbekir MS 95, fol. 271r; Taylor, 'The Disputation between a Muslim and a Monk of Bēt Ḥālē', 223.

14 Ibid.

15 Ibid.

16 Diyarbekir MS 95, fol. 270v; Taylor, 'The Disputation between a Muslim and a Monk of Bēt Ḥālē', 222.

17 Ibid.

18 Gerrit J. Reinink, 'Bible and Qur'an in Early Syriac Christian-Islamic Disputation', in M. Tamcke (ed.), *Christians and Muslims in Dialogue in the Islamic Orient of the Middle Ages* (Beirut, 2007), 65.

19 Diyarbekir MS 95, fol. 271r; Taylor, 'The Disputation between a Muslim and a Monk of Bēt Ḥālē', 224. This reference to Baḥīrā is likely the earliest mention in a Christian text. See Roggema, 'The Monk and the Arab Notable', 271.

20 On discussions of religious practice, both in *The Disputation* and in wider Christian–Muslim literature, see Charles Tieszen, *Cross Veneration in the Medieval Islamic World* (London, 2017); Charles Tieszen, 'Discussing Religious Practices', in D. Pratt and C. Tieszen (eds), *CMR* 15 (Leiden, 2020).

21 Diyarbekir MS 95, fol. 274v; Taylor, 'The Disputation between a Muslim and a Monk of Bēt Ḥālē', 240.

22 Diyarbekir MS 95, fol. 274v; Taylor, 'The Disputation between a Muslim and a Monk of Bēt Ḥālē', 240–1. A similar conception appears elsewhere in the account of *The Disputation*. While defending the Christian practice of venerating icons, crosses and the bones of martyrs, the monk made several appeals to precedents from the Hebrew Bible. In one such case, the monk referred to the book of Exodus and the pillar of fire (it is a pillar of light in the account of the debate) by which God led the Israelites. He did so in order to demonstrate that God existed in types. The pillar of light functioned as a type and so it could be said that God, not merely a created thing, saved the Israelites. According to the monk's retelling of the story, the pillar gave light to the Israelites and darkness to the pursuing Egyptians. In the same manner, just as light was given to 'those of the household', a term employed in order to refer to members of the Church, so darkness was given to 'outsiders', or 'unbelievers' (Diyarbekir MS 95, fol. 271v, 273v; Taylor, 'The Disputation between a Muslim and a Monk of Bēt Ḥālē', 226–7, 235; see also Taylor's comments on 'household' in 'The Disputation between a Muslim and a Monk of Bēt Ḥālē', 226–7, n. 159). Moreover, such divine light is paralleled by the monk with the 'way of life', a term synonymous in Syriac with salvation (Diyarbekir MS 95, fol. 272r; Taylor, 'The Disputation between a Muslim and a Monk of Bēt Ḥālē', 230; Taylor, 'The Disputation between a Muslim and a Monk of Bēt Ḥālē', 230, n. 170). In this sense, a distinction was made between those who could be a part of the household – the kingdom of God – and those who, no matter how close they might be to the kingdom or how near they may reside to it, were simply not a part of the household. On the last day, the monk adjured, Christ would say to these outsiders that he does not know them (Diyarbekir MS 95, fol. 271v; Taylor, 'The Disputation between a Muslim and a Monk of Bēt Ḥālē', 227. Cf. Lk. 13:25 and Mt. 7:23).

23 Ephrem the Syrian, *Hymns on Paradise*, trans. Sebastian Brock (Crestwood, 1990), 135 (VIII.11).

24 Cf. Penn, *Envisioning Islam*, 73–4; Roggema, 'The Monk and the Arab Notable', 271.

25 Jack Tannous, *Syria between Byzantium and Islam*, PhD diss., Princeton University (2010), 407–29. See also Christian Sahner, *Christian Martyrs under Islam* (Princeton, 2018), 34–5.

26 As quoted in Sahner, *Christian Martyrs under Islam,* 34. See also Sahner, *Christian Martyrs under Islam*, 53.

27 See ibid., 78–9 for Sahner's comments on how martyrologies functioned to demonstrate the power and familiarity of *individuals* who converted to Islam and then apostatized. These comments are important clarifications on the matters of conversion and apostasy, though it is important to emphasize that what I am considering above is the nature of conversions to Islam, not the reasons for or nature of apostasy from Islam.

28 Ibid., 44.

29 See also Mark Swanson, 'Christian Perceptions of and Responses to Islam', in D. Pratt and C. Tieszen (eds), *CMR* 15 (Leiden, 2020); Fred MacGraw Donner, *Muhammad and the Believers* (Cambridge, MA, 2012).

30 Cf. Penn, *Envisioning Islam*, 115.

31 Ibid., 73–4, 112–15.

32 My thoughts here are derived, in part, from my essay, '"Can You Find Anything Praiseworthy in My Religion?"', in D. Pratt, J. Hoover, J. Davies and J. Chesworth (eds), *The Character of Christian-Muslim Encounter* (Leiden, 2015), 132–6.

33 Martin Heimgartner, 'Letter 59 (Disputation with the Caliph al-Mahdī)', in D. Thomas and B. Roggema (eds), *CMR* 1 (Leiden, 2009), 522.

34 Sidney Griffith, 'The Monk in the Emir's *Majlis*', in H. Lazarus-Yafeh, M. Cohen, S. Somekh and S. Griffith (eds), *The Majlis* (Wiesbaden, 1999), 54, 60.

35 Griffith, *The Church in the Shadow of the Mosque*, 77.

36 Heimgartner, 'Letter 59 (Disputation with the Caliph al-Mahdī)', 522–6.

37 Alphonse Mingana, 'Timothy's Apology for Christianity', in *Woodbrooke Studies: Christian Documents in Syriac, Arabic and Garshūni*, vol. 2 (Cambridge, 1928), 32.

38 Ibid., 33.

39 Ibid.

40 On the Muslim claim that the Bible predicts Muḥammad and on the connections between him and the *paraklētos* of St John's Gospel, see Sandra Toenies Keating, 'The Paraclete and the Integrity of Scripture', in C. Tieszen (ed.), *Theological Issues in Christian-Muslim Dialogue* (Eugene, 2018), 15–25.

41 Mingana, 'Timothy's Apology for Christianity', 33–5.

42 Ibid., 35. At this point, the Caliph raised the matter of *taḥrīf* and how biblical references to Muḥammad have been lost due to textual corruption. See Mingana, 'Timothy's Apology for Christianity', 35–6.

43 Ibid., 38–9.

44 Ibid., 61–2.

45 See ibid., 62 where the Caliph suggested that, in light of Timothy's assessment of Muḥammad, he 'should, therefore, accept the words of the Prophet'. The exact words of the Prophet that the Caliph referred to were 'That God is one and that there is no other one besides Him' (ibid.). But Timothy had already learned this, he claimed, in the Torah, the Prophets and the Gospel. His responses prompted a discussion of Trinitarian doctrine.

46 Ibid., 61–2.

47 Ibid., 62.

48 Ibid., 61–2.

49 David Thomas, 'Cultural and Religious Supremacy in the Fourteenth Century', *Parole de l'Orient* 30 (2005), 302–4; Samir K. Samir, 'The Prophet Muḥammad as Seen by Timothy I and Other Arab Christian Authors', in D. Thomas (ed.), *Syrian Christians under Islam* (Leiden, 2001), 93–6.

50 Penn, *Envisioning Islam*, 110.

51 Tieszen, *Cross Veneration*, 65. See also Herman G. B. Teule, 'Theodore bar Kōnī', in D. Thomas and B. Roggema (eds), *CMR* 1 (Leiden, 2009), 344.

52 Sidney H. Griffith, 'Answering the Call of the Minaret', in J. J. van Ginkel, H. L. Murre-van den Berg and T. M. van Lint (eds), *Redefining Christian Identity* (Leuven, 2005), 101–2. For a full examination of this tenth chapter, see Sidney H. Griffith, 'Chapter Ten of the *Scholion*', *Orientalia Christiana Periodica* 47 (1981), 158–88.

53 Translated by Griffith in 'Chapter Ten of the *Scholion*', 182.

54 Ibid., 183. Cf. Samir, 'The Prophet Muḥammad as Seen by Timothy I and Other Arab Christian Authors', 76.

55 Translated in Griffith, 'Chapter Ten of the *Scholion*', 183.

56 Translated in ibid., 177.

57 Sidney Griffith, 'The Prophet Muḥammad, His Scripture and His Message, According to the Christian Apologies in Arabic and Syriac from the First Abbasid Century', in T. Fahd (ed.), *La vie du Prophète Mahomet* (Paris, 1983), 121.

58 Griffith, 'Chapter Ten of the *Scholion*', 177–8. On Timothy's 'Letter 40', see Barbara Roggema, 'To Sergius, Letter 40', in D. Thomas and B. Roggema (eds), *CMR* 1 (Leiden, 2009), 519–22.

59 Cf. Patriarch Timothy I where Moses is distinguished from Muḥammad by his miracles and the fact that Muḥammad changed Moses' law (i.e. the Torah). The prophet who was like Moses did not change his law, the apparent implication being that Christ did not change the Torah but built upon it. With this in mind, Timothy asserted, 'Muḥammad is not, therefore, like unto Moses' (Mingana, 'Timothy's Apology for Christianity', 51). However, on the second day of the debate – just a

few sections after this exchange in Timothy's account – the Patriarch favourably compares Moses and Muḥammad since both of them turned their followers away from idolatry and towards pure monotheism (Mingana, 'Timothy's Apology for Christianity', 61). So there were ways, for Timothy, in which Muḥammad could be like Moses and ways in which he was decidedly not like him.

60 Ibid., 50.

61 Cf. Tieszen, '"Can You Find Anything Praiseworthy in My Religion?"'

4 Muḥammad as a carnal warrior and scheming ruler

1 See Dominique Iogna-Pratt and John Tolan, 'Peter of Cluny', in D. Thomas and A. Mallett (eds), *CMR* 3 (Leiden, 2011), 604–5.

2 Sandra Keating, 'Manipulation of the Qur'an in the Epistolary Exchange between al-Hāshimī and al-Kindī', in M. Beaumont (ed.), *Arab Christians and the Qur'an from the Origins of Islam to the Medieval Period* (Leiden, 2018), 64.

3 On the related literary issues, including the difficulty of dating the text, see Laura Bottini, 'The Apology of Al-Kindī', in D. Thomas and B. Roggema (eds), *CMR* 1 (Leiden, 2009), 585–94. See also Keating, 'Manipulation of the Qur'an in the Epistolary Exchange between al-Hāshimī and al-Kindī', 51–2 and 52, n. 5.

4 Bottini, 'The Apology of Al-Kindī', 585.

5 See Keating, 'Manipulation of the Qur'an in the Epistolary Exchange', 54. See also Samir Khalil Samir, 'La version latine de l'Apologie d'al-Kindi (vers 830 ap. J.-C) et son original arabe', in M. Penelas, P. Roisee and C. Aillet (eds), *¿Existe una identidad mozárabe?* (Madrid, 2007).

6 Keating, 'Manipulation of the Qur'an in the Epistolary Exchange', 52.

7 See Sandra Keating, 'Abū Rā'iṭa l-Takrītī', in D. Thomas and B. Roggema (eds), *CMR* 1 (Leiden, 2009), 567–81.

8 Keating, 'Manipulation of the Qur'an in the Epistolary Exchange', 52–3.

9 Bottini, 'The Apology of Al-Kindī', 588–9.

10 Al-Kindī, *Risāla*, as quoted and translated in Anton Tien, 'The Apology of Al-Kindi', in N. A. Newman (ed.), *The Early Christian-Muslim Dialogue* (Hatfield, 1993), 388. Newman has provided his own revisions to this translation based upon Tien's draft. See Bottini, 'The Apology of Al-Kindī', 590.

11 Al-Kindī, *Risāla*, 388–9.

12 Ibid., 426.

13 Ibid.

14 Ibid., 426–7, 441.

15 Ibid., 430.

16 Ibid., 439–40.

17 Ibid., 432.

18 Ibid. A. J. Wensinck lists a handful of these traditions in *A Handbook of Early Muhammadan Tradition* (Leiden, 1927), 158.

19 Ṣaḥīḥ al-Bukhārī 5.268.

20 See Ibn Sa'd, *Kitāb al-ṭabaqāt al-kabīr*, 1.1.139. But on this description and the 'religious resonance of the number' in which it takes on symbolic meaning, see D. A. Spellberg, *Politics, Gender, and the Islamic Past* (New York, 1994), 216, n. 5. See also Khaṭīb al-Taibrīzī, *Mishkāt al-Maṣābīḥ*, 4.42.24.

21 On the polemical strategy of disgust, see Alexandra Cuffel, *Gendering Disgust in Medieval Religious Polemic* (Notre Dame, 2007); William Ian Miller, *The Anatomy of Disgust* (Cambridge, MA, 1997).

22 Al-Kindī, *Risāla*, 432–3.

23 Ibid., 434–5. On the number of Muḥammad's marriages, see Clinton Bennett, *In Search of Muhammad* (London, 1998), 249–52.

24 Al-Kindī, *Risāla*, 432.

25 Ibid., 428–9.

26 Ibid., 435

27 Ibid., 429.

28 Ibid., 438–9.

29 Ibid., 441–2. The story is related in a number of Islamic traditions and told in Muḥammad's biography. See *The Life of Muhammad*, ed. A. Guillaume (Karachi, 1967), 516.

30 Al-Kindī, *Risāla*, 442.

31 Ibid., 443.

32 Ibid., 444–5.

33 Krisztina Szilágyi, 'A Prophet like Jesus?', *Jerusalem Studies in Arabic and Islam* 36 (2009), 154–9.

34 E.g., al-Kindī, *Risāla*, 432, 446, 449.

35 Ibid., 448.

36 It could also be the case that a scribe copying al-Kindī's text has inserted this interpretation. On the manuscript witness of the *Risāla*, see Bottini, 'The Apology of Al-Kindī', 589–91; P. S. van Koningsveld, 'The Apology of Al-Kindī', in T. L. Hettema and A. van der Kooij (eds), *Religious Polemics in Context* (Assen, 2004). For the Latin text, see the edition and translation by J. Yolles and J. Weiss in *Medieval Latin Lives of Muhammad* (Cambridge, MA, 2018).

37 Samir, 'The Prophet Muḥammad as Seen by Timothy I and Other Arab Christian Authors', in D. Thomas (ed.), *Syrian Christians under Islam* (Leiden, 2001), 82.

38 Al-Kindī, *Risāla*, 438. Despite al-Kindī's presentation, there was an entire genre of literature, the *dalā'il al-nubuwwa* (proofs of prophethood), which sought to robustly defend Muḥammad's prophethood. See, for example, the likely

contemporaneous *Kitāb al-dīn wa-l-dawla* (*The Book of Religion and Empire*) by the Christian convert to Islam ʿAlī l-Ṭabarī (d. 860). David Thomas, "Alī l-Ṭabarī', in D. Thomas and B. Roggema (eds), *CMR* 1 (Leiden, 2009), 672–4.

39 See van Koningsveld, 'The Apology of Al-Kindī', 83. See also ibid., 81.

40 Herman G. B. Teule, 'Dionysius bar Ṣalībī', in D. Thomas and A. Mallett (eds), *CMR* 3 (Leiden, 2011), 669. As Teule notes, the text is part of a larger series of refutations against other non-Christian and Christian communities. In this way, it may have been a part of a heresiographical work. Teule, 'Dionysius bar Ṣalībī', 667.

41 Sidney Griffith, 'Disputes with Muslims in Syriac Christian Texts', in B. Lewis and F. Niewohner (eds), *Religionsgespräche im Mittelalter* (Wiesbaden, 1992), 269. Bar Ṣalībī is also notable for his use of Islamic sources. See Bert Jacobs, 'Preliminary Considerations on Dionysius bar Ṣalībī's Islamic Sources', *Hugoye* 21/2 (2018), 357–89.

42 Teule, 'Dionysius bar Ṣalībī', 668–9.

43 Dionysius bar Ṣalībī, *A Response to the Arabs*, ed. and trans. J. P. Amar. Corpus Scriptorum Christianorum Orientalium, vols 614 (Syriac edition)/615 (English translation) (Louvain, 2005), 9/10. The deceitful Muslims were Sunnīs. Bar Ṣalībī added that they believed as Arius did since they said that the Word of God and the Spirit were created. See Dionysius bar Ṣalībī, *A Response to the Arabs*.

44 Ibid., 2/2.

45 Ibid.

46 Ibid., 2–3/3.

47 Ibid., 3–4/3–4.

48 Ibid., 75–8/67–71.

49 Ibid., 79–81/72–4.

50 Later on, Bar Ṣalībī addressed alleged appearances of Muḥammad in the Bible. For example, he disputed the notion that the figure riding on a camel in Isa. 21:7 was, according to Muslim interpretation, a foretelling of Muḥammad. See Dionysius bar Ṣalībī, *A Response to the Arabs*, 91–2/84–5. He also addressed the question of the Paraclete's identity in Dionysius bar Ṣalībī, *A Response to the Arabs*, 85–6/78–9.

51 Ibid., 84/77.

52 Ibid., 86/79.

53 Ibid., 86–7/79.

54 Ibid., 87/80.

55 Ibid.

56 Ibid., 105/97.

57 Ibid., 105–6/97.

58 Ibid., 106/97.

59 Ibid., 106/98 and translated in Barbara Roggema, *The Legend of Sergius Baḥīrā* (Leiden, 2009), 483, n. 84. Amar's translation here is not accurate: 'marriage to

seventy women? For you say [there are] seventy women for each of you; and the [genital] organ of each one of you is seventy miles [long]' (ibid., 98). Amar amends the text here to something that is less explicit.

60 See the discussion in Chapter 1.

61 Jane Idleman Smith and Yvonne Yazbeck Haddad, *The Islamic Understanding of Death and Resurrection* (Oxford, 2002), 158–68.

62 Ṣoubḥī El-Ṣaleḥ, *La vie future selon le Coran* (Paris, 1986), 38–42. See also Smith and Haddad, *The Islamic Understanding of Death and Resurrection*, 10–11, 164; Christian Lange, *Paradise and Hell in Islamic Traditions* (Cambridge, 2015).

63 See a similar line of reasoning in Szilágyi, 'A Prophet like Jesus?'

64 Dionysius bar Ṣalībī, *A Response to the Arabs*, 107/98.

65 Ibid., 106/98.

66 Michael Philip Penn asks a similar question in *Envisioning Islam* (Philadelphia, 2015), 113, but for Penn the question is why Syriac texts in general are kinder with respect to Muḥammad than non-Syriac ones. As should be clear, however, the tension exists within the world of Syriac texts (even in the eighth and ninth centuries) without having to compare them to texts in other languages and/or from other Christian traditions. Cf. Barbara Rogemma's comments in her review of *Envisioning Islam* in *Islam and Christian-Muslim Relations* 28/1 (January 2017), 117–19.

67 On demographic changes from Christianity to Islam, see Richard Bulliet, *Conversion to Islam in the Medieval Period* (Cambridge, MA, 1979); Christian Sahner, *Christian Martyrs under Islam* (Princeton, 2018); Jack Tannous, *The Making of the Medieval Middle East* (Princeton, 2018); A. C. S. Peacock, ed., *Islamisation* (Edinburgh, 2017).

68 Similarly, Jacobs notes the relationship between the increased production of apologetic and polemical literature and more distinct boundary lines between religious communities. See Jacobs, 'Preliminary Considerations on Dionysius bar Ṣalībī's Islamic Sources', 358.

5 Muḥammad as an anti-saint

1 Eulogius, *Memoriale sanctorum*, II.1.2, p. 398 and trans. John Tolan, *Saracens* (New York, 2002), 87.

2 Eulogius, *Memoriale sanctorum*, II.1.2, p. 398.

3 Cordoban clergy even convened a council in the summer of 852, which resulted in a condemnation of future martyrdom attempts. Their efforts were not successful in deterring future martyrs. See Charles Tieszen, *Christian Identity amid Islam in Medieval Spain* (Leiden, 2013), 40.

4 See Christian Sahner, *Christian Martyrs under Islam* (Princeton, 2018), 218.

5 Charles Tieszen, 'Christians under Muslim Rule, 650–1200: Christians in Muslim Spain', in David Thomas (ed.), *Routledge Handbook on Christian-Muslim Relations* (London, 2018), 76.

6 For the relevant bibliography on the martyrs, see Charles Tieszen, *Christian Identity amid Islam in Medieval Spain* (Leiden, 2013), 37–8, n. 66. See also Juan Pedro Monferrer-Sala, 'Mitografia hagiomartirial', in M. Fierro (ed.), *De muerte violenta. Política, religión y violencia en Al-Andalus* (Madrid, 2004), 415–50; Sahner, *Christian Martyrs under Islam*, 140–59. For commentary and a new translation of Eulogius' works, along with Alvarus' *vita* of Eulogius, see Kenneth Baxter Wolf, *The Eulogius Corpus* (Liverpool, 2019).

7 Jessica A. Coope, *The Martyrs of Córdoba* (Lincoln, 1995), 40–1.

8 For just a few of many examples, see Eulogius, *Memoriale sanctorum*, I.pref.1–2, pp. 366–7, I.6–7, pp. 374–6, I.20, pp. 383–5; II.2, p. 402, II.4, pp. 403–4; III.7.3, p. 444, III.12, p. 454, III.16, pp. 455–6; Eulogius, *Documentum martyriale*, 15, p. 469, 18, p. 470.

9 '*Taceam sacrilegum illud et totis catholicorum auditibus immane facinus respuendum, quod de beatissima uirgine mundi regina, sancta et uenerabili Domini et Saluatoris nostri genitrice Maria canis impurus dicere ausus est. Protestatus enim est – salua loquor reuerentia tantae uirginis – quod eius foret in saeculo uenturo ab se uiolanda uirginitas*'. Eulogius, *Memoriale sanctorum*, I.7, p. 376.

10 Quoted in Aliah Schleifer, *Mary the Blessed Virgin of Islam* (Louisville, 1997), 63.

11 Quoted in ibid., 64.

12 Kenneth Baxter Wolf, 'Eulogius of Córdoba and His Understanding of Islam'. Available at www.academia.edu/20312136/Eulogius_of_Córdoba_and_His_Understanding_of_Islam (accessed 5 February 2019), 17. See also Jane I. Smith and Yvonne Y. Haddad, 'The Virgin Mary in Islamic Tradition and Commentary', *Muslim World* 79/3–4 (July/October 1989), 161–87. Other scholars, including myself at one point, explained this claim by Eulogius as the priest's own invention. See John Tolan, *Saracens* (New York, 2002), 93; Tieszen, *Christian Identity amid Islam in Medieval Spain*, 139.

13 See Tieszen, *Christian Identity amid Islam in Medieval Spain*, 85–94.

14 See Paulus Alvarus, *Indiculus luminosus*, 21, 293–5.

15 See Tieszen, *Christian Identity amid Islam in Medieval Spain*, 87–8. For a treatment of the *Risāla*, see Chapter 4 above.

16 For more analysis on this aspect of Eulogius' and Alvarus' works, see Tieszen, *Christian Identity amid Islam in Medieval Spain*, 99–144; Kenneth Baxter Wolf, 'Muḥammad as Antichrist in Ninth-Century Córdoba', in M. D. Meyerson and E. D. English (eds), *Christians, Muslims and Jews in Medieval and Early Modern Spain* (Notre Dame, 2000).

17 John Tolan adopts the same nomenclature in reference to Embrico of Mainz's twelfth-century *Vita Mahumeti*. See Tolan's *Sons of Ishmael* (Gainesville, 2008), 1–18. For the *Vita Mahumeti*, see Julian Yolles and Jessica Weiss, eds, *Medieval Latin Lives of Muhammad* (Cambridge, MA, 2018), 24–101 and for commentary, see John Tolan, 'Embrico of Mainz', in D. Thomas and A. Mallett (eds), *CMR* 3 (Ledien, 2011), 592–5.

18 Eulogius, *Liber apologeticus martyrum*, 15, p. 483. See also Paulus Alvarus, *Vita Eulogii*, III.9, trans. and ed. C. M. Sage, *Paul Albar of Cordoba* (Washington, DC, 1943), 199–200; Eulogius, *Epistula tertia ad Wiliesindum*, 1–2, pp. 497–8. For more on the *vita* of Muḥammad, including one of its Latin manuscripts and an English translation, see Kenneth B. Wolf, 'The Earliest Latin Lives of Muḥammad', in M. Gervers and R. J. Bikhazi (eds), *Conversion and Continuity* (Toronto, 1990), 96–9. A slightly revised version of Wolf's translation appears in Yolles and Weiss, eds, *Medieval Latin Lives of Muhammad*, 2–7. See also John Tolan, 'Istoria de Mahomet', in D. Thomas and B. Roggema (eds), *CMR* 1 (Leiden, 2009), 721–2.

19 Eulogius, *Liber apologeticus martyrum*, 16, pp. 483–6. It also appears in the Codex of Roda as a part of the ninth-century *Prophetic Chronicle*, for which see Chapter 6.

20 Wolf, 'The Earliest Latin Lives of Muḥammad', 91.

21 Ibid., 16, p. 484.

22 The Cow (*al-Baqarah*) and the Spider (*al-'Ankabūt*) are chapters 2 and 29 in the Qur'ān. Chapters 27 and 7 refer to hoopoes and frogs. For the ways in which these animals were fixed by the author into the Latin Western tradition, instead of the qur'anic context, as a means for denigrating Muḥammad, see Ulisse Cecini, 'Latin Christianity Engaging the Qur'an', in D. Pratt and C. Tieszen (eds), *CMR* 15 (Leiden, 2020), 229–31.

23 Eulogius, *Liber apologeticus martyrum*, 16, p. 485.

24 '*Cumque mulier illa displicita esset in oculis Zeit et eam repudiasset, sociauit eam prophetae suo coniugium, quod ceteris in exemplum et posteris fidelibus id agree cupientibus non sit in peccatum*'. Ibid.; translated from Wolf in Yolles and Weiss, eds, *Medieval Latin Lives of Muhammad*, 7.

25 Janna Wasilewski, 'The "Life of Muhammad" in Eulogius of Córdoba', *Early Medieval Europe* 16/3 (2008), 343–5.

26 Eulogius, *Liber apologeticus martyrum*, 16, pp. 485–6.

27 Similar biographical details about Muḥammad's death appear in Petrus Alfonsi's (d. c. 1116) *Dialogi contra Iudeos*, a text for which Alfonsi depended upon al-Kindi. See Petrus Alfonsi, *Dialogi contra Iudeos* 5, pp. 162–3. For his use of al-Kindi, see Tieszen, *Christian Identity amid Islam in Medieval Spain*, 194.

28 Krisztina Szilágyi, 'A Prophet Like Jesus?', *Jerusalem Studies in Arabic and Islam* 36 (2009), 131–71. See also Franz R. Franke, 'Die freiwilligen Märtyrer von

Cordova und das Verhältnis des Mozarabes zum Islam (nach den Schriften von Speraindeo, Eulogius und Alvar)', *Spanische Forschungen der Görresgesellschaft* 13 (1953), 58–9.

29 Eulogius, *Liber apologeticus martyrum*, 16, p. 484.

30 Nicetas of Byzantium, 'Confutatio dogmatum Mahomedis', ed. J. P. Migne, in *Patrologia Graeca*, vol. 105 (Paris, 1862), 708A.

31 Ibid., 776B and 784C. See also Christos Simelidis, 'The Byzantine Understanding of the Qur'anic Term "*al-Ṣamad*" and the Greek Translation of the Qur'an', *Speculum* 86/4 (October 2011), 897–900; Daniel J. Sahas, '"Holysphyros"? A Byzantine Perception of "The God of Muhammad"', in Y. Y. Haddad and W. Z. Haddad (eds), *Christian-Muslim Encounters* (Gainesville, 1995), 109–11.

32 See Craig L. Hanson, 'Manuel I Comnenus and the "God of Muhammad"', in J. Tolan (ed.), *Medieval Christian Perceptions of Islam* (London, 2000), 63–4.

33 Christian Høgel, 'An Early Anonymous Greek Translation of the Qur'ān', *Collectanea Christiana Orientalia* 7 (2010), 73–4.

34 See John Lamoreaux, 'Refutations of the Saracens by Bishop Theodore of Ḥarrān, Called Abū Qurrah, as Reported by John the Deacon', in D. Thomas and B. Roggema (eds), *CMR* 1 (Leiden, 2009), 474–6.

35 Theodore Abū Qurrah, 'Refutation of the Saracens', in J. C. Lamoreaux (ed.), *Theodore Abū Qurrah* (Provo, 2005), 224. Lamoreaux uses a variant reading where *sphuropēktos* is read in 'Opuscula', ed. J. P. Migne, in *Patrologia Graeca*, vol. 97 (Paris, 1865), 1545C. See Simelidis, 'The Byzantine Understanding of the Qur'anic Term "*al-Ṣamad*" and the Greek Translation of the Qur'an', 912–13.

36 Peter Schadler, *John of Damascus and Islam* (Leiden, 2018), 205–6; Simelidis, 'The Byzantine Understanding of the Qur'anic Term *"al-Ṣamad"* and the Greek Translation of the Qur'an', 889–90, 893–5.

37 See John of Seville, 'Item epistola Ioannis Spalensis Albaro directa', 9, pp. 200–1.

38 '*Direximus uobis illam adnotatjonem Mammetis heretici*'. Ibid., 8, p. 200.

39 Ann Christys, *Christians in Al-Andalus,* (London, 2002), 63–4.

40 Edward P. Colbert, *The Martyrs of Córdoba*, PhD dissertation, The Catholic University of America (1962), 156–7.

41 John of Seville, 'Item epistola Ioannis Spalensis Albaro directa', 9, pp. 200–1. Translation adapted from Robert G. Hoyland, *Seeing Islam as Others Saw It* (Princeton, 1997), 513.

42 Abū Ja'far Muḥammad ibn Jarīr al-Ṭabarī, *Tārīkh al-rusul wa-l-mulūk*, vol. 8, trans. M. Fishbein (New York, 1997), 1–4.

43 According to one tradition, after Muḥammad had seen Zaynab she was inexplicably made unattractive to other men. In this way, Muḥammad's marriage to her was a welcome event after Zayd divorced her. See al-Ṭabarī, *Tārīkh al-rusul wa-l-mulūk*, vol. 8, 4.

44 John of Damascus, *Peri haireseōn*, ch. 100, ed. and trans. P. Schadler (Leiden, 2018), 228 (Greek)/229 (English translation); and D. Sahas (Leiden, 1972), 138 (Greek)/139 (English translation).
45 Al-Kindī, *Risāla*, as quoted and translated in Anton Tien, 'The Apology of Al-Kindi', in N. A. Newman (ed.), *The Early Christian-Muslim Dialogue* (Hatfield, 1993), 432–3.
46 For some consideration of how Christians viewed marriage in Islamic milieus where marriage and family life could be viewed differently, see Lev E. Weitz, *Between Christ and Caliph* (Philadelphia, 2018). See also Kecia Ali, *The Lives of Muhammad* (Cambridge, MA, 2014), 114–54.
47 See David Powers, *Muḥammad Is Not the Father of Any of Your Men* (Philadelphia, 2009), 39–40, 48, 271 n. 40.
48 See, e.g. Ibn Sa'd, *Kitāb al-ṭabaqāt al-kabīr*, 1.1, p. 124. See also Hoyland, *Seeing Islam as Others Saw It*, 513, n. 208.
49 Tolan uses this term in his 'A Life of Muḥammad from Fifteenth-Century Spain', *Jerusalem Studies in Arabic and Islam* 36 (2009), 425–38.

6 Muḥammad as a tainted vessel of Christ

1 '*ab hominibus Deum colentibus et caelestia lura fatentibus compendiosa morte perempti sunt*'. Eulogius, *Liber apologeticus martyrum*, 3, pp. 477–8. See also ibid., 12, pp. 481–2.
2 George, a monk from Jerusalem who travelled to Spain and became a martyr, described Muḥammad, according to Eulogius' account, as a 'disciple of Satan' (*discipulo Satanae*). See Eulogius, *Memoriale sanctorum*, II.10.33, p. 430.
3 For Bishop Saul's letter, see *Item rescriptum Sauli Episcopi Albaro directum*, pp. 222–4. Also, see the analysis in Christian Sahner, *Christian Martyrs under Islam* (Princeton, 2018), 220; Charles Tieszen, *Christian Identity amid Islam in Medieval Spain*, (Leiden, 2013), 147–68.
4 See John Tolan, 'Tultusceptru de libro domni Metobii', in D. Thomas and A. Mallett (eds), *CMR* 2 (Leiden, 2010), 83–4.
5 See Ann Christys, *Christians in Al-Andalus* (London, 2002), 63. Osius was a controversial figure for his temporary affirmation of Arianism, but this need not inform his appearance in the 'Tultusceptru' since he was a generally well-known cleric, especially in Iberia. As such, it is not necessarily remarkable that he appears in the 'Tultusceptru' outside of the author's apparent attempt to root his *vita* in the lore of Iberian ecclesiastical history.
6 'Tultusceptru de libro domni Metobii', in J. Yolles and J. Weiss (eds), *Medieval Latin Lives of Muhammad* (Cambridge, MA, 2018), 10–11. This is a slightly

revised version of Kenneth Baxter Wolf's translation in 'The Earliest Latin Lives of Muḥammad', in M. Gervers and R. J. Bikhazi (eds), *Conversion and Continuity* (Toronto, 1990), 99–100.

7 'Tultusceptru', 10–11. At the first mention of the young monk's name the author wrote 'Ocim', but all subsequent references appear as 'Ozim'.

8 'Tultusceptru', 10–11. Intriguingly, one of the Cordoban martyrs, a monk named George who had travelled to Spain from Jerusalem, claimed in his denunciation of Muḥammad that 'the angel that appeared to your teacher and was transfigured into a spirit of light … was a demon' ('*illum angelum, qui eidem praeceptori uestro transfigurando se in spiritum lucis apparuit, daemonem credo fuisse*'). See Eulogius, *Memoriale sanctorum*, II.10.33, p. 430. But George went on to insult Muḥammad in very blatant terms: he was not only a disciple of Satan, as I point out in note 2 above, but also a servant of the Antichrist who was loyal to the devil (see Eulogius, *Memoriale sanctorum*, II.10.33, p. 430).

9 'Tultusceptru', 10–13.

10 Ibid., 12–13.

11 Ibid.

12 Ibid.

13 Ibid.

14 See chapters 109 and 23, respectively. Besides these two chapters, see, e.g. Q 3:28 for language relatively similar to that which the author of the 'Tultusceptru' employed.

15 See 'The Syriac Apocalypse of Pseudo-Methodius', trans. P. J. Alexander in *The Byzantine Apocalyptic Tradition* (Berkeley, 1985), 38. See also Benjamin Z. Kedar, *Crusade and Mission* (Princeton, 1984), 29 and Kenneth Baxter Wolf, 'Christian Views of Islam in Early Medieval Spain', in J. Tolan (ed.), *Medieval Christian Perceptions of Islam* (London, 1996), 101.

16 See the *Prophetic Chronicle*, 187r (viewable at http://bibliotecadigital.rah.es/dgbrah/i18n/catalogo_imagenes/grupo.cmd?path=1000124&presentacion=pagina&posicion=375&registrardownload=0). See also 'La crónica profética', ed. Manuel Gómez Moreno, in 'Las primeras crónicas de la Reconquista', *Boletín de la Real Academia de la Historia* 100 (1932), p. 624 and Wolf, 'Christian Views of Islam in Early Medieval Spain', 101.

17 Wolf also identifies a few of these shared features in his 'Counterhistory in the Earliest Latin Lives of Muhammad', in C. Gruber and A. Shalem (eds), *The Image of the Prophet between Ideal and Ideology* (Berlin, 2014), 22.

18 See Barbara Roggema, *The Legend of Sergius Baḥīrā* (Leiden, 2009), 298–301, 318–19.

19 See ibid., 301, n. 104 and Charles Tieszen, *Cross Veneration in the Medieval Islamic World* (London, 2017), 47. Alvarus also included a similar accusation in his

Indiculus luminosus, 25. See the related discussion in Tieszen, *Christian Identity amid Islam in Medieval Spain* (Leiden, 2013), 89.

20 See Roggema, 40–1, 47.

21 'Tultusceptru', 10–11.

22 Baxter's argument appears in 'The Earliest Latin Lives of Muḥammad', 95–6; 'Christian Views of Islam in Early Medieval Spain', 101–2; and 'Counterhistory in the Earliest Latin Lives of Muhammad', 22–6. For a similar argument applied to a different set of texts, see Charles Tieszen, '"Can You Find Anything Praiseworthy in My Religion?"', in D. Pratt, J. Hoover, J. Davies and J. Chesworth (eds), *The Character of Christian-Muslim Encounter* (Leiden, 2015).

23 Wolf, 'Counterhistory in the Earliest Latin Lives of Muhammad', 23.

24 Ibid.

25 Ibid., 24.

26 Ibid., 24–5.

27 See Zacarías García Villada, 'El códice de Roda recuperado', *Revista de Filología Española* 15 (1928), pp. 113–30; José María Lacarra, 'Textos navarros del Códice de Roda', *Estudios de edad media de la Corona de Aragón* 1 (1945), pp. 194–283; idem, 'Las geneaologías del Códice de Roda', *Medievalia* 10 (1992), pp. 213–16; and Helena de Carlos Villamarín, 'El Códice de Roda (Madrid, BRAH 78) como compilación de voluntad historiográfica', *Edad media: revista de historia* 12 (2011), pp. 119–42.

28 John Tolan, *Saracens* (New York, 2002), 98–9. See also Wolf, 'Counterhistory in the Earliest Latin Lives of Muhammad', 26, n. 50.

7 Muḥammad as a vanquished anti-hero

1 *Liber denudationis*, ed. and trans T. Burman (Leiden, 1994), 11.6, 368–9.

2 Ibid., 1.2, pp. 240–3.

3 David Thomas, "Alī l-Tabarī', in D. Thomas and B. Roggema (eds), *CMR* 1 (Leiden, 2009), 669. See also David Thomas, 'Conversion out of Principle', in A. C. S. Peacock (ed.), *Islamisation* (Edinburgh, 2017).

4 Mark N. Swanson, 'Būluṣ ibn Rajā'', in D. Thomas and A. Mallett (eds), *CMR* 2 (Leiden, 2010), 541–5. See also David Bertaina, 'Būluṣ ibn Rajā' on the History and Integrity of the Qur'ān', in M. Beaumont (ed.), *Arab Christians and the Qur'an from the Origins of Islam to the Medieval Period* (Leiden, 2018), 174–95. For more on conversion from and/or to Islam, see Richard Bulliet, *Conversion to Islam in the Medieval Period* (Cambridge, Massachusetts, 1979); Richard Bulliet, 'The Conversion Curve Revisited', in A. C. S. Peacock (ed.), *Islamisation* (Edinburgh, 2017), 69–79; Clint Hackenburg, *Voices of the Converted*, PhD dissertation, Ohio

State University (2015); and Christian Sahner, 'Swimming against the Current', *Journal of the American Oriental Society* 136/2 (April–June 2016), 265–84.

5 See Thomas E. Burman, *Religious Polemic and the Intellectual History of the Mozarabs, c. 1050–1200* (Leiden, 1994), 47–9, 55–62 and 225–8. See also Charles Tieszen, *Christian Identity amid Islam in Medieval Spain* (Leiden, 2013), 172–4.

6 Thomas Burman, 'Ramon Martí', in D. Thomas and A. Mallett (eds), *CMR* 4 (Leiden, 2012), 381–90.

7 Thomas Burman, 'Riccoldo da Monte di Croce', in D. Thomas and A. Mallett (eds), *CMR* 4 (Leiden, 2012), 689, 678–91.

8 Harvey Hames, 'Ramon Llull', in D. Thomas and A. Mallett (eds), *CMR* 4 (Leiden, 2012), 703–17.

9 See Burman, *Religious Polemic*, 46–9.

10 See ibid., 54–5.

11 *Liber denudationis*, 2.3, pp. 246–8. See also Burman, *Religious Polemic*, 49–50.

12 Sometimes referred to as 'Mozarabs' (from the Arabic *musta'rib* or *musta'rab*, meaning to make oneself like the Arabs or having assimilated Arab customs), Arabized Christian communities spoke Arabic and had adopted Arab cultural practices. In many ways, they were indistinguishable from Muslim communities in medieval Spain. The term is, nevertheless, a problematic one with reference to such communities that were actually quite diverse. See, in general, Tieszen, *Christian Identity amid Islam in Medieval Spain*, 15–16, but for more focused studies see especially Cyrille Aillet, *Les Mozarabes* (Madrid, 2010); Richard Hitchcock, *Mozarabs in Medieval and Early Modern Spain* (Hampshire, 2008).

13 *Liber denudationis*, 9.23, pp. 332–3. The author wrote that 'we are already in the fourth century' from Muḥammad's prediction that the earth's living creatures would pass away before 100 years. We arrive at a date between 1010 and 1132 if we assume that the Prophet said this within his prophetic career (c. 610–632) and add his 100 years plus the author's four centuries. See Tieszen, *Christian Identity amid Islam in Medieval Spain*, 172–3.

14 On the text's date and other issues of provenance, see Burman, *Religious Polemic*, 46–49, 215–29; Tieszen, *Christian Identity amid Islam in Medieval Spain*, 172–3.

15 For more on the text's audience, see Tieszen, *Christian Identity amid Islam in Medieval Spain*, 177–9.

16 I am grateful for David Bertaina who told me about his discovery of the connection between Ibn Rajā' and the *Liber denudationis*. He also shared with me his forthcoming Arabic edition and English translation of the *Kitāb al-Wāḍiḥ bi-l-Ḥaqq* and his forthcoming article, 'The Arabic Version of the *Liber denudationis*'.

17 Cf. n. 13 above. The relevant material for the date in the *Kitāb al-Wāḍiḥ bi-l-Ḥaqq* appears in 18.147.

18 Būluṣ ibn Rajā', *Kitāb al-Wāḍiḥ bi-l-Ḥaqq*, 1.12.

19 Compare ibid., 27.205–28.206 and *Liber denudationis*, 11.6, pp. 368–71.

20 Juan Pedro Monferrer-Sala, 'Conduits of Interaction. The Andalusi Experience', in D. Pratt and C. Tieszen (eds), *CMR* 15 (Leiden, 2020), 310–11. See also Bertaina, 'Arabic Versions of the *Liber Denudationis*'.

21 *Liber denudationis*, 1.2, pp. 242–3 and Ibn Rajā', *Kitāb al-Wāḍiḥ bi-l-Ḥaqq*, [Introduction].4.

22 *Liber denudationis*, 3.1, pp. 250–1 and Ibn Rajā', *Kitāb al-Wāḍiḥ bi-l-Ḥaqq*, 2.16–23.

23 *Liber denudationis*, 3.2, pp. 252–3. Ibn Rajā' is less explicit, though he did label the claims of the Qur'an 'lies' (*kadhab*) and referred to the way in which Muḥammad claimed to have been informed of such matters from God.

24 This is the language of the *Liber denudationis* (3.4, pp. 254–5), though the same argument appears in the *Kitāb al-Wāḍiḥ bi-l-Ḥaqq* (2.19–20).

25 *Liber denudationis*, 3.5, pp. 256–7.

26 To illustrate this, the texts employed the metaphor of a king who, before setting out, will send his messengers in order to announce his future arrival (ibid., 3.5, pp. 258–9; Ibn Rajā', *Kitāb al-Wāḍiḥ bi-l-Ḥaqq*, 2.23). The use of such king metaphors was common in Eastern Christian disputational literature, which itself drew upon patristic rhetoric. See Charles Tieszen, *Cross Veneration in the Medieval Islamic World* (London, 2017), 25–6 (and throughout); Barbara Roggema, 'Ḥikāyāt amthal wa-asmār. King Parables in Melkite Apologetic Literature', in R. Ebied and H. Teule (eds), *Studies on the Christian Arabic Heritage* (Leuven, 2004), 113–31.

27 The remark concerning miracles in this argument appears only in the *Liber denudationis* (3.5, pp. 256–7. See also 12.8–9, pp. 382–3).

28 *Liber denudationis*, 4.1, pp. 260–1 and Ibn Rajā', *Kitāb al-Wāḍiḥ bi-l-Ḥaqq*, 3.24–41.

29 *Liber denudationis*, 4.1, pp. 260–1 and Ibn Rajā', *Kitāb al-Wāḍiḥ bi-l-Ḥaqq*, 3.24–6. For the Islamic traditions, see Ṣaḥīḥ Muslim 1.34, Ṣaḥīḥ al-Bukhārī 23.1, which attribute the tradition to Abū Dharr (not, as was specifically mentioned in the text, Abū al-Dardā'; besides the similarity of their names, they were both companions of the Prophet, so the mistaken attribution is understandable).

30 *Liber denudationis*, 4.2, pp. 260–3 and Ibn Rajā', *Kitāb al-Wāḍiḥ bi-l-Ḥaqq*, 3.41.

31 *Liber denudationis*, 4.3, pp. 264–5 and Ibn Rajā', *Kitāb al-Wāḍiḥ bi-l-Ḥaqq*, 4.42–7.

32 See Bertaina, 'The Arabic Version of the *Liber Denudationis*'.

33 *Liber denudationis*, 4.3, pp. 264–5. These were the scribe's words, though the same argument appears in Ibn Rajā', *Kitāb al-Wāḍiḥ bi-l-Ḥaqq*, 6.50–7.

34 *Liber denudationis*, 4.4, pp. 264–5 and Ibn Rajā', *Kitāb al-Wāḍiḥ bi-l-Ḥaqq*, 6.51.

35 Cf. Ṣaḥīḥ al-Bukhārī 66.2 and Burman, 265, n. 2.

36 *Liber denudationis*, 4.5, pp. 266–7 and Ibn Rajā', *Kitāb al-Wāḍiḥ bi-l-Ḥaqq*, 6.52.

37 See Ṣaḥīḥ al-Bukhārī 1.2 and Ṣaḥīḥ Muslim 43.116–19.

38 *Liber denudationis*, 4.7, pp. 268–9. Cf. Ibn Rajā', *Kitāb al-Wāḍiḥ bi-l-Ḥaqq*, 6.51–2. On the accusation that Muḥammad had epilepsy, likely originating

with Theophanes the Confessor (d. 818) in his *Chronographia*, see Andrea Celli, '"Maometto cascava del male caduco"', in A. Barbieri (ed.), *Eroi dell'estasi* (Verona, 2017), 239–62. See also Błażej Cecota, 'Islam, the Arabs and Umayyad Rulers according to Theopanes the Confessor's Chronography', *Studia Ceranea* 2 (2012), p. 99.

39 *Liber denudationis*, 4.6, pp. 266–9 and Ibn Rajā', *Kitāb al-Wāḍiḥ bi-l-Ḥaqq*, 6.54.

40 *Liber denudationis*, 4.7, pp. 268–9. Cf. Ibn Rajā', *Kitāb al-Wāḍiḥ bi-l-Ḥaqq*, 6.54.

41 *Liber denudationis*, 12.7, pp. 382–3 and Ibn Rajā', *Kitāb al-Wāḍiḥ bi-l-Ḥaqq*, 30.229.

42 *Liber denudationis*, 4.7, pp. 268–9.

43 Tieszen, *Cross Veneration*, 44. As I discuss there, these authors also use the Black Stone in order to explain the Christian practice of venerating crosses. Muslims could hardly accuse Christians of worshiping the cross in light of the posture they took towards the Black Stone.

44 *Liber denudationis*, 11.2, pp. 366–7 and Ibn Rajā', *Kitāb al-Wāḍiḥ bi-l-Ḥaqq*, 26.197.

45 *Liber denudationis*, 11.2, pp. 366–7 and Ibn Rajā', *Kitāb al-Wāḍiḥ bi-l-Ḥaqq*, 26.197.

46 M.J. Kister, 'Ādam: A Study of Some Legends in *Tafsīr* and *Ḥadīth* Literature', in J. Kraemer (ed.), *Israel Oriental Studies*, vol. XIII (Leiden, 1993), 159; Ibn Qutaybah, *Ta'wīl mukhtalif al-ḥadīth*, trans. Che Amnah Bahari (Malaysia, 2009), 284.

47 Ibn Rajā', *Kitāb al-Wāḍiḥ bi-l-Ḥaqq*, 26.196–204.

48 *Liber denudationis*, 11.4, pp. 366–7.

49 Much of the material from *Liber denudationis* 8 appears to be drawn from Ibn Rajā', *Kitāb al-Wāḍiḥ bi-l-Ḥaqq*, 15.109–17.131.

50 *Liber denudationis*, 8.2–4, pp. 296–9.

51 Ibid., 8.5, pp. 300–1.

52 Ibid.

53 Ibid.

54 *Liber denudationis*, 8.5, pp. 300–1 (see also 3.4, 256–7) and Ibn Rajā', *Kitāb al-Wāḍiḥ bi-l-Ḥaqq*, 17.126–7.

55 *Liber denudationis*, 7.9–10, pp. 288–91 and Ibn Rajā', *Kitāb al-Wāḍiḥ bi-l-Ḥaqq*, 14.105–8.

56 *Liber denudationis*, 7.1–8, pp. 280–9 and Ibn Rajā', *Kitāb al-Wāḍiḥ bi-l-Ḥaqq*, 12.96–100.

57 As Burman explains, the confusion likely occurs because the scribe who translated the text from Arabic to Latin applied the term 'Jacobite', commonly used to refer to non-Chalcedonian, Miaphysite communities like the Copts, in light of the Arabic epithet (*al-qubṭiyah*) that usually accompanies her name. See Burman, *Religious Polemic*, 281n2.

58 *Liber denudationis*, 7.1, pp. 280–1 and Ibn Rajā', *Kitāb al-Wāḍiḥ bi-l-Ḥaqq*, 12.96–100.

59 See Burman, *Religious Polemic*, 283, n. 2.

60 *Liber denudationis*, 7.2, pp. 282–3.
61 *Liber denudationis*, 9, pp. 304–337 and Ibn Rajā', *Kitāb al-Wāḍiḥ bi-l-Ḥaqq*, 18.132–53.
62 *Liber denudationis*, 9.18, pp. 326–7. Cf. Ibn Rajā', *Kitāb al-Wāḍiḥ bi-l-Ḥaqq*, 18.142.
63 Tieszen, *Christian Identity amid Islam in Medieval Spain*, 258–9. See also Aziz al-Azmeh, 'Rhetoric for the Senses', *Journal of Arabic Literature* xxvi (1995), 215–31.
64 Ibn Rajā', *Kitāb al-Wāḍiḥ bi-l-Ḥaqq*, 18.143.
65 *Liber denudationis*, 9.20, pp. 328–9. Cf. Ibn Rajā', *Kitāb al-Wāḍiḥ bi-l-Ḥaqq*, 18.143.
66 *Liber denudationis*, 9.20, pp. 328–9.
67 Ibn Rajā', *Kitāb al-Wāḍiḥ bi-l-Ḥaqq*, 18.143.
68 *Liber denudationis*, 9.20, pp. 328–31.
69 Ibn Rajā', *Kitāb al-Wāḍiḥ bi-l-Ḥaqq*, 18.143.
70 See the discussion in Chapter 1 (for Baḥīrā) and Chapter 4 (for Bar Ṣalībī).
71 Paulus Alvarus, *Indiculus luminosus*, 23. Here, Alvarus draws upon Old Testament references (Ezek. 23.20 and Jer. 5.8) in order to make the lude accusation that Muslims were 'lustful horses or donkeys that bray' (*amissarii equi innientes seu rudentes asini*) and, just like Muḥammad, their genitals were like a donkey's and their ejaculation was like that of a horse. The comments are more explicit than the ones made by al-Kindī (see the discussion in Chapter 4), but they are similar insofar as they attribute animal-like characteristics to Muslim sexual anatomy and stamina. For a discussion of Alvarus, see Chapter 5.
72 *Liber denudationis*, 9.21, pp. 330–1 and Ibn Rajā, *Kitāb al-Wāḍiḥ bi-l-Ḥaqq*, 18.143.
73 E.g. texts such as Abū Ja'far Muḥammad al-Ṭabarī's (d. 923) *Tafsīr al-Qur'ān* drew upon a number of intellectuals including al-Ḥasan al-Baṣrī in order to explain Q 36:55, but without the details given in the *Kitāb al-Wāḍiḥ bi-l-Ḥaqq* or the *Liber denudationis*. Other sources, particularly *ṣifat al-jannah* literature, explain the passage as unmistakably describing sexual activity. See Waleed Ahmed, 'The Characteristics of Paradise (*Ṣifat al-Janna*)', in S. Günther and T. Lawson (eds), *Roads to Paradise*, vol. 2 (Leiden, 2017), 831.
74 Ibn Rajā', *Kitāb al-Wāḍiḥ bi-l-*Ḥaqq, 6.56 and Liber *denudationis*, 5.1, pp. 270–1.
75 As I noted in Chapters 1 (Baḥīrā) and 4 (Bar Ṣalībī), respectively, the long Arabic recension of the Baḥīrā legend referred to the generic physical dimensions of the houris (see *The Legend of Sergius Baḥīrā*, 482–3) and Bar Ṣalībī offered more specific and graphic detail (see Dionysius bar Ṣalībī, *A Response to the Arabs* 106/98).
76 This can be seen with regard to physical and sexual dimensions, but also with respect to divine punishment, for example, in al-Baghawī's (d. 1122) *Maṣābīḥ al-Sunnah* where 'the infidel takes 70 years to climb' a mountain. See Ṣoubḥi El-Ṣaleḥ, *La vie future selon le Coran* (Paris, 1986), 156. See also al-Azmeh, 228–9.

77 Maher Jarrar, 'Strategies for Paradise', in S. Günther and T. Lawson (eds), *Roads to Paradise*, vol. 1 (Leiden, 2017), 285. A similar theme in *ḥadīth* literature exists for descriptions of trees. In one example (e.g. Ṣaḥīḥ Muslim 53.7–9), a tree is so large that one can travel beneath it for a hundred years. See Roberto Tottoli, 'Muslim Eschatology and the Ascension of the Prophet Muḥammad: Describing Paradise in *Mi'rāj* Traditions and Literature', in S. Günther and T. Lawson (eds), *Roads to Paradise: Eschatology and Concepts of the Hereafter in Islam*, vol. 2, (Leiden, 2017), 869. See also a similar discussion among Muslims with respect to God's appearance, which, among those willing to reflect on this anthropomorphic matter, was assumed to be enormous. See Josef van Ess, *Theology and Society in the Second and Third Centuries of the Hijra*, vol. 4 (Leiden, 2018), 424–5, 442–3.

78 Jarrar, 'Strategies for Paradise', 285. See also Christian Lange, *Paradise and Hell in Islamic Traditions* (Cambridge, 2016), 138–9 and his discussion of horses in Paradise, the descriptions of which are exaggerated and fanciful, much like other animals such as birds that are as large as mules and covered with seventy thousand feathers.

79 See, e.g. Jalāl al-Dīn al-Suyūṭī, *Al-Budūr al-sāfira fī aḥwāl al-ākhira*, ed. M. al-Shāfi'ī (Beirut, 1996), 599. Many thanks to Juan Pedro Monferrer-Sala and Christian Lange who, in separate conversations, have helped me to sort out much of the references to the afterlife and connected issues here.

80 Burman, *Religious Polemic*, 329, n. 8.

81 Ṣaḥīḥ Muslim 53.63.

82 See *The Legend of Sergius Baḥīrā*, 482–3 and the discussion in Chapter 1.

83 *Liber denudationis*, 4.4, pp. 264–5 and Ibn Rajā', *Kitāb al-Wāḍiḥ bi-l-Ḥaqq*, 6.51.

84 E.g. *Sunan Abī Dāwūd*, 11.1723–5, 2036 and *Muwaṭṭā Mālik*, 9.340–1, 344–5.

85 *Liber denudationis*, 9.20–1, pp. 328–31 and Ibn Rajā', *Kitāb al-Wāḍiḥ bi-l-Ḥaqq*, 18.144. Ibn Rajā' only mentioned John the son of Zechariah, whom he described as the best of the prophets and the final one; the *Liber denudationis* added Elijah, Daniel and Jeremiah.

86 *Liber denudationis*, 10, pp. 338–9 and Ibn Rajā', *Kitāb al-Wāḍiḥ bi-l-Ḥaqq*, 19.154–157.

87 *Liber denudationis*, 10.1, pp. 338–9 and Ibn Rajā', *Kitāb al-Wāḍiḥ bi-l-Ḥaqq*, 19.156.

88 *Liber denudationis*, 10.2, pp. 338–9 and Ibn Rajā', *Kitāb al-Wāḍiḥ bi-l-Ḥaqq*, 19.157.

89 *Liber denudationis*, 10.5–6, pp. 343–5. Cf. Ibn Rajā', *Kitāb al-Wāḍiḥ bi-l-Ḥaqq*, 19.156 and 20.159.

90 *Liber denudationis*, 10.6, pp. 344–5 and Ibn Rajā', *Kitāb al-Wāḍiḥ bi-l-Ḥaqa*, 20.162.

91 *Liber denudationis*, 10.7, pp. 344–7 and Ibn Rajā', *Kitāb al-Wāḍiḥ bi-l-Ḥaqq*, 20.159.

92 *Liber denudationis*, 10.7, pp. 346–7. Cf. Ibn Rajā', *Kitāb al-Wāḍiḥ bi-l-Ḥaqq*, 20.159.

93 *Liber denudationis*, 10.5–6, pp. 343–5. The *Kitāb al-Wāḍiḥ bi-l-Ḥaqq* included a discussion of Christ's miraculous birth (21.168–22.178), but not in the same way as it appears in this section of the *Liber denudationis*.

94 *Liber denudationis*, 10.13, pp. 354–5 and Ibn Rajā', *Kitāb al-Wāḍiḥ bi-l-Ḥaqq*, 21.170.

95 *Liber denudationis*, 10.13, pp. 354–5 and Ibn Rajā', *Kitāb al-Wāḍiḥ bi-l-Ḥaqq*, 21.169–71. Instead of 'clay', Ibn Rajā' has 'dust' (*turābā*).

96 Intriguingly, Muḥammad is portrayed in the exact opposite manner by Thomas Carlyle (d. 1881) in his *On Heroes, Hero-Worship and the Heroic in History* (London, 1897), 42–77, where he affirms Muḥammad's prophethood.

97 Thomas Burman, 'Riccoldo da Monte di Croce', in D. Thomas and A. Mallett (eds), *CMR* 4 (Leiden, 2012), 688–9.

98 Ibid., 689.

99 For more on Luther and Islam, see Adam S. Francisco, *Martin Luther and Islam* (Leiden, 2007).

100 Thomas C. Pfotenhauer, *Islam in the Crucible* (Kearney, 2002).

8 Muḥammad as a powerless Prophet to the Arabs

1 Paul of Antioch, *Letter to a Muslim Friend*, trans. S. Griffith in S. Noble and A. Treiger (eds), *The Orthodox Church in the Arab World* (DeKalb, 2014), 220. A partial Arabic edition that corresponds to *The Letter from the People of Cyprus* (more on this text below) appears in Rifaat Ebied and David Thomas, *Muslim-Christian Polemic during the Crusades* (Leiden, 2005), 54–146. An Arabic edition and French translation appear in Paul Khoury, *Paul d'Antioche évêque Melkite de Sidon (XIIe s.)* (Beyrouth, 1964), 59–83 (Arabic) and 169–87 (French).

2 See David Thomas, 'Paul of Antioch', in D. Thomas and A. Mallett (eds), *CMR* 4 (Leiden, 2012), 80. See also David Thomas, 'Paul of Antioch's *Letter to a Muslim Friend* and *the Letter from Cyprus*', in D. Thomas (ed.), *Syrian Christians under Islam* (Leiden, 2001), 203–4; Samir Khalil Samir, 'Notes sur la "Lettre à un Musulman de Sidon" de Paul d'Antioche', *Orientalia Lovaniensia Periodica* 24 (1993), 180–90.

3 Alexander Treiger argues that the recipient of some of Paul's other treatises was a sheikh named Abū l-Surūr al-Tinnīsī. He suggests the same sheikh may have been the Muslim friend to whom Paul wrote the letter under discussion here, though such a conclusion cannot be certain. See Alexander Treiger, 'Paul of Antioch's *Responses to a Muslim Sheikh*', in D. Bertaina, S. Keating, M. Swanson and A. Treiger (eds), *Heirs of the Apostles* (Leiden, 2018), 336–7.

4 Paul of Antioch, *Letter to a Muslim Friend*, 220. On the Christian use in Arabic texts of *'alayhi al-salām* ('peace be upon him') as an honorific in reference to Muḥammad, see Samir Khalil Samir, 'The Prophet Muḥammad as Seen by Timothy I and Other Arab Christian Authors', in D. Thomas (ed.), *Syrian Christians*

under Islam (Leiden, 2001), 91. It conforms to Muslim usage, but does not imply conformity to Muslim views of the Prophet.

5 Paul of Antioch, *Letter to a Muslim Friend*, 220.

6 Ibid.

7 Ibid., 220–1.

8 Ibid., 221. For the Arabic, see Khoury, *Lettre aux Musulmans*, 61. Even before Paul of Antioch, it was common among Jewish and Christian authors to base the validity of a prophet on his message being heard in different languages and among different nations. See Sidney Griffith, 'The Gospel in Arabic', *Oriens Christianus* 69 (1985), 165; Camilla Adang, *Muslim Writers on Judaism and the Hebrew Bible* (Leiden, 1996), 163–5. Muslim intellectuals spent a great deal of time addressing this point in defence of Muḥammad. Ibn Qutayba (d. 889), for example, argued that the miraculous nature of the Qur'ān, which made its translation impossible, was part of its superiority to other divine revelations like the Gospel or the Torah. See Adang, *Muslim Writers on Judaism and the Hebrew Bible*, 169–70.

9 Thomas, 'Paul of Antioch's *Letter to a Muslim Friend* and *The Letter from Cyprus*', 207.

10 Cf. the remarks made about *The Letter from the People of Cyprus* (more on which below) by David Thomas, 'Cultural and Religious Supremacy in the Fourteenth Century', *Parole de l'Orient* (2005), 320.

11 According to the *shahādah*, the central Islamic creed, Muḥammad is the *rasūlu llāh*, the messenger of God. More than just a prophet (*nabī*), Muḥammad was the Seal of the Prophets (*khātam al-nabīyīn*) and God's Final Messenger (*rasūl*) sent with a final revelation.

12 A *dhimmī* was a non-Muslim, usually a monotheist, member of the *ahl-al-dhimmah* who was governed according to *dhimmah* regulations. These regulations developed over time, varied greatly and were applied inconsistently. In general, however, they were institutionalized in what came to be known as the Pact of 'Umar. See A. S. Tritton, *The Caliphs and their Non-Muslim Subjects* (London, 1930); Daniel Clement Dennet Jr, *Conversion and the Poll Tax in Early Islam* (Cambridge, MA, 1950); C. E. Bosworth, 'The Concept of *Dhimma* in Early Islam', in B. Braude and B. Lewis (eds), *Christians and Jews in the Ottoman Empire*, vol. 1 (New York, 1982); Bernard Lewis, *The Jews of Islam* (Princeton, 1984).

13 See Ibn Sahl in 'Iyad ibn Musa, *Muhammad Messenger of Allah*, trans. A. A. Bewley (Granada, 2006), 410, 434–5. See also Janina M. Safran, *Defining Boundaries in al-Andalus* (Ithaca, 2013), 96–7. For Ibn Sahl, see Delfina Serrano Ruano, 'Ibn Sahl', in D. Thomas and A. Mallett (eds), *CMR* 3 (Leiden, 2011), 211–13.

14 Paul of Antioch, *Letter to a Muslim Friend*, 221.

15 Thomas, 'Paul of Antioch's *Letter to a Muslim Friend* and *The Letter from Cyprus*', 207.

16 Paul of Antioch, *Letter to a Muslim Friend*, 222.

17 Ibid., 230.

18 Thomas comes to the same conclusion in 'Paul of Antioch's *Letter to a Muslim Friend* and *The Letter from Cyprus*', 208.

19 It was perhaps for this reason that the parable is removed from *The Letter from the People of Cyprus*, more on which appears below. It is also interesting to note al-Qarāfī's rejection of the comparison in his response to Paul's letter. For him, it did 'not make any sense'. Al-Qarāfī as quoted in Diego R. Sarrió Cucarella, *Muslim-Christian Polemics across the Mediterranean* (Leiden, 2014), 123. Again, on al-Qarāfī, see below.

20 Paul of Antioch, *Letter to a Muslim Friend*, 233. The conclusion also appears a bit earlier:

> It does not befit [God's] justice to demand on the day of resurrection that any people should have followed a messenger whom He had not sent to them, nor had they happened upon his book in their own language, neither by themselves or by way of a herald preceding him'. Christians, then, need not 'follow this messenger [i.e., Muḥammad], nor jettison what we have in our possession [i.e., the Gospel].

See ibid., 225.

21 Ebied and Thomas, eds, *Muslim-Christian Polemic during the Crusades*, 18, 23–7. On al-Dimashqī's *Reply to the Letter of the People of Cyprus*, see David Thomas, 'Ibn Abī Ṭālib al-Dimashqī', in D. Thomas and A. Mallett (eds), *CMR* 4 (Leiden, 2012), 798–801. For Ibn Taymiyya's *The Correct Answer to Those who Have Changed the Religion of Christ*, see Jon Hoover, 'Ibn Taymiyya', in D. Thomas and A. Mallett (eds), *CMR* 4 (Leiden, 2012), 824–44. For more on the possible identity of the author from Cyprus, see David Thomas, '*The Letter from the People of Cyprus*', in D. Thomas and A. Mallett (eds), *CMR* 4 (Leiden, 2012), 769 and Thomas, 'Cultural and Religious Supremacy in the Fourteenth Century', 312–14.

22 *The Letter from the People of Cyprus*, ed. and trans. R. Ebied and D. Thomas, in *Muslim-Christian Polemic during the Crusades* (Leiden, 2005), 56–9.

23 Ibid., 60–1, 64–5, 84–5, 122–3.

24 Ibid., 144–5.

25 Ibid., 146–7.

26 For the ways in which the author altered Christological statements in the *Letter to a Muslim Friend*, alterations that suggest he was more than likely Nestorian, see Alexander Treiger, 'The Christology of the *Letter from the People of Cyprus*', *Journal of Eastern Christian Studies* 65/1–2 (2013), 21–48.

27 *The Letter from the People of Cyprus*, 54–5.

28 Ibid., 114–15.

29 Thomas, 'Paul of Antioch's *Letter to a Muslim Friend* and *The Letter from Cyprus*', 217.
30 *The Letter from the People of Cyprus*, 54–5.
31 Q 26:198–9; 2:151; 3:164; 28:46; 32:3; 36:6.
32 *The Letter from the People of Cyprus*, 56–9.
33 Paul of Antioch, *Letter to a Muslim Friend*, 221.
34 Thomas, 'Paul of Antioch's *Letter to a Muslim Friend* and *The Letter from Cyprus*', 217.
35 *The Letter from the People of Cyprus*, 62–3.
36 Thomas, 'Paul of Antioch's *Letter to a Muslim Friend* and *The Letter from Cyprus*', 217. For ways in which this passage may reflect the author's Nestorian tradition, see Treiger, 'The Christology of the *Letter from the People of Cyprus*'.
37 See, e.g. *The Letter from the People of Cyprus*, 74–83.
38 Paul of Antioch, *Letter to a Muslim Friend*, 227–9.
39 *The Letter from the People of Cyprus*, 96–123.
40 Thomas, 'Paul of Antioch's *Letter to a Muslim Friend* and *The Letter from Cyprus*', 219.
41 *The Letter from the People of Cyprus*, 122–3.
42 Thomas, 'Paul of Antioch's *Letter to a Muslim Friend* and *The Letter from Cyprus*', 219.
43 Thomas, 'Cultural and Religious Supremacy in the Fourteenth Century', 320.
44 Ibid., 312.
45 Ibid., 312 and 314.
46 Thomas arrives at a similar conclusion in ibid., 319.
47 Thomas, 'Paul of Antioch's *Letter to a Muslim Friend* and *The Letter from Cyprus*', 221.
48 Ibid.
49 Paul of Antioch, *Letter to a Muslim Friend*, 234.
50 For more on al-Qarāfī and his response, see Sarrió Cucarella, especially pp. 100–40. Given the nature of *al-Ajwiba*, it would seem that Paul's assessment of Muḥammad, despite the precedent for it in Maliki jurisprudence, found no favour with al-Qarāfī.
51 As quoted in ibid., 101. It must be noted, as Sarrío Cucarella deduces, that both al-Qarāfī and Paul essentially spoke past one another since they began 'from very different theological points of departure' and, as a result, 'evaluate[d] the religion of the other from within their own frames of reference, which they [took] as axiomatic and universal'. See ibid., 100 and 139.
52 Paul of Antioch, *Letter to a Muslim Friend*, 233; *Lettre aux Musulmans*, 59.
53 See Thomas's commentary in 'Paul of Antioch's *Letter to a Muslim Friend* and *The Letter from Cyprus*' 205. On '*i'tibār*', see Angelika Brodersen, 'Reflection and

Deliberation', in J. D. McAuliffe (ed.), *Encyclopaedia of the Qur'ān*, vol. 4 (Leiden, 2004), 394.

54 Thomas, 'Paul of Antioch's *Letter to a Muslim Friend* and *The Letter from Cyprus*', 205.

55 Paul of Antioch, *Letter to a Muslim Friend*, 234.

56 See Thomas, 'Paul of Antioch's *Letter to a Muslim Friend* and *The Letter from Cyprus*', 205; Thomas, 'Paul of Antioch', in D. Thomas and A. Mallett (eds), *CMR* 4 (Leiden, 2012), 81.

57 Thomas, 'Cultural and Religious Supremacy in the Fourteenth Century', 312.

58 For more on the Muslim authors' attitudes towards *The Letter from the People of Cyprus*, see David Thomas, 'Christian-Muslim Misunderstanding in the Fourteenth Century', in M. Haddad, A. Heinemann, J. L. Meloy and S. Slim (eds), *Towards a Cultural History of the Mamluk Era* (Beirut, 2010); Ebied and Thomas, *Muslim-Christian Polemic during the Crusad*, 23–35.

59 Ibn Taymiyya, *Al-jawāb al-ṣaḥīḥ li-man baddala dīn al-Masīḥ*, ed. and trans. Thomas Michel in *A Muslim Theologian's Response to Christianity* (Ann Arbor, 1985), 141.

60 Cf. Thomas, 'Cultural and Religious Supremacy in the Fourteenth Century', 312, 314 and 320–1 and Ebied and Thomas, *Muslim-Christian Polemic during the Crusad*, 13–19.

9 Muḥammad as a Prophet and colonial goad for persecutors

1 On the spread of Fisher's story, see Justin Meggitt, 'Mary Fisher', in D. Thomas and J. Chesworth (eds), *CMR* 8 (Leiden, 2016), 368–9.

2 It continued to be used in support of religious freedom ideals well beyond the seventeenth century. See the book note for Oscar Straus's (d. 1926) book *Roger Williams: The Pioneer of Religious Liberty* (New York, 1894) in which Fisher's story is used to remind readers that 'the humane principle of toleration had been learned and practiced earlier than in Christian countries'. 'Quakers, Puritans and Turks', *The New York Times*, 10 June 1894.

3 George Fox, *George Fox* (Philadelphia, 1909), 57.

4 Ibid.

5 Ibid., 59.

6 Ibid., 59, n. 58.

7 Ibid. See also William C. Braithwaite, *The Beginnings of Quakerism* (London, 1912), 57; Bernadette Andrea, *Women and Islam in Early Modern English Literature* (Cambridge, 2007), 57.

8 For more on the charge of epilepsy, see the discussion in Chapter 7.

9 For more on the links between Fox and his views of Islam and the Qur'an, see Justin Meggitt, 'George Fox', in D. Thomas and J. Chesworth (eds), *CMR* 8 (Leiden, 2016), 523–34.

10 Meggitt, 'Mary Fisher', 367.

11 Justin J. Meggitt, *Early Quakers and Islam* (Eugene, 2013), 12. See Joel 2.28.

12 Meggitt, *Early Quakers and Islam*, 14.

13 Ibid., 11–13.

14 Richard Bauman, *Let Your Words Be Few* (Cambridge, 1983), 43. See also Meggitt, *Early Quakers and Islam*, 9, 14.

15 According to William Sewel's account, Mary Fisher and Ann Austin were imprisoned upon their arrival to Boston, Massachusetts, in 1656 because the deputy governor overheard one of the women use the word 'thee' instead of 'you', the latter implying a distinction in social class. This was all the proof he needed to conclude that they were Quakers and in turn deliver the requisite punishment. See William Sewel, *The History of the Rise, Increase and Progress of the Christian People called Quakers* (Philadelphia, 1728), 157. See also Meggitt, *Early Quakers and Islam*, 14–15.

16 Ibid., 14–15, 50.

17 Ibid., 12–13.

18 Sylvia Brown, 'The Radical Travels of Mary Fisher: Walking and Writing in the Universal Light', in S. Brown (ed.), *Women, Gender and Radical Religion in Early Modern Europe* (Leiden, 2007), 39, 41–5, 47.

19 Ibid., 45.

20 George Fox, *The Journal of George Fox*, ed. J. L. Nickalls (Cambridge, 1952), 263.

21 Quoted in Brown, 'The Radical Travels of Mary Fisher', 41.

22 Thomas Aldam, Elizabeth Hooton, William Pears, Benjamin Nicholson, Jane Holmes and Mary Fisher, *False Prophets and False Teachers Described* (London, 1652), 3 as quoted in Kate Peters, *Print Culture and the Early Quakers* (Cambridge, 2005), 168.

23 As quoted in Peters, *Print Culture and the Early Quakers*, 168.

24 Brown, 'The Radical Travels of Mary Fisher', 44.

25 Quoted in Brown, 'The Radical Travels of Mary Fisher', 45.

26 Mabel Richmond Brailsford, *Quaker Women* (London, 1915), 129–30. See also Brown, 'The Radical Travels of Mary Fisher', 46; Meggitt, *Early Quakers and Islam*, 58.

27 George Bishop, *New England Judged by the Spirit of the Lord* (London, 1703), 23. See also Brailsford, *Quaker Women*, 124–9.

28 Bishop, *New England Judged by the Spirit of the Lord*, 23.

29 Ibid., 24.

30 Ibid.

31 Ibid.
32 Ibid., 24–5.
33 Meggitt argues that it seems unlikely Fisher knew nothing of Muḥammad. See Meggitt, 'Mary Fisher', 371. For Fox's knowledge of Islam, see Meggitt, 'George Fox', 527–34; Meggitt, *Early Quakers and Islam*, 57.
34 Justin Meggitt, 'John Perrot', in D. Thomas and J. Chesworth (eds), *CMR* 8 (Leiden, 2016), 377. Brown, 'The Radical Travels of Mary Fisher', 57, n. 50.
35 See John Perrot, *A Visitation of Love and Gentle Greeting of the Turk* (London, 1660). See also Meggitt, *Early Quakers and Islam*, 61, n. 297.
36 Perrot, *A Visitation of Love and Gentle Greeting of the Turk*, 21.
37 Bishop, *New England Judged by the Spirit of the Lord*, 24.
38 Cf. Perrot, *A Visitation of Love and Gentle Greeting of the Turk*, 3.
39 In Brown, 'The Radical Travels of Mary Fisher', 52–4, she reflects on the nature of Fisher's encounter with the Sultan as purely an 'irenical exchange between Christianity and Islam' (52), a view she bases on a recollection of the meeting Fisher included in a letter written to Friends from London in 1659. Fisher's description of the event does not include any details about what she said to the Sultan or the exchange about Muḥammad. Fisher only commented on the Sultan's nobility and kind treatment of her, the fondness she had developed for Turks and the hope she had that God would, in time, raise the 'royall seed' that was already within them (the letter is quoted in its entirety in Brown, 'The Radical Travels of Mary Fisher', 53). The notion that the Turks already had within them God's Light conforms to standard Quaker views. Fisher's assessment that the Turks seemed 'more near truth then [*sic*] many Nations' (Brown, 'The Radical Travels of Mary Fisher', 53) reflected the way in which Quakers judged non-Christians less harshly than Christians (for which, see below). But the hope Fisher nourished that the Light would grow, by God's will, in Turks suggests that, while her meeting with the Sultan was a means by which to answer 'to that of God in everyone', to use Fox's words, her meeting in Adrianople may have had more than just irenic exchange in mind. Similarly, Andrea sees in Fisher's remarks about Muḥammad an 'embrace of cultural alterity'. See Andrea, 61. But, as Meggitt points out (Meggitt, 'Mary Fisher', 372–3), such a view does not account for the differences in how Quakers and Muslims viewed prophethood. And, as Fisher's own remarks made clear, she still saw Jesus as the standard by which prophethood was measured regardless of the legitimacy she may have granted to Muḥammad who could only function as a prophet to the extent that Fisher and other Quakers did.
40 Brown, 'The Radical Travels of Mary Fisher', 49–50.
41 Timothy Marr, *The Cultural Roots of American Islamicism* (Cambridge, 2006), 3–4.
42 Bishop's account of this event appears in Bishop, *New England Judged by the Spirit of the Lord*, 99–101. See also Meggitt, *Early Quakers and Islam*, 61–2.

43 Brown, 'The Radical Travels of Mary Fisher', 56–8. Cf. Gerard Croese's account of the meeting, written well after Bishop's text, which portrayed the Sultan as a 'Monster of a Man' along with other unbecoming descriptions. See Gerard Croese, *The General History of the Quakers* (London, 1696), 275–6. For analysis, see Brown, 'The Radical Travels of Mary Fisher', 60.

44 Bishop, *New England Judged by the Spirit of the Lord*, 24.

45 For a similar kind of conscription of Muḥammad, this time in the context of colonialism and the New World, see Manuel da Nóbrega's (d. 1570) sixteenth-century *Diálogo da Padre Nóbrega sobre a conversão do gentio* in which Islam, a religion of the Old World, was compared to indigenous religious beliefs in Brazil. In the *Diálogo*, Muslims (*mouros*) are said to 'believe in Muḥammad' (*crêem em Mafamede*) who is described as vicious and vile (*vicioso e torpe*), a womanizer and a proponent of a 'bestial sect' (*bestial seita*). He used sorcery in order to acquire followers. Such views were surely drawn from information common in Portugal, though Muḥammad's use of sorcery is intriguing. Significantly here, however, is that Muḥammad is used as a goad to encourage and justify Jesuit mission among indigenous groups in Brazil. For the text, see Serafim Leite, *Diálogo sobre a conversão do gentio pelo P. Manuel da Nóbrega* (Lisboa, 1954), 64 (original text)/92 (modern Portuguese edition). For commentary, see Eneida Ribeiro, 'Manuel da Nóbrega', in D. Thomas and J. Chesworth (eds), *CMR* 7 (Leiden, 2015), 816–19.

10 Muḥammad as a redundant Gabriel and missionary conscript

1 Akintunde E. Akinade, 'Islamic Challenges in African Christianity', in O. Kalu (ed.), *African Christianity* (Pretoria, 2005).

2 See *The Life of Muhammad*, trans. A. Guillaume (Karachi, 2007), 150–3. See also John Azumah, 'Patterns of Christian-Muslim Encounters in Sub-Saharan Africa', in D. Pratt, J. Hoover, J. Davies and J. Chesworth (eds), *The Character of Christian-Muslim Encounter* (Leiden, 2015), 382–4.

3 See J. Spencer Trimingham, *History of Islam in West Africa* (New York, 1962). See also Lamin Sanneh, *The Crown and the Turban* (Oxford, 1997); David Robinson, *Muslim Societies in African History* (Cambridge, 2004); Nehemia Levtzion and Randall L. Pouwells (eds), *The History of Islam in Africa* (Athens, OH, 2000); and Rüdiger Seesemann, 'Sufism in West Africa', *Religion Compass* 4/10 (October 2010), 606–14.

4 Crowther spelled his Yoruba name as 'Adjai', but the modern spelling is most commonly used in the relevant literature. See Andrew F. Walls, 'The Legacy of Samuel Ajayi Crowther', *International Bulletin of Missionary Research* 16/1 (January 1992), 20, n. 1.

5 Andrew F. Walls, *The Cross-Cultural Process in Christian History* (Maryknoll, 2002), 154.
6 Walls, 'The Legacy of Samuel Ajayi Crowther', 15.
7 Ibid.
8 Samuel Crowther and James Frederick Schön, *Journals of the Rev. James Frederick Schön and Mr. Samuel Crowther, Who, with the Sanction of Her Majesty's Government, Accompanied the Expedition up the Niger* (London, 1842), 373.
9 Ibid., 374.
10 Ibid., 375–8.
11 Ibid., 378–80.
12 Ibid., 182.
13 Ibid., 183.
14 Ibid.
15 Walls, 'The Legacy of Samuel Ajayi Crowther', 15.
16 Andrew F. Walls, *The Missionary Movement in Christian History* (Maryknoll, 1996), 102.
17 Walls, *The Cross-Cultural Process in Christian History*, 139.
18 Walls, 'The Legacy of Samuel Ajayi Crowther', 16.
19 Ibid., 16, 19.
20 Ibid., 16, 18. See also Stephen Ney, 'Samuel Ajayi Crowther and the Age of Literature' *Research in African Literatures* 46/1 (Spring 2015), 37–52; Stephen Ney, 'Samuel Ajayi Crowther's Journeys in Christian and Islamic Book History', *Social Sciences and Mission* 32 (2019), 31–53.
21 Samuel Crowther and John Christopher Taylor, *The Gospel on the Banks of the Niger* (London, 1859), 56.
22 Ibid.
23 Ney, 'Samuel Ajayi Crowther and the Age of Literature', 46. See also J. D. Y. Peel, *Religious Encounter and the Making of the Yoruba* (Bloomington, 2000), 187–8.
24 On the relative restrictions of using evidence arising from journals, see Alison Fitchett Climenhaga, 'Heathenism, Delusion and Ignorance: Samuel Crowther's Approach to Islam and Traditional Religion', *Anglican Theological Review* 96/4 (Fall 2014), 665. See also ibid., 665, n. 13 and the corresponding bibliography.
25 CMS, CA 2/031/116, journal, quarter ending March 25, 1853, p. 3.
26 CMS, CA 2/031/121, journal, quarter ending March 25, 1855, p. 8.
27 Ibid., pp. 8–9.
28 Fitchett Climenhaga, 'Heathenism, Delusion and Ignorance', 665.
29 Samuel Crowther, *Experiences with Heathens and Mohammedans in West Africa* (London, 1892).
30 Ibid., 5–6.
31 Ibid., 6.

32 Ibid., 7.
33 Ibid., 7–8.
34 Ibid., 8. George Sale (d. 1736) is perhaps best known for his translation of the Qur'ān into English with an introduction: *The Koran, Commonly Called The Alcoran of Mohammed, Translated into English Immediately from the Original Arabic; with Explanatory Notes, Taken from the Most Approved Commentators To Which is Prefixed A Preliminary Discourse* (London, 1734).
35 Crowther, *Experiences with Heathens and Mohammedans in West Africa*, 8.
36 Ibid. Crowther's Arabic reference here is to the resurrection and its corresponding Day of Judgment. See Q 75, which bears the title *Sūrah al-Qiyāmah*.
37 Crowther, *Experiences with Heathens and Mohammedans in West Africa*, 8.
38 Ibid., 8–9.
39 Ibid., 9. See also ibid., 22.
40 Ibid., 27.
41 Ibid.
42 Ibid., 30.
43 Ibid. Crowther also believed that Protestants were uniquely gifted, and perhaps divinely destined, to push back against the spread of Islam in West Africa. This was, in part, because 'The worshipping of images and the doctrine of transubstantiation,' presumably referring to Roman Catholic practices known to him, 'are great stumbling-blocks to the Mohammedans, and the Church which teacheth them is very unfit to bring those people over.' See ibid., 58–9.
44 Ibid., 15 (emphasis in original). Part of the 'erroneous' nature of Islam, for Crowther, was that it allowed its followers 'fascinating allurements' (23) and forced Muslims to depend on their own merits for salvation (6).
45 Ibid., 16. See also ibid., 29.
46 Ibid., 17. See also Crowther and Taylor, *The Gospel on the Banks of the Niger*, 233–4.
47 Crowther, *Experiences with Heathens and Mohammedans in West Africa*, 17. See also G. O. Gbadomọṣi, 'The Imamate Question among Yoruba Muslims', *Journal of the Historical Society of Nigeria* vi/2 (December 1972), 234.
48 Crowther, *Experiences with Heathens and Mohammedans in West Africa*, 17.
49 Ibid.
50 Ibid.
51 Ibid., 18.
52 Ibid.
53 Ibid., 19.
54 Ibid., 19–20.
55 Ibid., 20.
56 Ibid.

57 In the account Crowther gave in *The Gospel on the Banks of the Niger*, Muslims, though perhaps not converted, were completely satisfied with Crowther's response that Muḥammad came well after Christ and so did not appear in the Bible. See Crowther and Taylor, *The Gospel on the Banks of the Niger*, 161.

58 He also includes passages from the introduction to George Sale's English translation of the Qur'ān. See Crowther, *Experiences with Heathens and Mohammedans in West Africa*, 58–60.

59 Ibid., 30. See also ibid., 30–1, 33, 34. It may be that Crowther was drawn to Gabriel by reading the introductory matter to Sale's Qur'ān, part of which he includes in his *Experiences with Heathens and Mohammedans in West Africa*. In Sale's 'Preliminary Discourse', he consistently links Muḥammad, divine revelation and the angel Gabriel. See, e.g. Sale, 47, 50, 60, 64–5. Cf. John Tolan, *Faces of Muhammad* (Princeton, 2019), 163–8.

60 Quoted in P. R. McKenzie, *Inter-religious Encounters in West Africa* (Leicester, 1976), 24.

61 Crowther and Taylor, *The Gospel on the Banks of the Niger*, 171. See also Fitchett Climanhaga, 673.

62 Ibid.

63 Quoted in McKenzie, 70.

64 Fitchett Climenhaga, 'Heathenism, Delusion and Ignoran', 673.

65 Ibid., 679.

66 Shown and quoted in Peel, 88–9. See also Stephen Ney, *Ancestor, Book, Church*, PhD dissertation, University of British Columbia (2010), 25–6.

11 Muḥammad as a signpost for fellow pilgrims

1 Lamin Sanneh, *Summoned from the Margin* (Grand Rapids, 2012), 18–19.

2 Lamin Sanneh, *Piety and Power* (Maryknoll, 1996), 29.

3 Ibid., 30.

4 Sanneh, *Summoned from the Margin*, 101.

5 Ibid., 103–21 and 241–52.

6 Ibid., xiv–xv.

7 Lamin Sanneh, 'Muḥammad, Prophet of Islam, and Jesus Christ, Image of God', *International Bulletin of Missionary Research* 8/4 (October 1984), 169–74.

8 This essay appears as Chapter 2, 'Muḥammad's Significance for Christians', in Sanneh, *Piety and Power*.

9 Sanneh, 'Muhammad, Prophet of Islam', 169.

10 Ibid.

11 Ibid.

12 Ibid.
13 Ibid., 170.
14 Ibid.
15 Ibid.
16 Sanneh, 'Muḥammad's Significance for Christians', 38.
17 Ibid., 38.
18 Ibid., 32.
19 Ibid.
20 Ibid., 38.
21 Ibid., 48.
22 Ibid.
23 Ibid., 48–9.
24 Ibid., 49–50.
25 Ibid., 50.
26 Ibid. For more on translatability, see Lamin Sanneh, *Translating the Message* (Maryknoll, 2008).
27 Sanneh, 'Muhammad, Prophet of Islam', 170.
28 See ibid.
29 Ibid.
30 Ibid.
31 Ibid.
32 Ibid.
33 Ibid., 171.
34 Ibid.
35 Ibid., 172.
36 Ibid., 174.
37 Sanneh, 'Muhammad, Prophet of Islam', 174.

Conclusion

1 Constantine Bacha (Qusṭanṭīn Bāshā), *Mujādalat al-anbā Jirjī l-rāhib al-Simʿānī maʿthalāthat shuyūkh min fuqahāʾ al-Muslimīn bi-ḥaḍrat al-amīr Mushammar al-Ayyūbī* (Beirut, 1932), 23–4; Alex Nicoll, 'Account of a Disputation between a Christian Monk and Three Learned Mohammedans on the Subject of Religion', *Edinburgh Annual Register ad annum 1816* 9 (1820), 411. This last phrase – 'like Christ and the apostles' – is an odd phrase and one wonders if it represented the type of thing Muslims would have said in the debate or if the author of the account has placed it in their mouths so that Jirjī could build off of it a foil in his response. In fact, the Muslim claim is not merely that Muḥammad did what Christ and the

apostles did, but that what was achieved through him was something not done after Christ and the apostles.

2 Bacha, *Mujādalat al-anbā Jirjī l-rāhib al-Simʿānī maʿthalāthat shuyūkh min fuqahāʾ al-Muslimīn bi-ḥaḍrat al-amīr Mushammar al-Ayyūbī*, 24; Nicoll, 'Account of a Disputation between a Christian Monk and Three Learned Mohammedans on the Subject of Religion', 411. For a similar assessment from another Melkite monk, see the ninth-century response from Ibrāhīm al-Ṭabarānī to the emir ʿAbd al-Raḥmān al-Ḥāshimī. Abraham is a bit more generous, conceding that Muḥammad not only led the Arabs but was also more specifically 'a king with whom God was pleased and in whom and through whom He fulfilled His promise to Abraham concerning Ishmael'. Muḥammad was, nevertheless, not a prophet according to Ibrāhīm. See Giacinta Būlus Marcuzzo, ed., *Le dialogue d'Abraham de Tibériade avic ʿAbd al-Raḥmān al-Ḥāshimī à Jérusalem vers 820* (Rome, 1986), 320–1; K. Szilágyi, trans., 'The Disputation of the Monk Abraham of Tiberias', in S. Noble and A. Treiger (eds), *The Orthodox Church in the Arab World, 700–1700* (DeKalb, 2014), 99. For more on the monk Ibrāhīm and his disputation, see Mark N. Swanson, 'The Disputation of the Monk Ibrāhīm al-Ṭabrānī', in D. Thomas and B. Roggema (eds), *CMR* 1 (Leiden, 2009), 876–81.

3 Bacha, *Mujādalat al-anbā Jirjī l-rāhib al-Simʿānī maʿthalāthat shuyūkh min fuqahāʾ al-Muslimīn bi-ḥaḍrat al-amīr Mushammar al-Ayyūbī*, 24; Nicoll, 'Account of a Disputation between a Christian Monk and Three Learned Mohammedans on the Subject of Religion', 411–12.

4 Bacha, *Mujādalat al-anbā Jirjī l-rāhib al-Simʿānī maʿthalāthat shuyūkh min fuqahāʾ al-Muslimīn bi-ḥaḍrat al-amīr Mushammar al-Ayyūbī*, 41–2; Nicoll, 'Account of a Disputation between a Christian Monk and Three Learned Mohammedans on the Subject of Religion', 418. See also Bacha, *Mujādalat al-anbā Jirjī l-rāhib al-Simʿānī maʿthalāthat shuyūkh min fuqahāʾ al-Muslimīn bi-ḥaḍrat al-amīr Mushammar al-Ayyūbī*, 29–35; Nicoll, 'Account of a Disputation between a Christian Monk and Three Learned Mohammedans on the Subject of Religion', 414–15.

5 Bacha, *Mujādalat al-anbā Jirjī l-rāhib al-Simʿānī maʿthalāthat shuyūkh min fuqahāʾ al-Muslimīn bi-ḥaḍrat al-amīr Mushammar al-Ayyūbī*, 98; Nicoll, 'Account of a Disputation between a Christian Monk and Three Learned Mohammedans on the Subject of Religion', 437.

6 Bacha, *Mujādalat al-anbā Jirjī l-rāhib al-Simʿānī maʿthalāthat shuyūkh min fuqahāʾ al-Muslimīn bi-ḥaḍrat al-amīr Mushammar al-Ayyūbī*, 98; Nicoll, 'Account of a Disputation between a Christian Monk and Three Learned Mohammedans on the Subject of Religion', 437–8.

7 Bacha, *Mujādalat al-anbā Jirjī l-rāhib al-Simʿānī maʿthalāthat shuyūkh min fuqahāʾ al-Muslimīn bi-ḥaḍrat al-amīr Mushammar al-Ayyūbī*, 98–9; Nicoll, 'Account of a

Disputation between a Christian Monk and Three Learned Mohammedans on the Subject of Religion', 438.

8 'Beyond aversion' is a phrase I employ to describe assessments that, while they may stop short of endorsing another religious view, nevertheless demonstrate more nuance than mere denunciation or antagonism. In this way, though they may not constitute admiration, they might be seen as at least 'beyond aversion'. See my essay '"Can You Find Anything Praiseworthy in My Religion?"', in D. Pratt, J. Hoover, J. Davies and J. Chesworth (eds), *The Character of Christian-Muslim Encounter* (Leiden, 2015). My use of the phrase draws upon Mark Swanson's 'Beyond Prooftexting', *The Muslim World* 88/3–4 (July–October 1998), 297–319.

9 This persistent oversight is also noted by Annemarie Schimmel in 'The Prophet Muḥammad as a Centre of Muslim Life and Thought', in A. Schimmel and A. Falatūri (eds), *We Believe in One God* (New York, 1979) and by Clinton Bennett in 'Christian perceptions of Muḥammad', in D. Pratt and C. Tieszen (eds), *CMR* 15 (Leiden, 2020).

10 See the brief description by Laura Bottini 'The Apology of al-Kindī', in D. Thomas and B. Roggema (eds), *CMR* 1 (Leiden, 2009), 587–90.

11 John Tolan comes to a similar conclusion in his examination of Muḥammad in sources from western Europe. See his *Faces of Muhammad* (Princeton, 2019), 3, 263.

Bibliography

Primary sources

ʿAbd al-Jabbār. *Critique of Christian Origins*, ed. and trans. G. S. Reynolds and S. K. Samir (Provo, 2010).

al-Kindī, ʿAbd al-Masīḥ ibn Isḥāq. *Risāla*, ed. and trans. A. Tien, 'The Apology of Al-Kindi', in N. A. Newman (ed.), *The Early Christian-Muslim Dialogue: A Collection of Documents from the First Three Islamic Centuries (632–900 A.D.)* (Hatfield, 1993), 381–553.

al-Kindī, ʿAbd al-Masīḥ ibn Isḥāq. *Risāla*, ed. and trans. J. Yolles and J. Weiss, 'Apology of al-Kindī, in *Medieval Latin Lives of Muhammad* (Cambridge, MA, 2018).

al-Ṭabarī, Abū Ja'far Muḥammad ibn Jarīr. *Tārīkh al-rusul wa-l-mulūk*, vol. 8, trans. M. Fishbein (New York, 1997).

Aldam, Thomas, Elizabeth Hooton, William Pears, Benjamin Nicholson, Jane Holmes and Mary Fisher. *False Prophets and False Teachers Described* (London, 1652).

Alfonsi, Petrus. *Dialogi contra Iudeos*, trans. I. M. Resnick, in *Petrus Alfonsi: Dialogue against the Jews* (Washington, DC, 2006).

Alvarus, Paulus. *Indiculus luminosus*, ed. I. Gil, in *Corpus scriptorum muzarabicorum*, vol. 1 (Madrid, 1973).

Alvarus, Paulus. *Vita Eulogii*, ed. and trans. C. M. Sage, in *Paul Albar of Cordoba: Studies on His Life and Writings* (Washington, DC, 1943).

Bacha, Constantine (Qusṭanṭīn Bāshā). *Mujādalat al-anbā Jirjī l-rāhib al-Sim ʿānī ma ʿthalāthat shuyūkh min fuqahā' al-Muslimīn bi-ḥaḍrat al-amīr Mushammar al-Ayyūbī* (Beirut, 1932).

Bishop, George. *New England Judged by the Spirit of the Lord* (London, 1703).

Būluṣ ibn Rajā'. *Kitāb al-Wāḍiḥ bi-l-Ḥaqq*, ed. and trans. D. Bertaina (forthcoming).

Carlyle, Thomas. *On Heroes, Hero-Worship, and the Heroic in History* (Philadelphia, 1897).

Croese, Gerard. *The General History of the Quakers Containing the Lives, Tenents, Sufferings, Tryals, Speeches and Letters of the Most Eminent Quakers, Both Men and Women* (London, 1696).

Crowther, Samuel. *Experiences with Heathens and Mohammedans in West Africa* (London, 1892).

Crowther, Samuel and James Frederick Schön. *Journals of the Rev. James Frederick Schön and Mr. Samuel Crowther, Who, with the Sanction of Her Majesty's Government, Accompanied the Expedition up the Niger* (London, 1842).

Crowther, Samuel and John Christopher Taylor. *The Gospel on the Banks of the Niger: Journals and Notices of the Native Missionaries Accompanying the Niger Expedition of 1857–1859* (London, 1859).

Dionysius bar Ṣalībī. *A Response to the Arabs*, ed. and trans. J. P. Amar. Corpus Scriptorum Christianorum Orientalium, vols 614/615 (Louvain, 2005).

'The Disputation of Ibrāhīm al-Ṭabarānī', trans. K. Szilágyi, in S. Noble and A. Trieger (eds), *The Orthodox Church in the Arab World, 700–1700: An Anthology of Sources* (DeKalb, 2014), 90–111.

Ephrem the Syrian. *Hymns on Paradise*, trans. S. Brock (Crestwood, 1990).

Eulogius. *Documentum martyriale*, ed. I. Gil, in *Corpus scriptorum muzarabicorum*, vol. 2 (Madrid, 1973).

Eulogius. *Epistula tertia ad Wiliesindum*, ed. I. Gil, in *Corpus scriptorum muzarabicorum*, vol. 2 (Madrid, 1973).

Eulogius. *Memoriale sanctorum*, ed. I. Gil, in *Corpus scriptorum muzarabicorum*, vol. 2 (Madrid, 1973).

Fox, George. *George Fox: An Autobiography*, ed. R. M. Jones (Philadelphia, 1909).

Fox, George. *The Journal of George Fox*, ed. J. L. Nickalls (Cambridge, 1952).

Ibn Qutaybah. *Ta'wīl mukhtalif al-ḥadīth: An Annotated Translation*, trans. Che Amnah Bahari (Malaysia, 2009).

Ibn Sa'd, Abū 'Abd Allāh Muḥammad. *Kitāb al-ṭabaqāt al-kabīr*, ed. E. Sachau, in *Biographien Muhammeds, seiner Gefährten und der späteren Träger des Islams* (Leiden, 1905–40).

Ibn Taymiyya. *Al-jawāb al-ṣaḥīḥ li-man baddala dīn al-Masīḥ*, ed. and trans. Thomas Michel, in *A Muslim Theologian's Response to Christianity: Ibn Taymiyya's* Al-Jawab al-Sahih (Ann Arbor, 1985), 141.

John of Damascus. *Peri haireseōn*, ch. 100, ed. and trans. D. Sahas (Leiden, 1972).

John of Damascus. *Peri haireseōn*, ch. 100, ed. and trans. P. Schadler (Leiden, 2017).

John of Damascus. *Three Treatises on the Divine Images*, ed. and trans. A. Louth (Crestwood, 2003).

John of Seville. 'Item epistola Ioannis Spalensis Albaro directa', ed. I. Gil, in *Corpus scriptorum muzarabicorum*, vol. 1 (Madrid, 1973).

'La crónica profética', ed. M. Gómez Moreno, in 'Las primeras crónicas de la Reconquista: El ciclo de Alfonso III', *Boletín de la Academia de la Historia* (1932), 622–8.

Liber denudationis siue ostensionis aut patefaciens, ed. and trans. T. Burman (Leiden, 1994).

Marcuzzo, Giacinta Būlus, ed. *Le dialogue d'Abraham de Tibériade avic 'Abd al-Raḥmān al-Ḥāshimī à Jérusalem vers 820* (Rome, 1986).

Nicetas of Byzantium. *Confutatio dogmatum Mahomedis*, ed. J. P. Migne, in *Patrologia Graeca*, vol. 105 (Paris, 1862).

Nicoll, Alex. 'Account of a disputation between a Christian Monk and Three Learned Mohammedans on the Subject of Religion', *Edinburgh Annual Register ad annum 1816*, vol. 9 (1820), 405–42.

da Nóbrega, Manuel. *Diálogo do Padre Nóbrega sobre a conversão do gentio*, ed. S. Leite, in *Diálogo sobre a conversão do gentio pelo P. Manuel da Nóbrega* (Lisboa, 1954).

Paul of Antioch. *Letter to a Muslim Friend*, trans. S. Griffith, in S. Noble and A. Treiger (eds), *The Orthodox Church in the Arab World, 700–1700: An Anthology of Sources* (DeKalb, 2014), 216–51.

Paul of Antioch. *Lettre aux Musulmans*, ed. and trans. P. Khoury, in *Paul d'Antioche évêque Melkite de Sidon (XIIe s.)* (Beyrouth, 1964).

Perrot, John. *A Visitation of Love and Gentle Greeting of the Turk and Tender Trial of His Thoughts for God, and Proof of the Hearts of His Court, and the Spirits of the People Round about Him, in His Own Dominion, and the Inhabitants of the Earth that Are Borderers upon His Skirts, in Their Declared Religious Wayes … to which Is Annexed a Book Entituled, Immanuel the Salvation of Israel* (London, 1660).

'Quakers, Puritans and Turks', *New York Times*, 10 June 1894.

Saul. *Item rescriptum Sauli Episcopi Albaro directum*, ed. I. Gil in *Corpus scriptorum muzarabicorum*, vol. 1 (Madrid, 1973).

The Disputation between a Monk of Bēt Ḥālē and an Arab Notable, Diyarbakir Syriac MS 95, fols. 267r–274v.

The Disputation between a Monk of Bēt Ḥālē and an Arab Notable, ed. and trans. D. G. K. Taylor (Wiesbaden, 2015).

The Legend of Sergius Baḥīrā, ed. and trans. B. Roggema, in *The Legend of Sergius Baḥīrā: Eastern Christian Apologetics and Apocalyptic in Response to Islam* (Leiden, 2009).

The Letter from the People of Cyprus, ed. and trans. R. Ebied and D. Thomas, in *Muslim-Christian-Polemic during the Crusades* (Leiden, 2005).

Liber denudationis siue ostensionis aut patefaciens, ed. and trans. T. E. Burman in *Religious Polemic and the Intellectual History of the Mozarabs, c. 1050–1200* (Leiden, 1994).

The Life of Muhammad: A Translation of Ibn Ishaq's Sirat Rasul Allah, trans. A. Guillaume (Karachi, 2007).

Sale, George. *The Koran, Commonly Called the Alcoran of Mohammed, Translated into English Immediately from the Original Arabic; with Explanatory Notes, Taken from the Most Approved Commentators to Which Is Prefixed a Preliminary Discourse* (London, 1734).

Sanneh, Lamin. 'Muhammad, Prophet of Islam, and Jesus Christ, Image of God: A Personal Testimony', *International Bulletin of Missionary Research* 8/4 (October 1984), 169–74.

Sanneh, Lamin. 'Muḥammad's Significance for Christians: Biography, History and Faith', in L. Sanneh (ed.), *Piety and Power: Muslims and Christians in West Africa* (Maryknoll, 1996).

Sanneh, Lamin. *Summoned from the Margin: Homecoming of an African* (Grand Rapids, 2012).

Sewel, William. *The History of the Rise, Increase and Progress of the Christian People called Quakers: Intermixed with Several Remarkable Occurrences* (Philadelphia, 1728).

'The Syriac Apocalypse of Pseudo-Methodius', trans. P. J. Alexander in *The Byzantine Apocalyptic Tradition* (Berkeley, 1985).

al-Suyūṭī, Jalāl al-Dīn. *Al Budūr al-sāfira fī aḥwāl al-ākhira*, ed. M. al-Shāfi'ī (Beirut, 1996).

Theodore Abū Qurra. 'Opuscula', in J. P. Migne (ed.), *Patrologia Graeca*, vol. 97 (Paris, 1865), 1461–1602.

Theodore Abū Qurra. 'Refutation of the Saracens', in J. C. Lamoreaux (ed.), *Theodore Abū Qurrah* (Provo, 2005), 211–27.

'Tultusceptru de libro domini Metobii', in J. Yolles and J. Weiss (eds), *Medieval Latin Lives of Muhammad* (Cambridge, MA, 2018), 10–13.

Secondary sources

Accad, Martin. *Sacred Misinterpretation: Reaching across the Christian-Muslim Divide* (Grand Rapids, 2019).

Adang, Camilla. *Muslim Writers on Judaism and the Hebrew Bible: From Ibn Rabban to Ibn Hazm* (Leiden, 1996).

Ahmed, Waleed. 'The Characteristics of Paradise (*Ṣifat al-Janna*): A Genre of Eschatological Literature in Medieval Islam', in S. Günther and T. Lawson (eds), *Roads to Paradise*, vol. 2 (Leiden, 2017), 817–49.

Aillet, Cyrille. *Les Mozarabes. Islamisation, arabisation et christianisme en peninsula Ibérique (IXe–XIIe siècle)* (Madrid, 2010).

Akinade, Akintunde E. *Christian Responses to Islam in Nigeria: A Contextual Study of Ambivalent Encounters* (New York, 2014).

Akinade, Akintunde E. 'Islamic Challenges in African Christianity', in O. Kalu (ed.), *African Christianity: An African Story* (Pretoria, 2005), 117–39.

Alexander, Paul J. *The Byzantine Apocalyptic Tradition* (Berkeley, 1985).

Ali, Kecia. *The Lives of Muhammad* (Cambridge, MA, 2014).

Andrea, Bernadette. *Women and Islam in Early Modern English Literature* (Cambridge, 2007).

Andrae, Tor. *Die Person Muhammeds in Lehre und Glaube seiner Gemeinde* (Stockholm, 1917).

Anthony, Sean W. 'Fixing John Damascene's Biography: Historical Notes on His Family Background', *Journal of Early Christian Studies* 23/4 (2015), 607–27.

Anthony, Sean W. *Muhammad and the Empires of Faith: The Making of the Prophet of Islam* (Berkeley, 2020).

Anthony, Sean W. 'Muḥammad, the Keys to Paradise, and the *Doctrina Iacobi*: A Late Antique Puzzle', *Der Islam* 91/2 (2014), 243–65.

Anthony, Sean W. 'Who Was the Shepherd of Damascus? The Enigma of Jewish and Messianist Responses to the Islamic Conquests in Marwānid Syria and Mesopotamia', in P. Cobb (ed.), *The Lineaments of Islam: Studies in Honor of Fred McGraw Donner* (Leiden, 2012), 19–59.

Awad, Najib George. *Umayyad Christianity: John of Damascus as a Contextual Example of Identity Formation in Early Islam* (Piscataway, 2018).

Aydin, Mahmut. *Modern Western Christian Theological Understandings of Muslims since the Second Vatican Council* (Washington, DC, 2002).

al-Azmeh, Aziz. 'Rhetoric for the Senses: A Consideration of Muslim Paradise Narratives', *Journal of Arabic Literature* xxvi (1995), 215–31.

Azumah, John. 'Patterns of Christian-Muslim Encounters in Sub-Saharan Africa', in D. Pratt, J. Hoover, J. Davies and J. Chesworth (eds), *The Character of Christian-Muslim Encounter: Essays in Honour of David Thomas* (Leiden, 2015), 381–400.

Bauman, Richard. *Let Your Words Be Few: Symbolism of Speaking in Silence among Seventeenth-Century Quakers* (Cambridge, 1983).

Beaumont, Mark. 'Christians, Prophethood, and Muḥammad', in C. Tieszen (ed.), *Theological Issues in Christian-Muslim Dialogue* (Eugene, 2018), 26–41.

Beaumont, Mark, ed. *Arab Christians and the Qur'an from the Origins of Islam to the Medieval Period* (Leiden, 2018).

Bennett, Clinton. 'Christian Perceptions of Muḥammad', in D. Pratt and C. Tieszen (eds), *Christian-Muslim Relations. A Bibliographical History*, Vol. 15: *Thematic Essays (600–1600)* (Leiden, 2020), 153–79.

Bennett, Clinton. *In Search of Muhammad* (London, 1998).

Bennett, Clinton. *In Search of Understanding: Reflections on Christian Engagement with Muslims after Four Decades of Encounter* (Eugene, 2019).

Bertaina, David. 'The Arabic Version of the *Liber Denudationis*: How Fatimid Controversies shaped Medieval European Views of the Qur'an', forthcoming.

Bertaina, David. 'Būlus ibn Rajā' on the History and Integrity of the Qur'ān', in M. Beaumont (ed.), *Arab Christians and the Qur'an from the Origins of Islam to the Medieval Period* (Leiden, 2018), 174–95.

Bertaina, David. *Christian and Muslim Dialogues: The Religious Uses of a Literary Form in the Early Islamic Middle East* (Piscataway, 2011).

Bertaina, David, Sandra Toenies Keating, Mark N. Swanson and Alexander Treiger, eds. *Heirs of the Apostles: Studies on Arabic Christianity in Honor of Sidney H. Griffith* (Leiden, 2018).

Biale, David. 'Counter-History and Jewish Polemics against Christianity: The *Sefer toldot yeshu* and the *Sefer Zerubavel*', *Jewish Social Studies* 6 (1999), 130–45.

Blau, Joshua. 'A Melkite Arabic *Lingua Franca* from the Second Half of the First Millennium', *Bulletin of the School of Oriental and African Studies* 57/1 (1994), 14–16.

Bonta Moreland, Anna. *Muhammad Reconsidered: A Christian Perspective on Islamic Prophecy* (South Bend, 2020).

Bosworth, C. E. 'The Concept of *Dhimma* in Early Islam', in B. Braude and B. Lewis (eds), *Christians and Jews in the Ottoman Empire, Vol. 1: The Central Lands* (New York, 1982), 37–51.

Brailsford, Mabel Richmond. *Quaker Women, 1650–1690* (London, 1915).

Braithwaite, William C. *The Beginnings of Quakerism* (London, 1912).

Brockopp, Jonathan E., ed. *The Cambridge Companion to Muḥammad* (Cambridge, 2010).

Brodersen, Angelika. 'Reflection and Deliberation', in J. D. McAuliffe (ed.), *Encyclopaedia of the Qur'ān*, vol. 4 (Leiden, 2004), 393–4.

Brown, Syliva. 'The Radical Travels of Mary Fisher: Walking and Writing in the Universal Light', in S. Brown (ed.), *Women, Gender and Radical Religion in Early Modern Europe* (Leiden, 2007), 39–64.

Buaben, Jabal Muhammad. *The Image of the Prophet Muḥammad in the West: A Study of Muir, Margoliouth and Watt* (Leicester, 1996).

Bulliet, Richard. 'The Conversion Curve Revisited', in A. C. S. Peacock (ed.), *Islamisation* (Edinburgh, 2017), 69–79.

Bulliet, Richard. *Conversion to Islam in the Medieval Period: An Essay in Quantitative History* (Cambridge, MA, 1979).

Burman, Thomas E. *Religious Polemic and the Intellectual History of the Mozarabs, c. 1050–1200* (Leiden, 1994).

Cecini, Ulisse. 'Latin Christianity Engaging the Qur'an', in D. Pratt and C. Tieszen (eds), *Christian-Muslim Relations. A Bibliographical History*, Vol. 15: *Thematic Essays (600–1600)* (Leiden, 2020), 227–53.

Cecota, Błażej. 'Islam, the Arabs and Umayyad Rulers According to Theophanes the Confessor's Chronography', *Studia Ceranea* 2 (2012), 97–111.

Celli, Andrea. '"Maometto cascava del male caduco': Epilessia e profetismo islamico nella trattatistica storico-religiosa e medica in lingua italiana (Cinque–Seicento)', in A. Barbieri (ed.), *Eroi dell'estasi: Lo sciamanismo come artefatto culturale e sinopia letteraria* (Verona, 2017), 239–62.

Chase, Frederic H., trans. *St. John of Damascus: Writings* (Washington, DC, 1958).

Christys, Ann. *Christians in Al-Andalus (711–1000)* (London, 2002).

Colbert, Edward P. *The Martyrs of Córdoba (850–859): A Study of the Sources.* PhD dissertation, Catholic University of America (1962).

Cole, Juan. *Muhammad: Prophet of Peace amid the Clash of Empires* (New York, 2018).

Conticello, Vassa. 'Jean Damascène', in R. Goulet (ed.), *Dictionnaires des Philosophes Antiques*, Vol. 3 (Paris, 2005), 998–1012.

Coope, Jessica A. *The Martyrs of Córdoba: Community and Family Conflict in an Age of Mass Conversion* (Lincoln, 1995).

Crone, Patricia and Michael Cook. *Hagarism: The Making of the Islamic World* (Cambridge, 1977).

Cuffel, Alexandra. *Gendering Disgust in Medieval Religious Polemic* (Notre Dame, 2007).

Cyranka, Daniel. *Mahomet. Repräsentationen des Propheten in deutschsprachigen Texten des 18. Jahrhunderts* (Göttingen, 2018).

Dadoyan, Seta. *Islam in Armenian Intellectual Culture: Texts, Contexts, Dynamics* (Leiden, forthcoming).

Daniel, Norman. *Islam and the West: The Making of an Image* (Oxford, 2000).

de Carlos Villamarín, Helena. 'El Códice de Roda (Madrid, BRAH 78) como compilación de voluntad historiográfica', *Edad media: revista de historia* 12 (2011), 119–42.

De Cesare, Michelina. *The Pseudo-Historical Image of the Prophet Muḥammad in Medieval Latin Literature: A Repertory* (Berlin, 2012).

Dennet Jr, Daniel Clement. *Conversion and the Poll Tax in Early Islam* (Cambridge, MA, 1950).

Diaz y Diaz, Manuel C. 'Los textos antimahometanos más antiguos en codices Españoles', *Archives d'histoire doctrinale et littéraire du Moyen Age* 37 (1970), 149–68.

Dimmock, Matthew. *Mythologies of the Prophet Muhammad in Early Modern English Culture* (Cambridge, 2013).

Donner, Fred MacGraw. *Muhammad and the Believers: At the Origins of Islam* (Cambridge, MA, 2012).

Ebied, Rifaat. 'Dionysius bar Ṣalībī's Works in the Mingana Collection of Syriac and Arabic Manuscripts, with Special Emphasis on His Polemical Treatise "Against the Muslims" ', *Collectanea Christiana Orientalia* 8 (2011), 49–64.

Ebied, Rifaat. 'Prejudice and Polarization towards Christians, Jews and Muslims: "The Polemical Treatises" of Dionysius bar Ṣalībī', in M. Tamcke (ed.), *Christians and Muslims in Dialogue in the Islamic Orient of the Middle Ages* (Beirut, 2007), 171–83.

Ebied, Rifaat and David Thomas, eds. *Muslim-Christian Polemic during the Crusades:* The Letter from the People of Cyprus *and Ibn Abī Ṭālib al-Dimashqī's Response* (Leiden, 2005).

El-Ṣaleḥ, Ṣoubḥī. *La vie future selon le Coran* (Paris, 1986).

Fitchett Climenhaga, Alison. 'Heathenism, Delusion and Ignorance: Samuel Crowther's Approach to Islam and Traditional Religion', *Anglican Theological Review* 96/4 (Fall 2014), 661–81.

Fowden, Garth. *Before and after Muḥammad: The First Millennium Refocused* (Princeton, 2015).

Francisco, Adam S. *Martin Luther and Islam: A Study in Sixteenth-Century Polemics and Apologetics* (Leiden, 2007).

Franke, Franz R. 'Die freiwilligen Märtyrer von Codova und das Verhälnis des Mozarabes zum Islam (nach den Schriften von Speraindeo, Eulogius und Alvar)', *Spanische Forschungen der Görresgesellschaft* 13 (1953), 1–170.

Funkenstein, Amos. 'History, Counterhistory, and Narrative', in S. Friedlander (ed.), *Probing the Limits of Representation: Nazism and the 'Final Solution'* (Cambridge, 1992), 66–81.

Gbadomọşi, G. O. 'The Imamate Question among Yoruba Muslims', *Journal of the Historical Society of Nigeria* vi/2 (December 1972), 223–37.

Gero, Stephen. 'The Legend of the Monk Baḥīrā, the Cult of the Cross, and Iconoclasm', in P. Canivet and J.-P. Rey-Coquais (eds), *La Syrie de Byzance à l'Islam, VIIe-VIIIe siècles. Actes du colloque international, Lyon-Maison de l'Orient Méditerranéen, Paris-Institut du Monde Arabe, 11–15 September 1990* (Damascus, 1992), 47–57.

Ghaffar, Zishan. *Der historishe Muhammad in der islamischen Theologie: Zur Kriterienfrage in der Leben-Muhammad-Forschung* (Paderborn, 2018).

Gil, Moshe. 'The Story of Baḥīrā and its Jewish Versions', in H. Ben-Shammai (ed.), *Hebrew and Arabic Studies in Honour of Joshua Blau* (Tel Aviv, 1993), 193–210.

Gómez Moreno, Manuel. 'Las primeras crónicas de la Reconquista: El ciclo de Alfonso III', *Boletín de la Academia de la Historia* 100 (1932), 562–599.

Gottheil, Richard. 'A Christian Bahira Legend', *Zeitschrift für Assyriologie* 13 (1898), 189–242, 14 (1899), 203–68, 15 (1900), 56–102, 17 (1903), 125–66.

Griffith, Sidney H. 'Anastasios of Sinai, the *Hodegos*, and the Muslims', *Greek Orthodox Theological Review* 32/4 (1987), 341–58.

Griffith, Sidney H. 'Answering the Call of the Minaret: Christian Apologetics in the World of Islam', in J. J. van Ginkel, H. L. Murre-van den Berg and T. M. van Lint (eds), *Redefining Christian Identity: Cultural Interaction in the Middle East since the Rise of Islam* (Leuven, 2005), 91–126.

Griffith, Sidney H. *The Bible in Arabic: The Scriptures of the 'People of the Book' in the Language of Islam* (Princeton, 2013).

Griffith, Sidney H. 'Chapter Ten of the *Scholion*: Thedore Bar Kōnī's Apology for Christianity', *Orientalia Christiana Periodica* 47 (1981), 158–88.

Griffith, Sidney H. *The Church in the Shadow of the Mosque: Christians and Muslims in the World of Islam* (Princeton, 2008).

Griffith, Sidney H. 'The Church of Jerusalem and the "Melkites": The Making of an "Arab Orthodox" Christian Idenitty in the World of Islam, 750–1150 CE', in O. Limor and G.G. Stroumsa (eds), *Christians and Christianity in the Holy Land: From the Origins to the Latin Kingdoms* (Turnhout, 2006), 175–204.

Griffith, Sidney H. 'Disputes with Muslims in Syriac Christian Texts: From Patriarch John (d. 648) to Bar Hebraeus (d. 1286)', in B. Lewis and F. Niewohner (eds), *Religionsgespräche im Mittelalter* (Wiesbaden, 1992), 251–73.

Griffith, Sidney H. 'Disputing with Islam in Syriac: The Cae of the Monk of Bēt Ḥālē and a Muslim Emir', *Hugoye: Journal of Syriac Studies* 3/1 (2000), 29–54.

Griffith, Sidney H. 'Images, Islam and Christian Icons: A Moment in the Christian/ Muslim Encounter in Early Times', in P. Canivet and J.-P. Rey-Coquais (eds), *La Syrie de Byzance à l'Islam VIIe–VIIIe siècles. Actes du Colloque Inernational*

Lyon-Maisson de l'Orient Mediterranéen. Paris-Institut du Monde Arabe, 11–15 Septembre 1990 (Damscus, 1992), 121–38.

Griffith, Sidney H. 'John of Damascus and the Church in Syria in the Umayyad Era: The Intellectual and Cultural Milieu of Orthodox Christians in the World of Islam', *Hugoye: Journal of Syriac Studies* 11/2 (Summer 2008), 207–37.

Griffith, Sidney H. 'The Manṣūr Family and Saint John of Damascus: Christians and Muslims in Umayyad Times', in A. Borrut and F. M. Donner (eds), *Christians and Others in the Umayyad State* (Chicago, 2016), 29–51.

Griffith, Sidney H. '"Melkites", "Jacobites" and the Christological Controversies in Arabic in Third/Ninth-Century Syria', in D. Thomas (ed.), *Syrian Christians under Islam: The First Thousand Years* (Leiden, 2001), 9–55.

Griffith, Sidney H. 'The Monk in the Emir's *Majlis*: Reflections on a Popular Genre of Christian Literary Apologetics in Arabic in the Early Islamic Period', in H. Lazarus-Yafeh, M. Cohen, S. Somekh and S. Griffith (eds), *The Majlis: Interreligious Encounters in Medieval Islam* (Wiesbaden, 1999), 13–65.

Griffith, Sidney H. 'Muḥammad and the Monk Baḥīrā: Reflections on a Syriac and Arabic Text from Early Abbasid Times', *Oriens Christianus* 79 (1994), 146–74.

Griffith, Sidney H. 'The Gospel in Arabic', *Oriens Christianus* 69 (1985), 126–67.

Griffith, Sidney H. 'The Prophet Muḥammad, His Scripture and His Message, According to the Christian Apologies in Arabic and Syriac from the First Abbasid Century', in T. Fahd (ed.), *La vie du Prophète Mahomet: Colloque de Strasbourg (Octobre 1980)* (Paris, 1983), 99–146.

Griffith, Sidney H. 'The Qur'an in Christian Arabic Literature: A Cursory Overview', in M. Beaumont (ed.), *Arab Christians and the Qur'an from the Origins of Islam to the Medieval Period* (Leiden, 2018), 1–19.

Gruber, Christiane. *The Praiseworthy One: The Prophet Muhammad in Islamic Texts and Images* (Bloomington, 2018).

Gruber, Christiane and Frederick Colby, eds. *The Prophet's Ascension: Cross-Cultural Encounters with the Islamic Mi'raj Tales* (Bloomington, 2010).

Gruber, Christiane and Avinoam Shalem, eds. *The Image of the Prophet between Ideal and Ideology: A Scholarly Investigation* (Berlin, 2014).

Hackenburg, Clint. *Voices of the Converted: Christian Apostate Literature in Medieval Islam*. PhD dissertation, Ohio State University (2015).

Hanson, Craig L. 'Manuel I Comnenus and the "God of Muhammad": A Study in Byzantine Ecclesiastical Politics', in J. Tolan (ed.), *Medieval Christian Perceptions of Islam* (London, 2000), 55–82.

Henderson, John B. *The Construction of Orthodoxy and Heresy: Neo-Confucian, Islamic, Jewish, and Early Christian Patterns* (New York, 1998).

Henderson, John B. 'The Multiplicity, Duality, and Unity of Heresies', in W. J. van Bekkum and P. M. Cobb (eds), *Strategies of Medieval Communal Identity: Judaism, Christianity and Islam* (Leuven, 2004), 11–27.

Hitchcock, Richard. *Mozarabs in Medieval and Early Modern Spain: Identities and Influences* (Hampshire, 2008).

Høgel, Christian. 'An Early Anonymous Greek Translation of the Qur'ān: The Fragments from Niketas Byzantios' *Refutatio* and the Anonymous *Abjuratio*', *Collectanea Christiana Orientalia* 7 (2010), 65–119.

Hoyland, Robert G. 'The Earliest Christian Writings on Muḥammad: An Appraisal', in H. Motzki (ed.), *The Biography of Muhammad: The Issue of the Sources* (Leiden, 2000), 276–97.

Hoyland, Robert G. *Seeing Islam as Others Saw It: A Survey and Evaluation of Christian, Jewish and Zoroastrian Writings on Early Islam* (Princeton, 1997).

Hoyland, Robert G. 'Writing the Biography of the Prophet Muhammad: Problems and Solutions', *History Compass* 5 (2007), 1–22.

Hulmes, E. D. A. *Christian Attitudes to Islam: A Comparative Study of the Work of S.A. Crowther, E.W. Blyden and W.R.S. Miller in West Africa*. PhD dissertation, Oxford University (1980).

Jacobs, Bert. 'Preliminary Considerations on Dionysius bar Ṣalībī's Islamic Sources', *Hugoye: Journal of Syriac Studies* 21/2 (2018), 357–89.

Jarrar, Maher. 'Houris', in J. D. McAuliffe (ed.), *Encyclopaedia of the Qur'ān*, vol. 2 (Leiden, 2002), 456–58.

Jarrar, Maher. 'Strategies for Paradise: Paradise Virgins and Utopia', in S. Günther and T. Lawson (eds), *Roads to Paradise: Eschatology and Concepts of the Hereafter in Islam*, vol. 1 (Leiden, 2017), 271–94.

Kaegi, Jr., Walter Emil. 'Initial Byzantine Reactions to the Arab Conquest', *Church History* 38/2 (June 1969), 139–49.

Keating, Sandra Toenies. 'Manipulation of the Qur'an in the Epistolary Exchange between al-Hāshimī and al-Kindī', in M. Beaumont (ed.), *Arab Christians and the Qur'an from the Origins of Islam to the Medieval Period* (Leiden, 2018), 50–65.

Keating, Sandra Toenies. 'The Paraclete and the Integrity of Scripture', in C. Tieszen (ed.), *Theological Issues in Christian-Muslim Dialogue* (Eugene, 2018), 15–25.

Kedar, Benjamin Z. *Crusade and Mission: European Approaches toward the Muslims* (Princeton, 1984).

Kerr, David. 'Muhammad: Prophet of Liberation – a Christian Perspective from Political Theology', *Studies in World Christianity* 6/2 (2000), 139–74.

Kerr, David. 'Toward Christian Theological Recognition of the Prophethood of Muhammad', in Y. Y. Haddad and W. Z. Haddad (eds), *Christian-Muslim Encounters* (Gainesville, 1995), 426–46.

Khoury, Paul. *Paul d'Antioche évêque Melkite de Sidon (XIIe s.)* (Beyrouth, 1964).

Kidd, Thomas S. *American Christian and Islam: Evangelical Culture and Muslims from the Colonial Period to the Age of Terrorism* (Princeton, 2009).

Kister, M. J. 'Ādam: A Study of Some Legends in *Tafsīr* and *Ḥadīth* Literature', in J. Kraemer (ed.), *Israel Oriental Studies*, vol. XIII (Leiden, 1993), 113–62.

Lange, Christian, ed. *Locating Hell in Islamic Traditions* (Leiden, 2015).

Lange, Christian. *Mohammed: Perspectieven op de Profeet* (Amsterdam, 2017).

Lange, Christian. *Paradise and Hell in Islamic Traditions* (Cambridge, 2015).

Levtzion, Nehemia and Randall L. Pouwells, eds. *The History of Islam in Africa* (Athens, OH, 2000).

Levy-Rubin, Milka and Benjamin Z. Kedar. 'A Spanish Source on Mid-Ninth-Century Mar Saba and a Neglected Sabaite Martyr', in J. Patrich (ed.), *The Sabaite Heritage: The Sabaite Factor in the Orthodox Church* (Leuven, 2001), 63–72.

Lewis, Bernard. *The Jews of Islam* (Princeton, 1984).

Louth, Andrew. 'John of Damascus and the Making of the Byzantine Theological Synthesis', in J. Patrich (ed.), *The Sabaite Heritage in the Orthodox Church from the Fifth Century to the Present* (Leuven, 2001), 301–4.

Louth, Andrew. *St John Damascene: Tradition and Originality in Byzantine Theology* (Oxford, 2005).

Luchitskaja, Svetlana. 'The Image of Muhammad in Latin Chronography of the Twelfth and Thirteenth Centuries', *Pergamon* 26/2 (2000), 115–26.

Mack, Phyllis. *Visionary Women: Ecstatic Prophecy in Seventeenth-Century England* (Berkeley, 1992).

Madigan, Daniel. 'Jesus and Muḥammad, The Sufficiency of Prophecy', in M. Ipgrave (ed.), *Bearing the Word: Prophecy in Biblical and Qur'ānic Perspective* (New York, 2005), 90–9.

Marr, Timothy. *The Cultural Roots of American Islamicism* (Cambridge, 2006).

Marshall, David. 'Muḥammad in Contemporary Christian Theological Reflection', *Islam and Christian-Muslim Relations* 24/2) (2013), 161–72.

McKenzie, P. R. *Inter-religious Encounters in West Africa: Samuel Ajayi Crowther's Attitude to African Traditional Religion and Islam* (Leicester, 1976).

Meggitt, Justin J. *Early Quakers and Islam: Slavery, Apocalyptic and Christian-Muslim Encounters in the Seventeenth Century* (Eugene, 2013).

Melchert, Christopher. 'Bukhārī's *Kitāb tafsīr al-Qur'ān*', *Journal of the International Qur'anic Studies Association* 1 (2016), 149–72.

Michel, Thomas. *A Muslim Theologian's Response to Christianity: Ibn Taymiyya's* Al-Jawab al-Sahih (Ann Arbor, 1985).

Millar, Fergus. 'Hagar, Ishmael, Josephus, and the Origins of Islam', *Journal of Jewish Studies* 44 (1993), 23–45.

Miller, William Ian. *The Anatomy of Disgust* (Cambridge, MA, 1997).

Monferrer-Sala, Juan Pedro. 'Mitografia hagiomartirial. De muevo sobre los supuestos mártires Cordobeses del siglo IX', in M. Fierro (ed.), *De muerte violenta. Política, religión y violencia en Al-Andalus* (Madrid, 2004), 415–50.

Motzki, Harald, ed. *The Biography of Muhammad: The Issue of the Sources* (Leiden, 2000).

Ney, Stephen. *Ancestor, Book, Church: How Nigerian Literature Responds to the Missionary Encounter*, PhD dissertation, University of British Columbia (2010).

Ney, Stephen. 'Samuel Ajayi Crowther and the Age of Literature', *Research in African Literatures* 46/1 (Spring 2015), 37–52.

Ney, Stephen. 'Samuel Ajayi Crowther's Journey in Christian and Islamic Book History', *Social Sciences and Missions* 32 (2019), 31–53.

Papaconstantinou, Arietta, Neil McLynn and Danil L. Schwartz, eds. *Conversion in Late Antiquity: Christianity, Islam, and Beyond* (Surrey, 2015).

Papademetriou, George C. *Two Traditions, One Space: Orthodox Christians and Muslim in Dialogue* (Boston, 2011).

Parry, Kenneth. *Depicting the Word: Byzantine Iconophile Thoguht of the Eighth and Ninth Centuries* (Leiden, 1996).

Peacock, A. C. S., ed. *Islamisation: Comparitive Perspectives from History* (Edinburgh, 2017).

Peel, J. D. Y. *Religious Encounter and the Making of the Yoruba* (Bloomington, 2000).

Penn, Michael Philip. *Envisioning Islam: Syriac Christians and the Early Muslim World* (Philadelphia, 2015).

Penn, Michael Philip. *When Christians First Met Muslims: A Sourcebook of the Earliest Syriac Writings on Islam* (Berkeley, 2015).

Peters, Kate. *Print Culture and the Early Quakers* (Cambridge, 2005).

Pfotenhauer, Thomas C. *Islam in the Crucible: Can It Pass the Test?* (Kearney, 2002).

Popov, Radko. 'Speaking His Mind in a Multi-Cultural and Multi-Religious Society: John of Damascus and His Knowledge of Islam in Chapter 101 ("The Heresy of the Ishmaelites") of His Work Concerning Heresy', in G. C. Papademetrious (ed.), *Two Traditions, One Space: Orthodox Christians and Muslims in Dialogue* (Boston, 2011), 109–43.

Powers, David S. *Muḥammad Is Not the Father of Any of Your Men: The Making of the Last Prophet* (Philadelphia, 2009).

Pratt, Douglas and Charles Tieszen, eds. *Christian-Muslim Relations. A Bibliographical History*, Vol. 15: *Thematic Essays (600–1600)* (Leiden, 2020).

Reeves, Minou. *Muhammad in Europe: A Thousand Years of Western Myth-Making* (New York, 2000).

Reinink, Gerrit J. 'Bible and Qur'an in Early Syriac Christian-Islamic Disputation', in M. Tamcke (ed.), *Christians and Muslims in Dialogue in the Islamic Orient of the Middle Ages* (Beirut, 2007), 57–72.

Reynolds, Gabriel Said. 'Remembering Muḥammad', *Numen* 58 (2011), 188–206.

Robinson, David. *Muslim Societies in African History* (Cambridge, 2004).

Roggema, Barbara. 'A Christian Reading of the Qur'an: The Legend of Sergius-Baḥīrā and Its use of Qur'an and Sīra', in D. Thomas (ed.), *Syrian Christians under Islam: The First Thousand Years* (Leiden, 2001), 57–73.

Roggema, Barbara. 'Ḥikāyāt amthal wa-asmār. King Parables in Melkite Apologetic Literature', in R. Ebied and H. Teule (eds), *Studies on the Christian Arabic Heritage* (Leuven, 2004), 113–31.

Roggema, Barbara. *The Legend of Sergius Baḥīrā: Eastern Christian Apologetics and Apocalyptic in Response to Islam* (Leiden, 2009).

Roggema, Barbara. 'Muslims as Crypto-Idolaters – A Theme in the Christian Portrayal of Islam in the Near East', in D. Thomas (ed.), *Christians at the Heart of Islamic Rule: Church Life and Scholarship in 'Abbasid Iraq* (Leiden, 2003), 1–18.

Roggema, Barbara. Review of *Envisioning Islam: Syriac Christians and the Early Muslim World*, by Michael Philip Penn, *Islam and Christian-Muslim Relations* 28/1 (January 2017), 117–19.

Roggema, Barbara, Marcel Poorthuis and Pim Valkenberg, eds. *The Three Rings: Textual Studies in the Historical Trialouge of Judaism, Christianity and Islam* (Leuven, 2005).

Rubin, Uri. 'More Light on Muḥammad's Pre-existence: Qur'ānic and Post-Qur'ānic Perspectives', in A. Rippin and R. Tottoli (eds), *Books and Written Culture of the Islamic World: Studies Presented to Claude Gilliot on the Occasion of His 75th Birthday* (Leiden, 2015), 288–311.

Safran, Janina M. *Defining Boundaries in Al-Andalus: Muslims, Christians and Jews in Islamic Iberia* (Ithaca, 2013).

Sahas, Daniel J. 'The Art and Non-Art of Byzantine Polemics: Patterns of Refutation in Byzantine Anti-Islamic Literature', in M. Gervers and R. J. Bikhazi (eds), *Conversion and Continuity: Indigenous Christian Communities in Islamic Lands, Eighth to Eighteenth Centuries* (Toronto, 1999), 55–73.

Sahas, Daniel J. '"Holosphyros"? A Byzantine Perception of "The God of Muhammad"', in Y. Y. Haddad and W. Z. Haddad (eds), *Christian-Muslim Encounters* (Gainesville, 1995), 109–25.

Sahas, Daniel J. *John of Damascus on Islam: The 'Heresy of the Ishmaelites'* (Leiden, 1972).

Sahner, Christian. *Christian Martyrs under Islam: Religious Violence and the Making of the Muslim World* (Princeton, 2018).

Sahner, Christian. 'Swimming against the Current: Muslim Conversion to Christianity in the Early Islamic Period', *Journal of the American Oriental Society* 136/2 (April–June 2016), 265–84.

Samir, Samir K. 'La version latine de l'Apologie d'al-Kindi (vers 830 ap. J.-C) et son original arabe', in M. Penelas, P. Roisee and C. Aillet (eds), *¿Existe una identidad mozárabe? Historia, lengua y cultura de los Cristiano de al-Andalus (siglos IX–XII)* (Madrid, 2007), 33–82.

Samir, Samir K. 'Notes sur la "Lettre à un Musulman de Sidon' de Paul d'Antioche", *Orientalia Lovaniensia Periodica* 24 (1993), 179–95.

Samir, Samir K. 'The Prophet Muḥammad as Seen by Timothy I and Other Arab Christian Authors', in D. Thomas (ed.), *Syrian Christians under Islam: The First Thousand Years* (Leiden, 2001), 75–106.

Sanneh, Lamin. *The Crown and the Turban: Muslims and West African Pluralism* (Oxford, 1997).

Sanneh, Lamin. *Disciples of All Nations: Pillars of World Christianity* (Oxford, 2008).

Sanneh, Lamin. 'The Domestication of Islam and Christianity in African Societies', *Journal of Religion in Africa* 11/1 (1980), 1–12.

Sanneh, Lamin. *Translating the Message: The Missionary Impact on Culture* (Maryknoll, 2008).

Sanneh, Lamin. *West African Christianity: The Religious Impact* (Maryknoll, 1983).

Sarrió Cucarella, Diego R. *Muslim-Christian Polemics across the Mediterranean: The* Splendid Replies *of Shihāb al-Dīn al-Qarāfī (d. 684/1285)* (Leiden, 2014).

Schadler, Peter. *John of Damascus and Islam: Christian Heresiology and the Intellectual Background to Earliest Christian-Muslim Relations* (Leiden, 2018).

Schimmel, Annemarie. *And Muhammad Is His Messenger: The Veneration of the Prophet in Islamic Piety* (Chapel Hill, 1985).

Schimmel, Annemarie. 'The Prophet Muḥammad as a Centre of Muslim Life and Thought', in A. Schimmel and A. Falatūri (eds), *We Believe in One God: The Experience of God in Christianity and Islam* (New York, 1979), 35–61.

Schleifer, Aliah. *Mary the Blessed Virgin in Islam* (Louisville, 1997).

Seesemann, Rüdiger. 'Sufism in West Africa', *Religion Compass* 4/10 (October 2010), 606–14.

Shalem, Avinoam, ed. *Constructing the Image of Muhammad in Europe* (Berlin, 2013).

Shoemaker, Stephen J. *The Death of a Prophet: The End of Muhammad's Life and the Beginnings of Islam* (Philadelphia, 2012).

Siddiqui, Muzammil. 'Muslim and Byzantine Christian Relations: Letter of Paul of Antioch and Ibn Taymīyah's Response', *Greek Orthodox Theological Review* 31/1 (1986), 33–45.

Simeldis, Christos. 'The Byzantine Understanding of the Qur'anic Term *al-Ṣamad* and the Greek Translation of the Qur'an', *Speculum* 86/4 (October 2011), 887–913.

Smith, Jane Idleman and Yvonne Yazbeck Haddad. *The Islamic Understanding of Death and Resurrection* (Oxford, 2002).

Smith, Jane Idleman and Yvonne Yazbeck Haddad. 'The Virgin Mary in Islamic Tradition and Commentary', *Muslim World* 79/3–4 (July/October 1989), 161–87.

Spellberg, Denise A. *Politics, Gender, and the Islamic Past: The Legacy of 'A'isha bint Abi Bakr* (New York, 1994).

Spellberg, Denise A. *Thomas Jefferson's Qur'an: Islam and the Founders* (New York, 2013).

Stroumsa, Sarah. 'The Signs of Prophecy. The Emergence and Early Development of a Theme in Arabic Theological Literature', *Harvard Theological Review* 78 (1985), 101–14.

Suermann, Harald. "Muhammad in Christian and Jewish Apocalyptic Expectations', *Islam and Christian-Muslim Relations* 18/2 (2007), 15–21.

Swanson, Mark. 'Christian Perceptions of and Responses to Islam', in D. Pratt and C. Tieszen (eds), *Christian-Muslim Relations. A Bibliographical History*, Vol. 15: *Thematic Essays (600–1600)* (Leiden, 2020), 73–97.

Szilágyi, Krisztina. 'A Prophet like Jesus? Christians and Muslims Debating Muḥammad's Death', *Jerusalem Studies in Arabic and Islam* 36 (2009), 131–71.

Szilágyi, Krisztina. *After the Prophet's Death: Christian-Muslim Polemic and the Literary Images of Muhammad*. PhD dissertation, Princeton University (2014).

Szilágyi, Krisztina. 'Muḥammad and the Monk: The Making of the Christian Baḥīrā Legend', *Jerusalem Studies in Arabic and Islam* 34 (2008), 169–214.

Tamcke, Martin, ed. *Christians and Muslims in Dialogue in the Islamic Orient of the Middle Ages* (Beirut, 2007).

Tannous, Jack. *The Making of the Medieval Middle East: Religion, Society, and Simple Believers* (Princeton, 2018).

Tannous, Jack. *Syria between Byzantium and Islam: Making Incommensurables Speak*. PhD dissertation, Princeton University (2010).

Taylor, David G. K. 'The Disputation between a Muslim and a Monk of Bēt Ḥālē: Syriac Text and Annotated English Translation', in S. Griffith and S. Grebenstein (eds), *Christsein in der islamischen Welt: Festschrift für Martin Tamcke zum 60. Geburtstag* (Wiesbaden, 2015), 187–242.

Teule, Herman. 'Paul of Antioch's Attitude towards the Jews and the Muslims. His *Letter to the Nations and the Jews*', in B. Roggema, M. Poorthuis and P. Valkenberg (eds), *The Three Rings: Textual Studies in the Historical Trialogue of Judaism, Christianity and Islam* (Leuven, 2005), 91–110.

Thomas, David. 'Christian-Muslim Misunderstanding in the Fourteenth Century: The Correspondence between Christians in Cyprus and Muslims in Damascus', in M. Haddad, A. Heinemann, J. L. Meloy and S. Slim (eds), *Towards a Cultural History of the Mamluk Era* (Beirut, 2010), 13–30.

Thomas, David. 'Conversion Out of Principle: 'Ali b. Rabban al-Tabari (d. c. 860) and 'Abdallah al-Tarjuman (d. c. 1430), Two Converts from Christianity to Islam', in A. C. S. Peacock (ed.), *Islamisation* (Edinburgh, 2017), 56–68.

Thomas, David. 'Cultural and Religious Supremacy in the Fourteenth Century: *The Letter from Cyprus* as Interreligious Apologetic', *Parole de l'Orient* 30 (2005), 298–322.

Thomas, David. 'Paul of Antioch's *Letter to a Muslim Friend* and *The Letter from Cyprus*', in D. Thomas (ed.), *Syrian Christians under Islam: The First Thousand Years* (Leiden, 2001), 203–21.

Thomas, David. 'With the Qur'an in Mind', in M. Beaumont (ed.), *Arab Christians and the Qur'an from the Origins of Islam to the Medieval Period* (Leiden, 2018), 131–49.

Thomas, David, Barbara Roggema, Alex Mallett, and John Chesworth, eds. *Christian-Muslim Relations. A Bibliographical History* (Leiden, 2009–).

Thomson, Robert W. 'Armenian Variations on the Bahira Legend', *Harvard Ukrainian Studies* 3–4/2 (1979–80), 884–95.

Thomson, Robert W. 'Muhammad and the Origin of Islam in Armenian Literary Tradition', in *Studies in Armenian Literature and Christianity* (Aldershot, 1994), 829–58.

Tieszen, Charles. *A Textual History of Christian-Muslim Relations: Seventh–Fifteenth Centuries* (Minneapolis, 2015).

Tieszen, Charles. '"Can You Find Anything Praiseworthy in My Religion?" Religious Aversion and Admiration in Medieval Christian-Muslim Relations', in D. Pratt, J. Hoover, J. Davies and J. Chesworth (eds), *The Character of Christian-Muslim Encounter: Essays in Honour of David Thomas* (Leiden, 2015), 126–44.

Tieszen, Charles. *Christian Identity amid Islam in Medieval Spain*. Leiden, 2013.

Tieszen, Charles. 'Christians under Muslim Rule, 650–1200: Christians in Muslim Spain', in D. Thomas (ed.), *Routledge Handbook on Christian-Muslim Relations* (London, 2018), 75–9.

Tieszen, Charles. *Cross Veneration in the Medieval Islamic World: Christian Identity and Practice under Muslim Rule* (London, 2017).

Tieszen, Charles. 'Discussing Religious Practices', in D. Pratt and C. Tieszen (eds), *Christian-Muslim Relations: A Bibliographical History*, Vol. 15: *Thematic Essays (600–1600)* (Leiden, 2020), 489–513.

Tieszen, Charles. 'From Invitation to Provocation: "Holy Cruelty" as Christian Mission in Ninth-Century Córdoba', *Al-Masāq* 24/1 (April 2012), 21–33.

Tieszen, Charles. 'Re-planting Christianity in New Soil: Arabized Christian Religious Identity in Twelfth-Century Iberia', *Islam and Christian-Muslim Relations* 22/1 (January 2011), 57–68.

Tieszen, Charles, ed. *Theological Issues in Christian-Muslim Dialogue* (Eugene, 2018).

Tolan, John. 'A Life of Muḥammad from Fifteenth-Century Spain', *Jerusalem Studies in Arabic and Islam* 36 (2009), 425–38.

Tolan, John. *Faces of Muhammad: Western Perceptions of the Prophet of Islam from the Middle Ages to Modernity* (Princeton, 2019).

Tolan, John. *Saracens: Islam in the Medieval European Imagination* (New York, 2002).

Tolan, John. *Sons of Ishmael: Muslims through European Eyes in the Middle Ages* (Gainesville, 2008).

Tottoli, Roberto. 'Muslim Eschatology and the Ascension of the Prophet Muḥammad: Describing Paradise in *Mi'rāj* Traditions and Literature', in S. Günther and T. Lawson (eds), *Roads to Paradise: Eschatology and Concepts of the Hereafter in Islam*, vol. 2 (Leiden, 2017), 858–90.

Treiger, Alexander. 'The Christology of the *Letter from the People of Cyprus*', *Journal of Eastern Christian Studies* 65/1–2 (2013), 21–48.

Treiger, Alexander. 'Paul of Antioch's *Responses to a Muslim Sheikh*', in D. Bertaina, S. Keating, M. Swanson and A. Treiger (eds), *Heirs of the Apostles: Studies on Arabic Christianity in Honor of Sidney H. Griffith* (Leiden, 2018), 333–46.

Trimmingham, J. Spencer. *History of Islam in West Africa* (New York, 1962).

Tritton, A. S. *The Caliphs and their Non-Muslim Subjects: A Critical Study of the Covenant of 'Umar* (London, 1930).

van Doorn-Harder, Nellie. 'Who Is Muhammad to Christians? Revisiting the Question' *Studies in Interreligious Dialogue* 26/1 (2016), 57–74.

van Ess, Josef. *Theology and Society in the Second and Third Centuries of the Hijra: A History of Religious Thought in Early Islam*, vol. 4 (Leiden, 2018).

van Koningsveld, P.S. 'The Apology of Al-Kindī', in T. L. Hettema and A. van der Kooij (eds), *Religious Polemics in Context* (Assen, 2004), 69–84.

Walker, Joel Thomas. *The Legend of Mar Qardagh: Narrative and Christian Heroism in Late Antique Iraq* (Berkeley, 2006).

Walls, Andrew F. *The Cross-Cultural Process in Christian History* (Maryknoll, 2002).

Walls, Andrew F. 'The Legacy of Samuel Ajayi Crowther'. *International Bulletin of Missionary Research* 16/1 (January 1992), 15–21.

Walls, Andrew F. *The Missionary Movement in Christian History: Studies in the Transmission of Faith* (Maryknoll, 1996).

Wasilewski, Janna. 'The "Life of Muhammad" in Eulogius of Córdoba: Some Evidence for the Transmission of Greek Polemic to the Latin West', *Early Medieval Europe* 16/3 (2008), 333–53.

Weitz, Lev E. *Between Christ and Caliph: Law, Marriage, and Christian Community in Early Islam* (Philadelphia, 2018).

Wensinck, A. J. *A Handbook of Early Muhammadan Tradition* (Leiden, 1927).

Winter, Tim. 'Jesus and Muhammad: New Convergences', *Muslim World* 99 (January 2009), 21–38.

Wolf, Kenneth Baxter. 'Christian Views of Islam in Early Medieval Spain', in J. Tolan (ed.), *Medieval Christian Perceptions of Islam* (London, 1996), 85–108.

Wolf, Kenneth Baxter. 'Counterhistory in the Earliest Latin Lives of Muhammad', in C. Gruber and A. Shalem (eds), *The Image of the Prophet between Ideal and Ideology* (Berlin, 2014), 13–26.

Wolf, Kenneth Baxter. *The Eulogius Corpus: Translated with Introduction and Commentary* (Liverpool, 2019).

Wolf, Kenneth Baxter. 'Eulogius of Córdoba and His Understanding of Islam'. Available at www.academia.edu/20312136/Eulogius_of_Córdoba_and_His_Understanding_of_Islam (accessed 5 February 2019).

Wolf, Kenneth Baxter. 'Muḥammad as Antichrist in Ninth-Century Córdoba', in M. D. Meyerson and E. D. English (eds), *Christians, Muslims and Jews in Medieval and Early Modern Spain* (Notre Dame, 2000), 3–19.

Wolf, Kenneth Baxter. 'The Earliest Latin Lives of Muḥammad', in M. Gervers and R. J. Bikhazi (eds), *Conversion and Continuity: Indigenous Christian Communities in Islamic Lands, Eighth to Eighteenth Centuries* (Toronto, 1990), 89–101.

Yolles, Julian and Jessica Weiss, eds. *Medieval Latin Lives of Muhammad* (Cambridge, MA, 2018).

Index

A Response to the Arabs 52, 55, 88
A visitation of love and a gentle greeting of the Turk 117, 118
'Abd al-Jabbār 157
'Abd al-Malik ibn Marwān 22
Abraham 92, 99
Abū al-Dardā' 177
Abū Dharr 177
Abū Qurrah, Theodore 64, 160
Abū Rā'iṭa al-Takrītī 46
Abū l-Surūr al-Tinnīsī 181
Abū Ṭālib 7
Adrianople 109, 114, 118, 119, 187
Africa 121, 122, 123, 131
Ahl al-dhimmah 182
'Ā'ishah 83, 156
al-Ajwiba al-fākhira 'an al-as'ila al-fājira ('Splendid Replies to Insolent Questions') 105
Akbar 73, 184
Aleppo 1
'ālim 2, 3
Allāhu akbar 71, 73
Alvarus, Paulus 58–70, 74, 75, 88, 170, 174, 179
al-Andalus 5, 6, 97
Andalusī 97
angel 7, 11, 61, 62, 71, 73, 83, 111, 129, 131, 151, 174
Anglican 6, 123
Antichrist 59, 60, 65, 174
Antioch 1, 95
anti-hero 77, 92, 93, 145
anti-saint 57, 65, 68, 145
Aphrodite 26, 159
apocalypse, apocalyptic 11, 16, 17
Apocalypse of Pseudo-Methodius 72
Apostle(s) 2, 3, 21, 47, 54, 85, 91, 99, 102, 143, 144, 156, 192, 193
Arab(s) 10, 11, 12, 13, 14, 15, 16, 17, 22, 33, 35, 38, 41, 43, 47, 51, 61, 64, 65, 72, 73, 74, 76, 79, 85, 95, 96, 98, 100, 101, 105, 143, 144, 145, 151, 161, 176
Arabia, Arabians 7, 41, 102, 143
Arabized Christian(s) 6, 78, 79, 80, 88, 176
Arian, Arius 30, 160, 168, 173
Armenian 6, 12, 155
Atlantic Ocean 113, 114, 121, 123, 143
Austin, Ann 186
Awkbar 73
Axum 121

al-Baghawī 179
Baghdad 4, 38
Baḥīrā 4, 9–19, 35, 36, 42, 54, 63, 73, 88, 89, 145, 150, 163, 179
Banū Hāshim 73
Bar Ṣalībī, Dionysius 52–6, 88, 89, 145, 168, 179
barakah 134, 135, 137, 140, 142
Barbados 114
Barīd 88, 89, 90
Beckley, Beatrice 114
Berber 121
Berid imberid 87, 89
Bēt Ḥālē 33, 40, 41, 42, 43, 55, 145, 146, 147, 148
beyond aversion 146, 194
Bishop, George 119
Bishr ibn al-Barā' 49
Black Stone 84, 85, 178
Book of Common Prayer 130
Book of Scholia 41–3
Boston 114, 119, 186
boy 9, 11, 13, 18, 73, 145
Brazil 188
Britain 126
British 122
al-Bukhārī 27, 28
Butler's Lives of the Saints 138
Byzantine(s) 10, 21, 23, 153

camel 65, 67, 168
Carlyle, Thomas 181
catechumen 9, 17, 19
Cave of Ḥira 160
Chalcedonian(s) 1, 6, 9, 15, 178
Christ. *See* Jesus
Christology 3, 39, 148, 153, 183
Chronicle of Alfonso III 76
Chronographia 178
Church of England 6, 109
Church of the Holy Sepulchre (Church of the Anastasis) 158
Church Missionary Society (CMS) 123, 126
Clapham Sect 123
Codex of Roda 73, 75, 76
Collectio Toletana 46
colonial 5, 109, 118, 121, 143
Colonial America 119
Constantine V 21
Constantinople 21, 95, 96, 114, 115, 116, 130
Contra legem Saracenorum 93
Copt(s), Coptic 6, 9, 77, 80, 86, 178
Córdoba, Cordoban 57, 58, 60, 61, 67, 68, 69, 70, 74, 75, 80, 169, 174
corporeal 61, 63
Council of Chalcedon 153
counterhistory 9, 16, 17, 18, 19, 157
cow 11
creator 3
Croese, Gerard 188
Crowther, Samuel Ajayi 6, 121–32, 133, 145, 146, 151, 188, 190, 191
Cypriot, Cyprus 100, 101, 102, 103, 104, 105, 106, 107
Cyrene son of Manṣūr 158

da Nóbrega, Manuel 188
Damascus 22, 23, 100, 101, 106
Daniel 180
David 99
David the Oriental 78, 80
Dāwūd al-Iṣfahānī 78, 80
Derby 110, 111
dhimmah 182
dhimmī 97, 182
Diálogo da Padre Nóbrega sobre a conversão do gentio 188
al-Dimashqī, Muḥammad ibn Abī Ṭalib 100, 101, 106, 107
The Disputation between a Muslim and a Monk from Bēt Ḥālē 33–8, 150, 163
dog(s) 59, 63, 65, 68
Dominican 77, 80, 93
donkey(s) 10, 179
Dyer, Mary 119

East Syrian(s) 6, 9, 12, 13, 17, 33, 34, 38, 41, 43, 46, 51, 52, 55, 56, 77, 147, 155, 156
Eastern Christian(s) 6, 22, 61, 63, 64, 78, 88, 138, 177
Edirne 109
Egypt 80, 82, 121, 130
Egyptian(s) 163
Elijah 180
Embrico of Mainz 171
encyclopaedism, encyclopedia 24, 25
England 5, 109, 110, 112, 114, 118, 123
English 113, 115, 116, 123, 125, 129, 130, 190, 191
Ephrem the Syrian 35, 36, 148
epilepsy, epileptic 83, 85, 111, 177, 185
Epiphanius of Salamis 23, 25
Erribon 70, 71, 72, 73
Escim 73
Ethribum 72
Ethiopia 121
Eulogius 58–70, 74, 75, 149, 170, 173
Europe, European 4, 46, 101, 109, 112, 194
Exodus 163
Experiences with Heathens and Mohammedans in West Africa 126, 131
Explanatio simboli apostolorum 78

False prophets and false teachers described 113, 117
Father 13, 35
Fātiḥah 133
Fāṭima 59, 156
Fatimid 80, 82
Fisher, Mary 5, 6, 109–20, 145, 146, 151, 185, 186, 187
Fourah Bay College 123
Fox, George 110, 111, 113, 116, 186, 187
Freetown 127
friends 110, 111, 112, 114, 115, 187
Fulani 122

Gabriel 7, 11, 35, 61, 62, 83, 111, 121, 129, 131, 191
Gambia, The 133, 134, 135
George 173, 174
George of Cyprus 21, 157
German 93
Germanus 21
The Golden Legend: Readings of the Saints 138
Gospel(s) 10, 35, 36, 39, 50, 53, 81, 95, 121, 144, 162, 164, 165, 182
Greece 114
Greek 22, 29, 43, 64, 72, 93
Greek Orthodox 9, 153

Habar 26, 159
Hagar 10, 36, 53, 92
Hagarenes 24
Ḥajj 77, 80, 84
hamartiography 57, 60
Ḥanbalī 100
al-Ḥasan al-Baṣrī 87, 88, 89, 179
Hāshim, Hāshimite 15, 73
al-Ḥāshimī, ʿAbd al-Raḥmān 193
al-Hāshimī, ʿAbdallāh ibn Ismāʿīl 45, 46, 47, 50, 51, 148
Hebrew 39, 41, 85, 91, 103, 111, 147, 150, 163
Heraclius 23, 65
heresiarch 61
Historia de regibus Gothorum, Vandalorum et Suevorum 75–6
Historiarum adversum paganos libri VII 75
Holy Spirit 13, 35, 39, 40, 65, 85, 92, 103, 110, 111, 112, 114, 118, 129, 168
horse(s) 87, 88, 122, 179, 180
houris 14, 54, 89
hypostases, hypostasis 13, 52

Iberian Peninsula 4, 5, 57, 76, 173
Ibn ʿAbbās 84
Ibn Qutaybah 84, 182
Ibn Rajāʾ, Būluṣ 77, 79–93, 145, 147, 149, 176, 177, 180, 181
Ibn Sahl 97, 182
Ibn Taymiyya 100, 101, 106, 107, 157
Ibn ʿUmar 27
Ibrāhīm al-Ṭabarānī 193
Ilorin 129
ʿImrān 59
Iraq, Iraqī 33, 78, 80, 143
Ishmael 3, 72, 92, 143
Ishmaelite(s) 23, 24, 25, 26, 30, 72
Isidore of Seville 61, 65, 75
Israel 28
'Istoria de Mahomet' 61–7, 70, 74, 75, 76
Italy 77, 80, 95, 114
Izmir 114

Jacobite(s) 9, 33, 86, 178
Al-jawāb al-ṣaḥīḥ li-man baddala dīn al-Masīḥ 157
Jeremiah 180
Jerusalem 10, 22, 114, 158, 173, 174
Jesuit 188
Jesus 10, 12, 39, 42, 43, 50, 51, 53, 63, 72, 76, 79, 81, 82, 91, 92, 93, 99, 103, 104, 113, 116, 117, 118, 120, 125, 126, 128, 130, 131, 134, 135, 141, 144, 145, 146, 147, 150, 151, 163, 165, 180, 191, 192
Jew(s), Jewish 7, 10, 12, 13, 17, 18, 29, 42, 43, 49, 52, 97, 98, 114, 151, 155, 160, 162, 182
jinn 14
Jirjī 1–4, 143, 144, 145, 153, 192
Joel 111
John 36, 164
John V, Patriarch 158
John the Baptist 13, 22, 91, 180
John of Damascus 4, 21–31, 33, 62, 66, 67, 84, 145, 149, 158, 159, 160, 161
John of Seville 65–7, 70, 74
Joseph 62
Judaism 74

Kaʿb 10, 12, 13, 14
Kaʿbah 84
Kadhā wa-kadhā 14, 27, 28, 90
Khadījah 47
al-Kindī, ʿAbd al-Masīḥ ibn Isḥāq 45–51, 52, 55, 56, 60, 63, 66, 67, 145, 148, 167, 179
king(s) 10, 11, 15, 177
Kingdom of Kanem 121
Kitāb al-dīn wa-l-dawla (*The Book of Religion and Empire*) 168
Kitāb al-Wāḍiḥ bi-l-Ḥaqq (*Clarity in Truth*) 77, 79–93, 149, 176, 177, 179
The Koran, Commonly Called The Alcoran of Mohammed, Translated into English

Immediately from the Original Arabic; with Explanatory Notes, Taken from the Most Approved Commentators To Which is Prefixed A Preliminary Discourse 190

Latin 12, 43, 58, 72, 73, 75, 77, 78, 80, 87, 93, 167, 171, 178
Latin Christian(s) 6, 79
Latin Europe 4, 5
Lebanon 95
Leghorn 114
The Letter from the People of Cyprus 95, 100–7, 109, 145, 151, 181, 182, 183, 185
Letter to a Muslim Friend 95–107
Levant 114
Liber apologeticus martyrum 61
Liber denudationis siue ostensionis, aut patefacientem (*The Book of Denuding or Exposing, or The Discloser*) 77–93, 145, 147, 149, 176, 177, 178, 179, 180
light 2
Livorno 114
London 114, 187
Luke 35
Luther, Martin 93, 181

Maghreb 121
al-Mahdi, Caliph 38–41, 56, 164, 165
Mali Empire 121
al-Malik al-Ẓāhir Ghāzi ibn Yūsuf ibn Ayyūb 1, 2
Malik ibn Anas 97
Mālikī 97
al-Ma'mūn 46
Mande Songhey Empire 121
Mansour, Manṣūr 21, 22
Mar Sim'ān al-Barḥī 1
Mariolatry 128
Māriyah the Copt 86
Maronite 9
Martyr(s) 57, 58, 59, 61, 65, 68, 69, 74, 169, 170, 173, 174
Mary 12, 35, 59, 60, 62, 92, 128, 131, 149
Mary (daughter of 'Imrān) 59
Maṣābīḥ al-Sunnah 179
Maslama ibn 'Abd al-Malik 33
Massachusetts 114
mazīd 89
Mecca 7, 77, 78, 80, 84, 97, 121
Medina 72, 73
Mediterranean 4, 78, 80, 95, 96, 100, 109, 112, 121, 143
Mehmed IV, Sultan 109, 114, 115, 116, 117, 118, 119, 120, 187, 188
Melkite 1, 9, 15, 95, 143, 153, 160, 193
Messenger 1, 2, 7
Messiah 2, 42
Methodist(s) 6, 133, 134
Miaphysite 9, 178
miracle(s) 10, 46, 49, 50, 51, 53, 65, 82, 85, 177, 180
Mi'rāj 84
mission, missionary 6
monk(s) 1, 10, 18, 22, 26, 30, 33, 34, 35, 36, 40, 43, 51, 55, 73, 77, 80, 143, 144, 145, 146, 156, 158, 160, 162, 163, 173, 174, 193
Monophysite 33
monotheism, monotheist(s), monotheistic 12, 21, 23, 28, 30, 43, 51, 52, 53, 55, 74, 75, 84, 92, 98, 145, 147, 148, 166, 182
Moses 28, 33, 42, 43, 53, 59, 60, 85, 99, 165, 166
Mount Sinai 10, 15, 28
Mozarab(s) 176
Muḥammad al-Amīn 133
Muqātil ibn Sulaymān 67
Musk 1, 143, 144

Nestorian(s) 9, 33, 183, 184
New England 5, 109, 114, 119, 121, 143
New England Judged 119
New World 4, 143, 188
Nicetas of Byzantium 64
Niger River 123
Nigeria 122, 129, 133
North America 143

Ocim 73, 174
Old World 188
On Heroes, Hero-Worship and the Heroic in History 181
Osius 70, 71, 73, 173
Oṡogun 122
Ottoman Empire 5, 109, 114, 116, 117, 119
Ozim 70, 71, 73, 174

Pact of 'Umar 182
pagan(s), paganism 7, 17, 18, 28, 37, 41, 43, 69, 97, 98, 101, 150, 151
Palestine 80

Panarion 23
Paraclete (*paraklētos*) 12, 39, 155, 164, 168
paradise 11, 14, 36, 54, 59, 60, 87, 88, 89, 91, 105, 106, 146, 148, 149, 180
Paul 113, 160
Paul of Antioch 95–108, 109, 145, 151, 181, 182, 184
Paulus Orosius 75
Pēgē gnōseōs 23, 24, 25, 29, 30, 62, 66, 159
Perfectus 57, 58
Peri haireseōn 23, 24, 25, 26, 29, 159
Perrot, John 117
Peter the Venerable 46
Pfotenhauer, Thomas 93
Pharaoh 59
pilgrim(s), pilgrimage 10, 77, 78, 80, 133, 135, 142
polemic, polemical 12, 61, 64, 67, 78, 80, 106, 167
polytheism, polytheist(s) 10, 12, 30, 35, 40, 52, 55, 69, 84, 92
Pope 114
Portuguese 122
Prophetic Chronicle 73, 76
Protestant(s) 6, 131, 134, 190

Qāḍī 57, 97
al-Qarāfī, Shihāb al-Dīn Aḥmad ibn Idrīs 105, 107, 183, 184
Quaker(s), Quakerism 109–20, 145, 151, 186, 187
Quraysh 7, 73

Al-radd ʿalā l-Naṣārā (*Refuation of the Christians*) 77
Ramon Llull 78
Ramon Martí 77, 78
Roman Catholic(s) 128, 153
Reformed 6
Riccoldo da Monte di Croce 77, 93
Risāla 45–51, 56, 60, 66, 148
Risāla min ahl jazīrat Qubruṣ 157
River Gambie 133
River Jordan 13
Roman Catholic(s), Roman Catholicism 6, 128, 133, 134, 153, 190
Rome 6, 96, 114

Sabas 22
Ṣalāḥ al-Dīn 1
Sale, George 127, 190, 191
Sanneh, Lamin 6, 133–42, 145, 146, 147, 151
Saracen(s) 24, 73
Satan 57, 174
Saul 69, 173
Selby 113
Sergius. *See* Baḥīrā
Sewell, William 186
shahādah 2, 22, 72, 82, 128, 133, 135, 182
Shango 132
sharīʿah 100
shirk 136, 139
Sidon 95
Sierra Leone 123, 127, 133
Sinai 80
Sisebut 65
Smyrna 114, 130
Society of Friends 109, 110, 111, 112, 116, 117
Son, Son of God 3, 13, 103, 118, 119, 126, 128, 129, 131
South Carolina 118
Southwark 110
Spain 57, 61, 65, 70, 75, 76, 80, 145, 173, 174, 176
St Catherine's Monastery 80
Sub-Saharan Africa 121
Sufi 121
Syria(n) 33, 34, 45, 52, 73, 143, 146
Syriac 12, 33, 35, 38, 40, 43, 45, 52, 53, 54, 72, 153, 155, 163, 169

al-Ṭabarī 37, 179
al-Ṭabarī, ʿAlī Rabban 77, 168
Tafsīr al-Qur'ān 179
taḥrīf 164
takbīr 71
Tathbīt dalā'il al-nubuwwa 157
tawḥīd 36
Theodore bar Kōnī 41–3, 151
Theophanes the Confessor 178
Timothy I, Patriarch 38–43, 51, 52, 55, 56, 105, 141, 145, 146, 147, 150, 165, 166
Toledo 65, 78, 79, 80
Tomlinson, Richard and Elizabeth 113
Torah 39, 81, 97, 162, 165, 182

Trinitarian, Trinity 3, 34, 35, 36, 38, 39, 148, 150, 151, 165
'Tultusceptru de libro domni Metobii' 70–6, 151, 173, 174
Turk(s) 109, 115, 119, 187
Turkey 52, 109, 114, 117

UK 133
'ulamā' 1, 2, 3
Umayyad 22, 23
United States 133

Venice 114, 117
violence, violent 47, 50, 51, 82, 83, 85, 92, 147
virgin(s) 14, 59, 92
Visigoths 76
vita, *vitae* 60, 62, 65, 68, 70, 72, 74, 75, 76, 171, 173
Vita Mahumeti 171
vulture 61, 62, 65

warrior 45, 51, 55
Wesleyan 127
West Africa(n) 4, 121, 122, 123, 124, 125, 126, 127, 131, 132, 133, 143, 146, 190
West Syrian(s) 6, 9, 12, 13, 17, 43, 45, 46, 52, 55, 56, 156
Wilberforce, William 123
word 35, 39, 92, 103, 168
World Christianity 133, 134

Yale Divinity School 133
Yathrib 72
York 113, 114
York Castle 113
Yorkshire 109, 113
Yoruba 122, 123, 129, 188
Yorubaland 122, 132
youth. *See* boy

Ẓāhirite 78
Zayd 12, 13, 17, 26, 62, 66, 67, 172
Zaynab bint al-Ḥarith 49
Zaynab bint Jaḥsh 12, 27, 48, 57, 62, 66, 67, 86, 172
Zechariah 180

www.ingramcontent.com/pod-product-compliance
Lightning Source LLC
Chambersburg PA
CBHW072233290426
44111CB00012B/2070

* 9 7 8 1 3 5 0 1 9 1 2 5 9 *